Colin McEvedy · The New Penguin Atlas of Medieval History

Maps devised by the author
and drawn by David Woodroffe

Penguin Books

INTRODUCTION

My idea in compiling this atlas has been to show the unfolding of medieval history in Europe and the Near East as a continuous story. This makes it a different sort of book from most historical atlases, which tend to take countries one at a time and concentrate on their internal structures. There is none of this sort of detail here: no dissection of individual kingdoms, no descriptions of their administrative hierarchies. Instead, the emphasis is on showing what happened to the whole family of nations in the Europe–Near East area as the centuries progressed. These maps will not show you where the kings of France established their mints or the Cluniacs built their monasteries: what they are intended to give you is a picture of how old empires fell and new ones rose, and how, in Europe, a new society emerged that had the energy to break free from the geographical, intellectual and technical limitations that defined the medieval world.

The forty-seven maps that make up the atlas are arranged in six sections. The bulk of each section consists of five or six maps showing the political condition of the area at intervals that average forty years. At the end of each section there are two or more maps corresponding in date to the last political one: the first shows the boundaries of Christendom and, after the seventh century, Islam, the two defining cultures of the region; the second shows the development of the economy. Others, if there are any, deal with population changes and the exploration of the wider world.

Nearly all the maps in this atlas cover exactly the same area: Europe, North Africa and the Near East. This is a social as well as a geographical unit, defined by barriers that kept its members in and almost everyone else out. Its limits are shown in Figure 1. Starting with the Ural Mountains, the traditional frontier between Europe and Asia, the boundary line runs anti-clockwise via the Arctic Ocean, Atlantic and Sahara Desert to the Nile valley. From there it passes to the south coast of the Red Sea, then across the

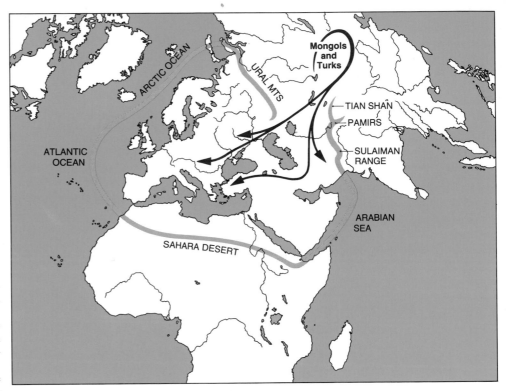

FIGURE I *The boundaries of the Europe–Near East area.*

Arabian Sea to reach the mountains that mark the divide between Iran and the Indian subcontinent. Some sections of this line were permeable. The Urals have never been a significant barrier to movement, sea lanes connecting the Near East with East Africa and India had been established in classical times, and there were a number of usable passes in the mountains dividing Iran and Central Asia from India. But very few people entered the Europe–Near East area by any of these routes: the only significant number of arrivals came through the Central Asian gap. Here, between the southern end of the Urals and the northern flank of the Central Asian massif, the way was

wide open. This was the portal of entry for the Turco-Mongol tribes that constituted the one important addition to the west's medieval mix.

Figure 2 shows the area actually used as the base map of the atlas. A few corners have been lopped off the area defined in Figure 1: the extreme north-east of European Russia, the northern part of the Scandinavian peninsula, Oman in Arabia, and Makran, the Iranian province nearest India. None of these has much to contribute to our story, being desolate, scantily inhabited places. The good fit is, of course, a function of the cartography: the projection has been chosen to make the best use of the space available.

Its only disadvantage is that whereas north, south, east and west are in the expected directions on the left-hand side of the base map, east starts lifting up from 3 o'clock towards 1 o'clock as you move towards the right. The lines of latitude and longitude that define the projection and create this effect are shown on the index map at the end of the book.

Figure 2 also shows the world as perceived in the west in the fourth century AD, when the sequence of maps begins. Almost nothing was known about Russia north of the steppe, and even the doyen of classical geographers, Claudius Ptolemy, thought Scandinavia was an island. On the other hand, he and his colleagues knew about the existence of the Canaries, which had been visited at the beginning of the Christian era, though not subsequently. They also knew a little more of Nubia than appears on the base map. About the east coast of Africa they were well informed: Arab traders regularly sailed as far as Zanzibar, returning with ivory and stories about the 'fountains of the Nile', which, whether truly inspired or just plain lucky, turned out to be surprisingly accurate. As to the Asian land mass, the extent (though not the shape) of India was correctly understood and there was outline knowledge of both Sri Lanka and the Malay peninsula. China was only dimly perceived, and, despite the fact that caravans had been travelling the Silk Road for more than 300 years, there was very little detail to the Roman map of inner Asia. There is no mention of Lake Balkhash in any classical source and considerable uncertainty about the separate nature of the Aral and Caspian seas.

We have now defined our board: let us look at the players. These constitute an almost endless list of political and religious groupings: tribes, empires, nation states, merchant principalities, nomadic herdsmen, peasant farmers, theocracies, feudal fiefs and personal hegemonies. The trick is to impose some order on them. In the last century and for much of this the preferred option would have been to group them according to race, Nordic versus Mediterranean for example, and there is still a certain attraction to the idea. After all, the major discontinuities in population that correspond to the boundaries of the Europe–Near East area mark the divisions between

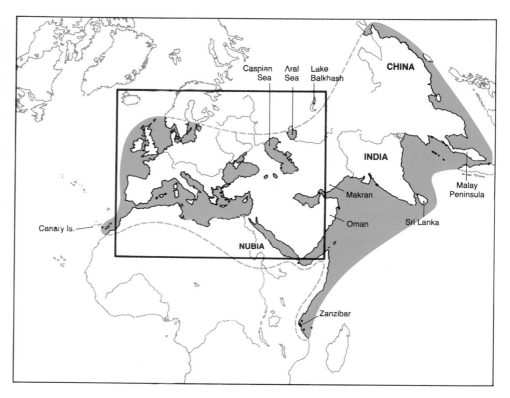

FIGURE 2 *The base map used in the atlas (black rectangle) and, in blue, the perimeter of the known world in AD 362.*

the major races of mankind, so why shouldn't the minor divisions within the area correspond to sub-racial distinctions along the lines of Nordics, Mediterraneans, and so on. The answer is that the only physical criterion for sub-racial distinctions, the determination of gene frequencies, leads to boundaries so fuzzy as to be almost useless. There just isn't the amount of physical difference between Germans and Italians, say, that the mind's eye picture of the typical German and the typical Italian would lead us to expect. In fact, the picture itself is phoney, being generated by images of the extreme, not the average. It would be a very difficult business indeed to sort 100

mixed Berliners and Venetians into different boxes if they weren't allowed to talk.

For speech is, of course, the necessary clue. Not only does it play an important role in the creation and maintenance of social units, it yields clear data about the place of each society in the evolutionary stream. As Dr Johnson said, 'languages are the pedigree of nations', and even in the medieval period, where information is often less complete than we would like, we can unravel the pedigree with very few uncertainties.

The essentials for classification used in the atlas are shown on Figure 3, which allocates a characteristic

3

shading or border to each of the major languages, with modifications appropriate to their historical development. Take the large circles first. They represent the linguistic groups visible on the first map in the atlas, dated AD 362. Most of them belong to the Indo-European family. Ranged across northern Europe are the Celts (vertically lined), the Teutons (with a border of dots) and the Balts and Slavs (diagonally lined in opposite senses). Below them are the two major languages of the Roman Empire, Latin and Greek, both left unshaded. In the east, the Iranian language group is horizontally lined, with Persian, the dominant speech in Iran itself, given a wider ruling than the outliers in the Caucasus (Alan) and Transoxiana (Kushan). Of the non-Indo-European languages, Finnish gets a grey tint, while Mongol and Turkic, which are closely related, have a border of small circles, open in the Mongol case, solid in the Turkic. Arabs and Berbers form another pair, not so closely related as Turks and Mongols but, like them, sharing social as well as linguistic traits: they are crosshatched, with the Berbers having the closer mesh. Three relatively minor peoples are represented by middle-size circles: the Armenians, Indo-European speakers whose language is distantly related to Greek, the Basques (whose first appearance is delayed till AD 476) and the Georgians. The last two are relicts of Europe's pre-Indo-European population, possibly related to each other, certainly not related to anyone else. All three are left unshaded.

This initial system of classification sees us through the first two sections of the atlas. Then, with the creation of the Frankish Empire, we have a chance to recast the conventions in a way that better serves the four remaining sections. The new languages that emerged during this period are displayed as ellipses on Figure 3. The ones that immediately concern us are English and German, both derived from the Teutonic stem, and French, Italian and Spanish, all evolved from Latin and hence known as Romance languages. These became the core languages of western Christendom, the social unit that is the main focus of interest in the later medieval period. All are left plain, which means that the dots that previously distinguished the Teutonic stock are now confined to one part of it, Scandinavia. As the Scandinavians were still playing up to the old Teutonic image and frightening the wits out of their Christian brethren in England and elsewhere, there is a rough justice to this. However, it does mean that in this section we are exchanging a purely linguistic classification for one which takes social factors into account. Another example of the same thing is the marking used for Magyar, the language of a Finnish tribe that moved on to the steppe and adopted the Turkic lifestyle. So long as the Magyars hold to this way of life they are given a border of circles (indicating their status as nomads) with a grey infilling (indicating their Finnish language). But once they move to Hungary and establish a settled kingdom, they exchange this special border for a simple outline and an overall tint. Similar, largely self-explanatory changes are made in the Turkic convention. Clans too small to be given a border of circles are shown as a single circle, flagged for attention. Settled states, like the Ottoman, are given an outline with half circles attached to it.

The new languages that appear from time to time in the remainder of the atlas are fitted into one or other of these systems. As from AD 1000, Russian is distinguished from the other Slav languages by a dashed version of the Slav diagonal shading. Kurdish states, which first appear on the same map, have the closer ruled version of the Iranian shading. Romanian and Albanian, two languages that appeared in the Balkans in the fourteenth century, are left plain. Romanian, derived from the Latin spoken by the Roman colonists of the region, belongs with the other Romance languages. Albanian has independent status within the Indo-European group: its probable ancestor is the Illyrian tongue spoken by the pre-Roman population. As to the cartographic conventions that cut across the linguistic classification, the most important is the use of a dotted border for the crusader states both in the Levant and in the Baltic. This is a conscious echo of the Teutonic *Völkerwanderung* but must not be taken to imply that the majority of the crusaders spoke Teutonic languages. In the Baltic they did, but in the Levant the dominant language – and culture – was French.[1]

As to the more usual conventions, it is perhaps

FIGURE 3 *Key to the system of shadings used in the atlas.*

1. Though there is no doubt about the status of Romanian, there is considerable controversy about its origins. Present-day Romanians claim to be the descendants of the Latin-speaking colonists planted in Dacia (modern Transylvania) in the first century AD. The problem with this idea is that there is no evidence for the survival of these colonies in the ten centuries between the overthrow of the Roman province in AD 270 and the first mention of Vlachs (Romance speakers) in Romania in AD 1230. Most people think that a more plausible origin for the Romanians lies in the Latin-speaking population south of the Danube, where Roman institutions struck deeper roots and survived for much longer. On this reconstruction, the Vlachs only moved into present-day Romania in the thirteenth century, when the nomads' grip on the region began to slacken.

Worth emphasizing in this connection is the fact that though the system of shadings used in the atlas distinguishes one language from another, it is not a reliable guide to the relationships between them. Not only is Romanian not related to Albanian, but Latin is not a close relative of Greek: it is much nearer to Celtic. Similarly, Kurdish is closer to Persian than it is to Alan.

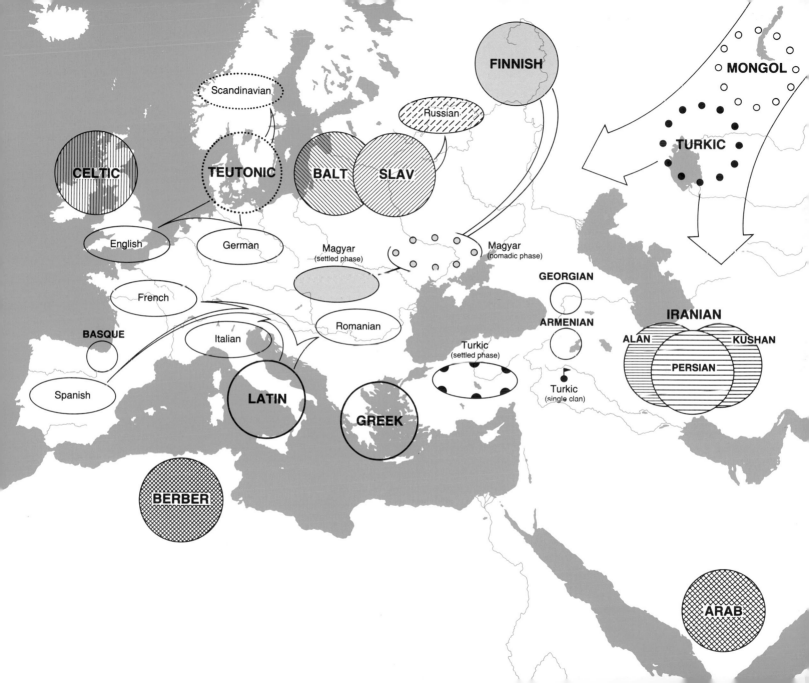

worth making a few points about their use in this atlas. Arrows nearly always mean migrations, not raids, i.e., what is moving is not just an army but a people. An exception to this rule is made for the Mongol campaigns of the thirteenth century, but this is made plain by the accompanying narrative and the use of a different sort of arrow. Towns are rarely shown on the political maps. Those that do appear meet one of two criteria: they are either sovereign political units (as Naples and Amalfi were in the eleventh century) or they have overseas political dependencies (as is the case with Pisa in the thirteenth century and Genoa in the fourteenth). Venice, of course, makes it on both counts. Size, however, is nothing to do with it, nor local self-government. The many important places in the German Empire that habitually looked after their own affairs and paid heed to the Imperial authorities only when they had to, are not featured on the political maps (if them, why not the Counts and Dukes who were equally independent minded?). Nor are such famous Italian cities as Milan and Florence, despite the fact that their revenues were greater than those of many sovereign states. Where these places will be found is on the half dozen maps that have towns (and trade routes) as their topic. On these the sole criterion is size. The towns are grouped in three categories: modest (populations in the range 15,000–22,000), medium (23,000–49,000) and large (50,000–125,000). I have used this system in preference to one of continuous grading by circle size because it is easier for the eye to take in and also because I believe that cities do pass from one category to another in a qualitative sense. Of course, the question begged is the one about how the population figures are obtained in the first place. I have published, with Richard Jones, an *Atlas of World Population History* (Penguin, 1978), which gives the sources for the overall population figures used in this book, and one day we hope to find a publishable format for the city database that we've compiled. In the interim you'll have to take the figures on trust, though if you feel anxious about them you should be able to get some reassurance from the standard authors on the subject.[2]

If these rules seem complicated, the reasoning behind them is simple: historical maps work best when they deal with one topic at a time. Hence the division between the maps in the main sequence, which show political units, and the maps which cover Christendom, towns and trade routes, and population. By the same token, none of the maps contains more than the minimum amount of geography, just a coastline and sufficient rivers and lakes to enable you to find your way around inside the main land mass. Such physical features as mountains and deserts, which govern the distribution of population and give nations their shape, have to be added by the reader's eye. It is important, then, to take the essentials of the physical geography on board at this stage. This, as the map opposite demonstrates, is not too hard a task. The zone of continuous population is confined to the area between the band of conifer forest occupying the north of Europe and the upper limit of the desert stretching across Africa and Arabia. Within this region are three separate worlds. The first is the area of crop land that constitutes the heart of Europe. Basically it consists of France, with Britain as an outlier; Germany, including the Low Countries and Denmark; and Poland and the core provinces of European Russia. Boxed off by mountains, but forming part of the same system, are northern Italy (between the Alps and the Apennines) and Bohemia (as outlined by the Böhmerwald, the Ore Mountains [Erzgebirge] and the Sudeten highlands). Hungary, defined on north and east by the arc of the Carpathians, is a borderland: in medieval times it was as often as not part of the nomads' domain.

This domain, the second of our three worlds, dominates the right-hand side of the map. Its essential element is the steppe, in the medieval period the habitat of Huns, Turks and Mongols. These nomadic herdsmen guided their flocks from one pasture to another within a grassland corridor that runs the length of Asia, enters Europe through the gap between the Urals and the Caspian, and then expands to take in all of south Russia and some of Hungary.

The third of the worlds we have to consider is made up of the countries bordering the Mediterranean. The south of Italy is the centre point of this ecosystem, which stretches from Spain to the Levant, lapping

2. Russell, J. C., *Medieval Regions and their Cities* (Bloomington, Ind., 1972), and *Late Ancient and Medieval Population*, Transactions of the American Philosophical Society, Vol. 43, No. 3 (Philadelphia, 1958). Beloch, K. J., *Bevölkerungsgeschichte Italiens*, 3 vols. (Berlin, 1937, 1939, 1961). Also, for the final map, De Vries, Jan, *European Urbanisation 1500–1800*, (London, 1984).

I don't myself believe that any town in the period covered by the towns and trade route maps (AD 528–1483) had a population of more than 125,000. If there is an exception the best bet would be fifteenth-century Cairo, which must have been at or near this limit. Rome in the late antique period was much bigger, but the rate of its decline (from 250,000 in the early fourth century to 125,000 in the early fifth) would have brought it into the medieval range well before AD 528.

FIGURE 4 *Physical features and land use.*

The map simplifies both. In the early Medieval period a great part of what is shown as crop land was wooded, and much remained so even after the clearances of the tenth–fourteenth centuries. The plateaus are schematic; the mountains of the desert zone and the oases at which its scanty populations collected have been omitted altogether.

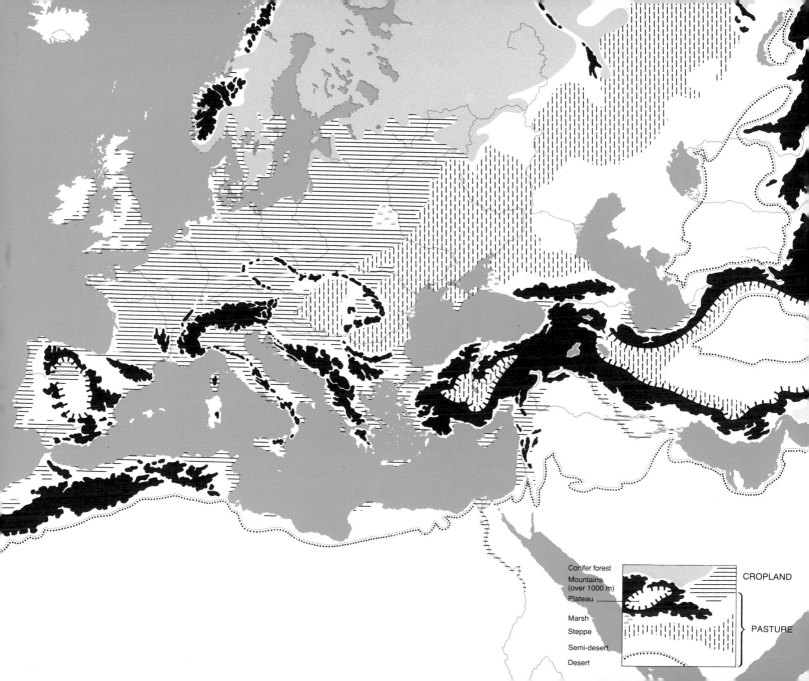

Conifer forest
Mountains (over 1000 m)
Plateau
Marsh
Steppe
Semi-desert
Desert

CROPLAND

PASTURE

over into the Atlantic in the case of Spain and Morocco, and to the Persian Gulf in the case of Iraq. It contains a mixture of crop-lands and pasture, often broken up into penny packets by mountain ranges that drop abruptly into the sea or by arid stretches where the only husbandry possible is that of the goat-herd. Egypt, attached to the southern edge of the zone, is a special case, a desert country brought to life by the Nile, the sole river to cross the Sahara. In the east, this world extends as far as the Iranian plateau, which contains stretches of steppe of interest to the Central Asian nomads and often occupied by them. From Azerbaijan, at the western end of the plateau, the nomads could easily move on to Ana-tolia, where there was equally attractive pasture on the central plain. Anatolia thus came to play the same borderland role between settled and nomadic worlds in Asia as Hungary did in Europe.

*

The starting and finishing posts for the medieval era are conventionally taken as the reign of Constantine the Great (the beginning of the fourth century AD) and the Voyages of Discovery (the end of the fifteenth century). This is almost exactly the same period that Gibbon covered in his *Decline and Fall of the Roman Empire*, and the questions posed by his narrative must be important to us. Why did the civilized world, which had triumphed over the barbarians in the centuries before Christ, start to contract not long after the Christian era began? Why did the Western Empire fall and why was the Eastern Empire able to survive for a further ten centuries? Did the end of the Western Empire matter to anyone except the tiny minority who formed its ruling caste? Were the Dark Ages really so dark? And had the high noon of empire really been so beneficent?

On the last question Gibbon had no doubts. As he put it, 'If a man were called to fix the period in the history of the world during which the condition of the human race was most happy and prosperous, he would, without hesitation, name that which elapsed from the death of Domitian to the accession of Com-modus.' For 'human race' substitute 'Mediterranean world', and for the regnal dates, which are not at everyone's fingertips these days, 'the second century AD', and you have a proposition that many histori-ans would still be willing to defend. The frontiers were secure, the civil order largely unchallenged, and the people free to pursue the arts of peace. There were black spots: the institution of slavery, a scarcely bearable social ill, though one that was perhaps less widespread than is generally thought, and the unhappy circumstances of Egypt, which the Romans always regarded as a country to plunder rather than a province to administer, and of Palestine, where the Jews refused to Romanize and suffered for it. But by and large the *pax Romana* worked. And the scale of it has to be impressive. The Empire encompassed an area that now requires the services of thirty-two separate governments (thirty-three if you count Cyprus twice). It contained a quarter of mankind, and the most literate and sophisticated quarter at that. And it was prudent about its defences, maintaining an army of a third of a million men even though no enemy in sight could muster a tenth of that number. It seems extraordinary that, a bare seventy years after the end of Gibbon's golden age, the Imperial system was to find itself in desperate trouble and that a second crisis a hundred years later would bring the western half, and Rome itself, to ruin.

With hindsight it is easy to see that the Western Empire was never as secure as it seemed. The rural folk who made up the bulk of its population had no need of the urban constructs that had evolved in Italy and the Hellenistic east: the cities, the seeds of the Empire's civilizing mission, withered away as soon as the winds blew cold, and most of them were deserted long before the barbarians put them to the torch. More to the point, the fiscal situation was always touch-and-go. A revenue failure underlay the hyper-inflation that made the third-century crisis so danger-ous, and the early fifth century generalissimo Stilicho was out of funds while he was still winning his battles – after one victory he had to strip the gold from Rome's most venerable temple to pay his troops. But if there is a single specific answer to the question of why Rome fell when it did, it has to be military. The legionaries were outclassed by the barbarians on the field of battle, which meant that the Empire had to look for the guards it needed among the very people who were bent on plundering it. The coincidence of the medieval period is not just with Gibbon's *Decline and Fall* but equally with Oman's 'Age of Cavalry'.

Why didn't the same forces bring down the eastern half of the Empire? Well, in the end they did, but the East was richer, could pay larger ransoms and hire larger armies. It had always been richer in the sense that its resources were more easily harvested by the central government, and once it had a central govern-ment of its own, which it acquired with the division of the Empire and the building of Constantinople, it was able to buy its way out of the troubles that felled the West. But its military capabilities were limited: the ranks of its armies were filled out with barbarians, and though it managed some considerable recoveries – restabilizations is perhaps a better word – after the first in-rushes of the Germans and Arabs, Bulgars and Turks, it was never able to measure up to the requirements of the Cavalry Age. Peasant societies don't readily produce armies of mounted men.

None the less, for all its contracting perimeter, the Eastern Empire must have seemed much the best place to be during the early medieval centuries. Pay no attention to recent attempts to play down the ter-rors and insecurities of the Dark Ages: they might have been fun for the bully boys, but for the vast majority of ordinary folk they were a disaster. Western society was brutalized and impoverished: intellectual life was stunted and many of the skills essential to civilization were lost. The only buildings with any pretensions to architecture were cobbled together from the ruins of classical structures. Such records as were attempted serve mainly to betray the dwindling horizons and rising superstition of the time. We don't know as much as we would like to about what went on during these centuries, but most of what we do know is bad.

From a low point that, it is now generally agreed, coincided with the reign of Charlemagne, the west gradually clawed its way back up to the light. It even managed to produce an answer to the problem of how to raise a cavalry force from a peasant society, the feudal system. The nomads were top of the class when it came to mounted warfare because they spent their lives in the saddle; feudal Europe developed a caste of landowners who devoted themselves just as whole-heartedly to the culture of the war-horse. For several centuries much of the wealth of the west was used to mount, equip and train the ruling classes so that they could function as heavy cavalry in the battles of the day. The preoccupation outlived the role's utility. Heraldic designs that identified the knight on the battlefield became the insignia of his social rank. The behaviour considered appropriate to his position was defined as chivalrous and made the subject of perhaps the most tedious of all literatures.

The creation of a class of horse junkies was not one of the most important aspects of the revival of the west. It was, however, something that the Chinese never managed to achieve, despite the fact that they faced an identical problem. Huns, Turks and Mongols harried China relentlessly, and on several occasions in the early medieval period succeeded in conquering the northern half of the country. Finally, in the thirteenth century, the Mongols overran the whole of it, adding a Genghizkhanid lineage, the Yuan, to the list of dynasties that have ruled China. Yet the best the Chinese could do to defend themselves from these onslaughts was to try to bribe the nearer tribes to fight for them or, failing that, to fight against each other.

Of course, in one way the Chinese did much better than either Rome or Byzantium: they always expelled or absorbed their conquerors and re-established their traditional empire. Because of its size, its geographical simplicity and its cultural homogeneity, China proved to be an unsinkable unit: the 50,000 villages of the Chinese Empire formed a single, self-repairing network, and there was never a chance that any piece of it would break off for long enough to develop a separate identity. Just the opposite is true of Rome. The Empire of the Caesars represented a summation of half a dozen different polities, each with its own language, history, culture and aspirations. For a moment in time, which roughly corresponds to the period when Italy was the most populous member of this group, Rome was able to bring them all under a single rule. But the unifying culture was imposed, not inherent: the Celts, Phoenicians, Egyptians, Berbers and Greeks had their own customs and their own gods; giving them Roman names was never more than window-dressing. Moreover, the demographic centre of gravity had not stopped permanently in Italy: it had merely rested there for a few centuries during its westward progression from the Near East via Greece and Rome to the Rhine. When it moved on, the Mediterranean world came apart, the northern shore adhering to western Europe, the southern shore to the Levant.

Voltaire, asked to explain Rome's fall, said 'it fell because all things fall'. This isn't as unhelpful as it sounds. On the long view, what has to be explained is not that the Empire fell apart, but why the bits never came together again. And the answer, as we have seen, is that the world on which it was built was breaking up. Continental Europe detached itself from the old order and developed an ethos of its own, while the Arabs created a new culture for the Near East and North African littoral. What survived of the Mediterranean polity – Spain, southern Italy, the Balkans and Anatolia – became a battleground between these two. The theme of the medieval centuries is not the decline and fall of the Roman Empire but the emergence of Islam and western Christendom.

It is a better theme than Gibbon's. For a westerner it is the supreme story of defeat turned into victory, but it is also much richer than that. It is a marvellous catalogue of vices and follies, cunning and credulity, greed, ambition and achievement. Plus a cast of thousands. Don't miss it.

Augustus, the first Roman Emperor (27 BC–AD 14), gave the Empire the simple frontiers it needed: a line of fortified posts along the Rhine and Danube to protect the European provinces, another running from the highlands of Armenia to the Red Sea to defend Roman Asia, and a third paralleling the edge of the Sahara and enclosing all the worthwhile bits of North Africa. Initially he had been more ambitious, dispatching expeditions up the Nile to Nubia and into Arabia as far as the Yemen, to see if these places would make useful additions to the Empire. It quickly became clear that they would not. He also attempted the conquest of Germany, a project that would have eliminated an important enemy and shortened the defensive line in Europe. However, the Germans weren't having it, and after losing three legions Augustus pulled back. Convinced now that there would be more pain than profit in further expansion, he advised his successors against enlarging the Empire in any direction.

On the whole they followed his advice. An exception was made in the case of Britain, the last bastion of a Celtic world that had once stretched from Spain to central Europe. Its conquest, complete except for the fringe territories of Ireland and Scotland, almost eliminated the Celts from the map. The Germans, by contrast, remained very much in evidence. The Romans did acquire a few territories on the far side of the Rhine and Danube, only to lose them again by the date of this map. However, if the Roman strategy in this theatre was essentially defensive, no one could call it unsuccessful. Despite increasing pressure from the fast-multiplying Germans, the frontier line was held. The German tribes had to turn east for their *Lebensraum*.

This advance, the first in a series of German 'drives to the east', got under way in the second century AD. Moving parallel to the Danube, the Germans occupied all the lands between Germany proper and the Black Sea; they then spread across the south of Russia, which became the stamping ground of the Goths, an offshoot of the Getes of Sweden. By the date of this map the Goths had split into two groups, the Visigoths (West Goths), who occupied the terri-tory between the Danube and the Dniester, and the Ostrogoths (East Goths), who based themselves on the lands between the Dniester and Don. The Ostrogoths adopted the horse-riding lifestyle developed by the Iranian peoples of the steppe, becoming adept at the use of the lance: their prowess won them a vast empire that stretched back to their original homeland on the shores of the Baltic. Under King Ermanarich they also resumed their eastward drive, advancing across the Don towards the Caucasus and Volga. This brought them into conflict with the Alans, descendants of the Scyths (the original Iranian steppe-dwellers), and with the Huns, a Turkish people who had recently moved into this area from Central Asia.

The Goths were the strongest of the Germans and the most adventurous; in Germany itself there was no nation of comparable power. To a large extent this weakness was political. The tribes continually quarrelled among and within themselves: kings with real authority were exceptional and usually ephemeral. The Romans found the Frankish and Alemannian confederations the most troublesome; the tribes in the next tier were of less concern, although the Angles and Saxons made themselves felt by raiding the coasts of Britain and Gaul. Beyond the Germans were the Slavs, many of them under Ostrogothic control but others visible on this map to the north of the Ostrogothic perimeter. Beyond the Slavs lay the sparsely inhabited world of forest and tundra which was the domain of the Finns.

In the east the Romans faced, not a roster of barbarian tribes, but a single state comparable in many ways to their own. The Persian Empire was neither as large nor as populous as the Roman — a reasonable guess would be that it contained 5 or 6 million people as against Rome's 40 to 45 million – and in some senses it was less sophisticated, but it had its own style and religion, Mazdaism, and an imperial tradition that could be traced back as far as the sixth century BC. Proud and prickly, the Shahs of Persia felt honour-bound to challenge Rome's position in Asia whenever opportunity offered. In such endeavours they could count on the support of their eastern kin, the Kushans, who held sway over modern Afghanistan, much of Transoxiana and some of the north-western provinces of India. But for all their efforts the frontier never shifted much, and when it did it was usually in Rome's favour. Over the years the Romans had strengthened their grip on the north of Mesopotamia (the land between the Euphrates and Tigris, modern Iraq) as well as retaining their overlordship of the highland kingdoms of Lazica, Iberia and Armenia.

If the Empire had much the same perimeter in the mid fourth century as in the first, it was in a social sense a very different structure. It was dominated by the army, whose ranks now provided most of the emperors. It had been converted to Christianity. And it had been split into two, with separate administrations (and usually different emperors) for the Latin-speaking west and the Greek-speaking east. However, these last two statements require some back-pedalling as regards the year 362, when there was only one emperor and he had just declared himself a pagan.

The emperor in question was Julian, the sole surviving member of the Constantinian dynasty. A competent general, Julian had decisively defeated the last Franco-Alemannic invasion of France, though he allowed some of the Franks to settle in Belgium, retaining their tribal organization while acknowledging the supremacy of Rome (358). This formula (the term *foederatii* was later applied to such tribes) was to be used increasingly in the next fifty years, but Julian probably regarded it as a temporary expedient, necessary because first internal dissensions and then Persian attacks required his presence and army in the east.

AD **362**

LAPPS

FINNS

HUNS

KUSHAN
PRINCIPALITIES

Norse

Swedes

Getes

SLAVS

Picts

Jutes

BALTS

Irish

Angles

Danes

Ostrogoths

Frisians

Saxons

Lombards

Alans

Franks

Thur

Siling
Vandals

Rugians

Abasgians

K. OF
IBERIA

Bur

Marco-
manni

Quadi

K. OF LAZICA

Alemanni

Asding
Vandals

Gepids

Visigoths

K. OF
ARMENIA

PERSIAN
EMPIRE

ROMAN EMPIRE

BERBERS

ARABS

NUBIA

YEMEN

key
Bur   Burgundians
Thur   Thuringians

After a promising start, Julian's expedition against Persia turned into a disaster. He himself was killed, and to save the army his successor had to sign away the eastern half of Roman Mesopotamia and the over-lordship of Iberia and Armenia (364). The new frontier was to prove a lasting one, though the Romans found it difficult to stop interfering in Armenia. Eventually, in 387, the Persians gave them back the western fifth of the country in return for a clear title to the remainder. This sounds like a poor bargain, but the Romans accepted it with relief, for by then it was essential to have peace on the eastern frontier. Their misfortunes there were only a moon-cast shadow of what was taking place in Europe.

In 372, the eastward expansion of the Ostrogoths provoked an explosive reaction from the Huns of the Volga steppe. The Ostrogothic cavalry was humiliated by the faster-moving Huns, whose mounted archers destroyed every force Ermanarich sent against them. As his Empire crumbled away the Huns rolled forward to the Danube, crushing the Visigoths and enslaving the Gepids, who had the misfortune to occupy the Hungarian steppe. There the Huns settled down with their flocks, lords of a pasture that stretched back to the Caspian. In three years they had obliterated a century of German expansion.

While the Gepids remained where they were as vassals of the Huns, many of the Goths applied to the Roman Empire for sanctuary. The Romans allotted them lands along the Danube frontier, but acted so overbearingly that by 378 the Visigoths had broken out in revolt against their new masters. The Eastern Emperor marched his army to Adrianople, which the Visigoths had attacked but failed to take. The next day he moved against the Visigothic camp a dozen miles to the north. Either he didn't know there was a group of Ostrogoths in the vicinity or he didn't think it important: he set no guard either in the morning, which he wasted in fruitless negotiations, or in the afternoon, when he allowed his army to be drawn into an assault on the wagon line that protected the Visigothic encampment. No sooner was the Roman army fully committed than the Ostrogoths appeared on its flank. There was no time to face about before the Roman formations were driven in on each other by the charge of the mailed Ostrogothic lancers. In a few minutes what had been an army turned into a helpless press of men, unable either to flee or to fight. The Goths cut them down mercilessly. Among the dead were the Emperor and almost his entire staff.

The battle of Adrianople marks the end of the old Roman army. Seven centuries earlier the first legions had marched out against the Sabines in the hills above Rome: now the tread of the infantry that had conquered the Mediterranean world would be heard no more. Cavalry had demonstrated that it was the decisive arm, and, unable to generate sufficient cavalry units of native stock, the Romans were forced to hire Germans or Huns to fight their battles for them. Consequently, it was not long before barbarian generals were wielding considerable political power. In the fifth century the men standing closest to the Emperors were more often Vandals, Goths or Franks than native Romans.

While Adrianople was an unmitigated disaster for the Romans, it turned out to be not much of a victory for the Goths. For all their prowess on the field the Goths were hopeless at sieges, and if they couldn't take fortified towns they couldn't build on their success. A mixture of diplomacy and blockade proved sufficient to get them back to their allocated lands for a generation. Then, in 395, under their newly elected King Alaric, they broke out again. This time they only agreed to desist from their plundering expeditions when they were offered lands in Epirus (north-west Greece), a position from which they could advance on either half of the Empire. In 401 Alaric decided that the West was the better option. He led the Visigothic host to the north of Italy, where he was confronted by the West's generalissimo, Stilicho the Vandal.

Stilicho had a multitude of problems. Both economically and militarily the Empire was living from hand to mouth, with bands of Germans on the loose in the frontier provinces and a Roman army that was rapidly wasting away. If Stilicho could pay the price, most of the Germans were happy to enlist in his forces, but he hadn't enough money to hire all of them: it was a matter of paying some, bribing others to stay out of it, and facing down the rest. As always in warfare between mercenary armies, battles were few and rarely sanguinary. A series of skirmishes would lead to a parley and then both sides usually backed off. This year's opponents could be next year's allies, and all you were trying to do was improve your prospects.

Stilicho was adept at this combination of positional warfare and negotiation. By 402 he had bundled the Visigoths back into Illyria (modern Yugoslavia), and in 405 he defeated an equally formidable invasion mounted by a coalition of Ostrogoths, Quadi and Asding Vandals that descended on Italy from the north. However, to defend Italy he was forced to strip the Rhine frontier of troops. The next year saw the formation of the most intimidating combination yet. Probably stimulated by pressure from the Huns, entire tribes began moving westward parallel to the upper Danube. The major actors in this drama were the Marcomanni and Quadi (collectively known as Suevi) and the Asding and Siling Vandals, but the coalition included a clan of Alans displaced from the Caucasus. Its target was the now defenceless province of Gaul. On the last day of 406 the leading elements of this host crossed the frozen Rhine at Mainz.

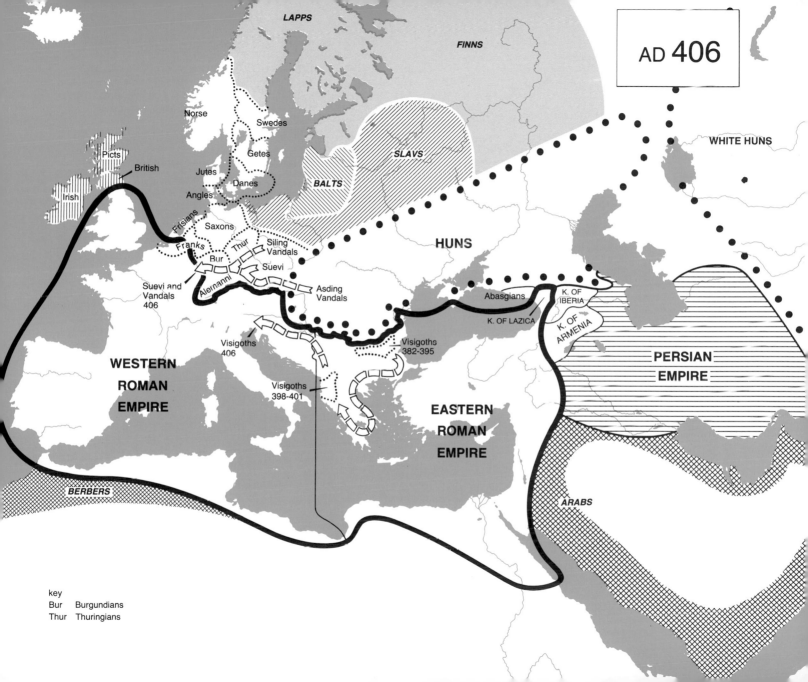

AD 406

LAPPS

FINNS

WHITE HUNS

Norse

Swedes

Getes

SLAVS

Jutes

Danes

BALTS

Picts

British

Angles

Irish

Frisians

Saxons

HUNS

Franks

Thur

Siling
Vandals

Bur

Suevi

Suevi and
Vandals
406

Alemanni

Asding
Vandals

Abasgians

K. OF
IBERIA

K. OF LAZICA

K. OF
ARMENIA

PERSIAN
EMPIRE

WESTERN
ROMAN
EMPIRE

Visigoths
406

Visigoths
382-395

Visigoths
398-401

EASTERN
ROMAN
EMPIRE

BERBERS

ARABS

key
Bur   Burgundians
Thur   Thuringians

There was no Roman army available to oppose the barbarian hordes that swarmed over Gaul in 407; the wretched provincials' only hope of deliverance lay in the garrison of Britain, which had revolted and set up an emperor of its own. This would-be champion of the Roman order did indeed cross the Channel with his troops, and ostensibly it was to pacify the province that Rome itself appeared to have abandoned, but, in reality, all he was interested in was seeking support for his usurped imperial title. He neither confronted the Alans, Vandals and Suevi as they completed their leisurely pillage of Gaul, nor contested the advances the Franks, Burgundians, and Alemanni had made on the left bank of the Rhine. In fact the only significant result of his bid for power was that Britain too was now ungoverned and undefended. In the end he was easily captured and executed by a Roman force that would have been better employed elsewhere (411), while Britain slipped out of the Roman orbit into Celtic anarchy. The Alans, Vandals and Suevi had meanwhile moved on to Spain where they battened on the lands in the south and west.

In 408 Stilicho was murdered on the orders of the Western Emperor Honorius, who had grown mistrustful of his ambition. Immediately, the Italian core of the Empire, for which so much had been sacrificed, was forfeit. Not that the Germans had any thought of destroying the Empire: it had existed for so long that everyone assumed it would go on forever. What the barbarian warlords wanted was imperial grants and commissions, lands for their followers and positions for themselves. First to state his price was King Alaric of the Visigoths, and now that Stilicho no longer stood guard over Italy he was able to present his demands at the gates of Rome.

Honorius was not too impressed by this. The western emperors hadn't resided at Rome for more than a hundred years: they were usually to be found at Milan, which the soldier emperors of the fourth century used as their headquarters. Honorius, who wasn't a fighting man, preferred Ravenna, which was ringed about with marshes and lagoons in a way which made it effectively impregnable. Alaric could hold

Rome to ransom if he wanted to, but Honorius wasn't going to let him step into Stilicho's shoes.

Alaric got his ransom: 5,000 lbs of gold, 30,000 lbs of silver, 4,000 garments of silk and 3,000 of fur, and 3,000 lbs of pepper. Then, as Honorius remained unmoved, he set up a puppet emperor. This didn't work either, so the Visigothic king marched on Rome again and put it to the sack. It wasn't a vicious affair as these things go – the Goths only spent three days in the city – and in practical terms it didn't alter the situation significantly. But, whether Pagan or Christian, the citizens of the Empire were dismayed by the news. The unthinkable had happened, and who could say what further disasters the future would bring?

Alaric tried to make amends. If he was going to rule Rome he had to guarantee its food supply, which meant obtaining control of the grain-growing lands in Africa. He led his army to the toe of Italy but, lacking a fleet, couldn't manage the crossing to Sicily, let alone Africa. Thwarted, he turned back, perhaps intending to confiscate the necessary shipping from the seaports on his line of march. But with the journey barely begun, he fell ill and died. Legend has it that he and his treasure lie beneath the River Busento, which his retainers diverted for the purpose, but since much of the bed of the Busento is exposed throughout the year this seems an unlikely tale.

Alaric's successor, his brother-in-law Athaulf, was no more successful than Alaric in his efforts to wring a settlement from Honorius. He finally abandoned Italy in favour of southern Gaul, where he tried to legitimize the Visigothic regime by forcibly marrying the Emperor's sister, captured during the Italian campaign. At the wedding Athaulf spoke wistfully of his desire to see Roman and Goth live together in harmony, Gothic sword defending Roman law, but Honorius was implacable, and the Visigoths, starved of supplies, had to move on again. They went to Spain where, after another abortive attempt to reach Africa, they finally signed up as Roman *foederatii*. In return for clearing Spain of Rome's enemies they would get lands in Gaul.

This bargain was honoured by both sides. The Visigoths broke up the Siling Vandal and Alan settlements before leaving for Gaul: the fact that the

Asding Vandals and Suevi were left in possession of the north-west doesn't seem to have perturbed the Romans, who were eager to see the Visigoths reach the territory allocated to them. In a sense the whole saga was a success for the Romans, who, without fighting a battle, had managed to achieve a technically acceptable solution of the problem posed by the Visigothic invasion. The reality was different. The Goths now had a kingdom that was independent in every way that mattered. And their marches and countermarches had shown the world that the Roman state could no longer protect the lives and property of its citizens.

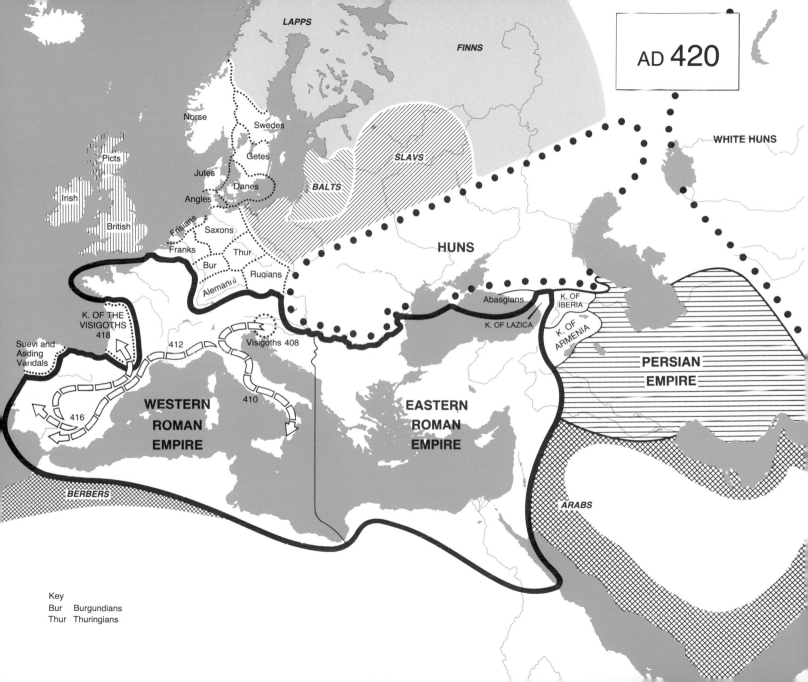

LAPPS

FINNS

AD 420

WHITE HUNS

Norse

Swedes

Getes

SLAVS

Picts

Jutes

BALTS

Irish

Danes

British

Angles

Frisians

Saxons

Franks

Thur

HUNS

Bur

Alemanii

Ruqians

Abasgians

K. OF
IBERIA

K. OF THE
VISIGOTHS
418

K. OF LAZICA

K. OF
ARMENIA

PERSIAN
EMPIRE

Suevi and
Asding
Vandals

412

Visigoths 408

416

410

WESTERN
ROMAN
EMPIRE

EASTERN
ROMAN
EMPIRE

BERBERS

ARABS

Key
Bur   Burgundians
Thur   Thuringians

For fifty years after their advance to the Danube, the Huns were remarkably quiet: raiding parties appeared occasionally in Germany and the Balkans, and some clans hired themselves out to the Romans from time to time, but essentially the tribes kept to the pastures they had won in the 370s. All this changed when Attila became king. First he united the different Hun tribes under his rule (433–44), then he instituted a policy of annual plundering expeditions. It was difficult enough to tell where he would strike next; putting together an army that could stop him – remember that he had two of the most formidable German tribes, the Ostrogoths and Gepids, riding in his train – was almost impossible.

Initially Attila concentrated on the Eastern Empire. He soon forced it to its knees and then made sure it stayed there by obtaining the surrender of the frontier zone on the right bank of the Danube. Deprived of its defences, the Empire had no option but to pay a tribute that eventually rose to 2,100 lbs of gold a year.

Attila then turned west. He had already raided as far as the Rhine, where, in 436, he inflicted such a devastating defeat on the Burgundians that they abandoned their capital, Worms, and didn't stop running till they reached Savoy. (The memory of this catastrophe forms the culminating episode in the lay of the Niebelungen, the most famous of German epics.) Now he tightened his grip on the west German tribes: the Alemanni, the Franks of the Rhine valley, and the Thuringians. Then in 451 he invaded Gaul.

Although the dwindling regiments of the Western Empire could not be expected to mount a successful defence against Attila on their own, the western generalissimo Aetius managed to put together a coalition that was capable of making a stand. The backbone of the army was provided by the Visigoths. Other contingents were supplied by the Burgundians of Savoy and the Franks of north-east Gaul, while Aetius contributed such troops as still remained in Roman service. On the approach of the allied force, Attila fell back from Orleans, the westernmost point reached by any of the Altaian conquerors, and the two sides met at the Campus Mauriacus in the valley of the Seine.

The fight was hard but inconclusive. Attila failed to draw the wary allied troops from their line of battle, and neither the Huns nor their German confederates were able to drive them out of it. The Visigothic king was killed – it was said by an Ostrogothic lance – but his men stood firm. For the first time in his career Attila had been checked. Aetius, 'the last of the Romans', had saved Gaul from the sort of devastation inflicted on the Balkans.

Attila probably didn't take his setback too seriously, for the next year he made a successful foray into northern Italy. However, the battle of the Campus Mauriacus did mark a watershed of sorts, for in the winter of 452–3 the Hun king died, and the Empire he passed on to his too-numerous sons was destroyed by a German revolt. Led by the Gepids, the Germans crushed their overlords at the battle of the river Nedao (454: somewhere in Hungary but the exact site is unknown).

While the Mediterranean world had been preoccupied with the threat from the north, another enemy penetrated to its heart. The Asding Vandals emerged from the north-western corner of Spain, picked up such remnants of the Siling Vandals and Alans as remained in the south and, in 429, crossed to North Africa. Their King Gaiseric had his followers counted at the embarkation point, presumably to see how much shipping was needed; the total of men, women and children came to 80,000, which can probably be taken as a representative figure for a migrating tribe of the period. The Vandal expedition was a success: the Romans ceded the western provinces to Gaiseric in 435, and then, in 442, allowed him to exchange them for the much more important central zone equivalent to modern Tunisia.

Gaiseric's advance was achieved by a mixture of factional alliances (the shipping for the expedition was supplied by a prefect of Africa temporarily in revolt against Rome), aggressive warfare (he seized Carthage in 439) and blackmail (the Romans wanted at all costs to maintain the supply of grain to the city of Rome). It ended with him ensconced in the West's second city, master of the western Mediterranean's most important fleet and of its sole reliable source of surplus wheat.

Britain, forgotten by Rome, was raided by almost everyone else – Picts, Irish, Angles, Saxons, Jutes and Frisians. The Jutes even began a permanent settlement in the south-east (449). It is possible that they were encouraged to do so by pressure from the Danes, who were edging into Jutland at about this time; alternatively, the Danes may simply have moved in after the Jutes had left.

The Persian Empire had so far escaped the sort of problems that had brought the Romans low. A few Hun incursions via the Caucasus are recorded, but there was no sustained assault from the Russian steppe and no invasion of migrating peoples. However, in the 440s movements among the tribes of Central Asia brought a new group, the White Huns, into Transoxiana. The Kushans retreated into Afghanistan, leaving the eastern provinces of the Persian Empire exposed to the attentions of the newcomers.

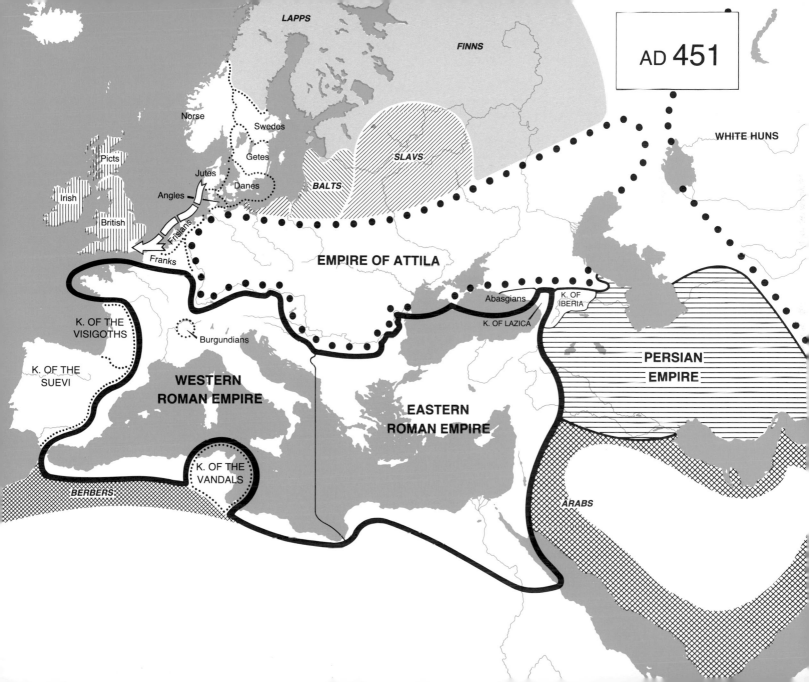

AD 451

LAPPS

FINNS

WHITE HUNS

Norse

Swedes

Getes

Jutes

Angles

Danes

Picts

Irish

British

Frisians

Franks

SLAVS

BALTS

EMPIRE OF ATTILA

Abasgians

K. OF
IBERIA

K. OF LAZICA

PERSIAN
EMPIRE

K. OF THE
VISIGOTHS

Burgundians

K. OF THE
SUEVI

WESTERN
ROMAN EMPIRE

EASTERN
ROMAN EMPIRE

K. OF THE
VANDALS

BERBERS

ARABS

After the disaster at the Nedao, some of the Huns remained for a few years in Hungary, raiding the Eastern Empire. When they found that even this was beyond their strength, they followed their brethren who had returned to the Russian steppe (470). On the shores of the Sea of Azov, the two contingents, known as Kutrigurs and Utigurs, bickered over the sorry remnants of the Empire of Attila. Next to them, in the Crimea, a pocket of Ostrogoths survived as a memento of Ermanarich's equally vanished glory.

The collapse of Attila's empire enables us to get our first proper perspective on the Slavs. In earlier maps anything up to half of them have been hidden from view, unwilling tributaries of Ostrogoth or Hun. Here we can see their full range. This has been enhanced at its western end by the German movement into the Roman Empire, for whenever a German tribe decided to try its luck on the far side of the Roman frontier the Slavs edged forward into the vacant space. Slowly but steadily, ingloriously but persistently, the Slavs were enlarging their share of the continent.

By this time the German offensives had brought the western half of the Roman Empire to the point of extinction. Most active were the Visigoths who, in the 470s, pushed the boundaries of their Gallic kingdom out towards the Loire and Rhône. They also conquered all of Spain except for the parts held by the Suevi and the aboriginal and almost inaccessible Basques. As to the rest of Gaul, the Burgundians took the Rhône valley, while the Franks and Alemanni divided the north-east between them. That left the north-west of the country: most of it was held by a Roman patrician, Syagrius, the rest by British chieftains who had fled their troubled island and established themselves in what was subsequently to be known as Brittany, i.e. Little Britain.

While the Roman Empire in Gaul crumbled away piecemeal, the Italian centre was extinguished by a simple administrative act. In 476 the *de facto* ruler of the peninsula, a German general named Odoacer, decided to dispense with the puppet emperors toted round by his predecessors. By offering a formal, entirely meaningless submission to Constantinople he obtained the blessing of the eastern authorities. The puppet western emperor of the day, the poignantly named Romulus Augustulus, was duly dismissed, and Odoacer became King of Italy.[1]

Before the Western Empire lost the last of its land, it had lost its command of the sea. The fleet which the Vandal King Gaiseric had found in the harbour of Carthage enabled him to dominate the Mediterranean: he held its seaports to ransom and snatched its islands from the Romans' failing grasp. The Balearics, Corsica, Sardinia and Sicily were incorporated in the Vandal kingdom: annual raiding parties brought back the spoils of both West and East. The Vandal sack of Rome in 455 was far more thorough and business-like than Alaric's: among the plunder, it is said, was the famous seven-branched candlestick that Titus had seized at the sack of Jerusalem nearly 400 years previously. But Gaiseric steered clear of unprofitable confrontations, yielding all but a fraction of Sicily to Odoacer when pressed. And though his expeditions bruised Constantinople's interests they did not fundamentally harm it. The Germans who worried the Eastern Empire most were the Ostrogoths, who invaded the Balkans in 475 and then reoccupied the old Visigothic settlement area along the lower Danube.

1. Romulus Augustulus is usually billed as the last emperor of the West, but technically that title belongs to a previous puppet, Julius Nepos, who had escaped to Dalmatia and whose authority was recognized there until his death in 480.

Officially, the extinction of the western half restored the unity of the Empire, but it is useful to retain the term Eastern Roman Empire as a reminder of the many differences between the classical Empire of Rome and the later Empire of Constantinople.

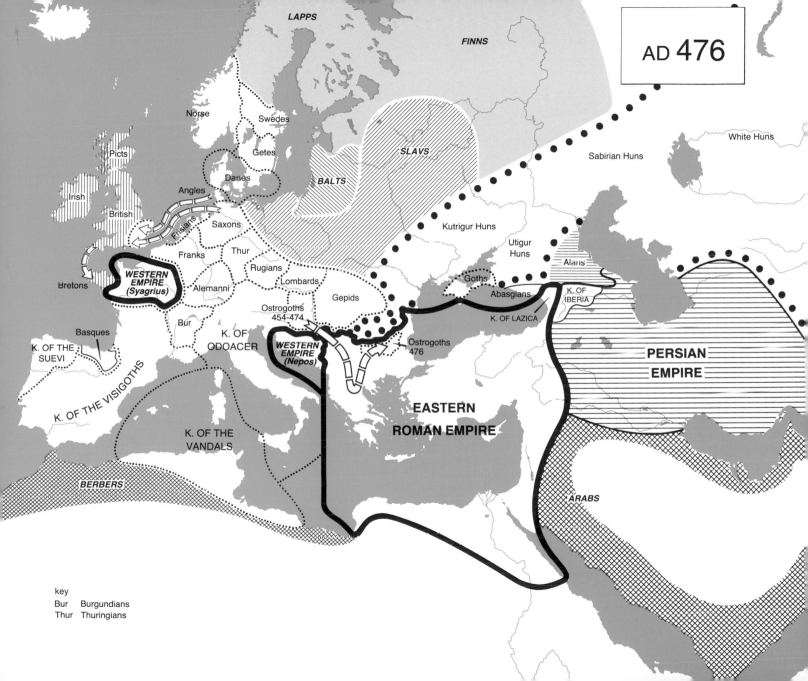

AD 476

LAPPS

FINNS

Norse

Swedes

Picts

Getes

Irish

Danes

British

Angles

Frisians

Saxons

SLAVS

BALTS

Sabirian Huns

White Huns

Kutrigur Huns

Utigur Huns

Alans

Bretons

Franks

Thur

Rugians

Lombards

Goths

Abasgians

K. OF
IBERIA

Alemanni

Gepids

K. OF LAZICA

WESTERN
EMPIRE
(Syagrius)

Basques

Bur

Ostrogoths
454-474

K. OF
ODOACER

WESTERN
EMPIRE
(Nepos)

Ostrogoths
476

PERSIAN
EMPIRE

K. OF THE
SUEVI

K. OF THE VISIGOTHS

EASTERN
ROMAN EMPIRE

K. OF THE
VANDALS

BERBERS

ARABS

key
Bur   Burgundians
Thur   Thuringians

King Odoacer of Italy proved a vigorous ruler. He annexed Dalmatia on the death of Nepos (480), and when the Rugians crossed the Danube from Bohemia he defeated them so crushingly that they vanish from history (487: their place in Bohemia was taken by a confederacy of Suevic remnants, the Bavarians). But, though these victories of Odoacer were welcomed by the Italian provincials whose security they sustained, they were poorly received at Constantinople: the East Romans had no wish to see an already powerful German state extend its frontiers still further. Too weak to challenge Odoacer themselves, they found a willing tool in Theodoric the Ostrogoth. It was a smart move: whether Theodoric won or lost, the Roman Empire would be rid of one unruly set of *foederatii*. In the event it was Odoacer who lost. After a hard-fought war and some judicious treachery, Theodoric emerged the master of an enlarged Italian Kingdom (493). The new Gothic power was established just in time to prevent the collapse of the old.

By assassinating some of his rivals and executing the remainder for their share in such wrongdoing, Clovis of Tournai made himself sole King of the Franks. He also greatly enlarged the Frankish domain. In 486 he drove Syagrius from the Roman quarter of Gaul and incorporated this territory in his kingdom. In 496 and again in 505 he defeated the Alemanni and forced them to submit to Frankish rule. Finally, at the Battle of Vouillé, he crushed the Visigoths (507). The Visigothic King was among the slain, and the Franks took over nearly all the Visigothic lands north of the Pyrenees.[1]

At this point Theodoric intervened. First he defeated the Burgundians, who had used the opportunity presented by the Visigoths' downfall to occupy the coastland east of the Rhône. This area, Provence, he annexed to the Ostrogothic state. Then he placed the matching province on the far side of the Rhône, Septimania, under his protection, thus preserving it for the Visigoths.

Clovis died in 511. That same year the demoralized Visigoths conferred the crown of the West Gothic realm on Theodoric. This created a Gothic empire of impressive dimensions, a solid block of territory running from Spain via Mediterranean France to Italy and Illyria. Certainly Gothic prestige had never been higher: it proved sufficient to make the Vandals give up their toe-hold in Sicily without argument. The contrast with the disunity of the Frankish kingdom, which Clovis had divided between his four sons, seemed particularly striking. But the reality was different. The two Gothic kingdoms remained entirely distinct, and in neither had the ruling class put down much in the way of roots. The Franks, on the other hand, were integrating successfully into Gallo-Roman society, and their sense of identity survived the dynastic partition. In fact the Frankish state wasn't really divided: it was regarded as a single realm ruled by four kings.

The Angles and Saxons were now well established in Britain. One consequence of this was that the part they held became known as Angle-land, ultimately England. They seem to have had little trouble displacing the Britons: the only check they suffered was at Mount Badon, somewhere in the south-west, some time around 490. This tiny event – it can't have been more than a skirmish – was later blown up into a major victory, one of a series said to have been won by a British hero named Arthur. And this was only the beginning: Celtic minstrels steadily reworked the story until they had an entirely imaginary King Arthur conquering all England and much of the Continent too.

In 484, while attempting to defend the eastern provinces from the annual inroads of the White Huns, the Persian king lost his life and his army. Iran lay open to the victors, who, in true nomad fashion, contented themselves with a measure of control and an immoderate tribute. Luckily, their attentions were increasingly directed to India, the gateway to which had been in their hands since their elimination of the Kushans of Afghanistan (*c.* 460). Persia breathed again, but softly.

1. At some stage Clovis received the homage of the Bretons, as the British of Brittany can now be called, but their attachment to the Frankish state proved purely nominal.

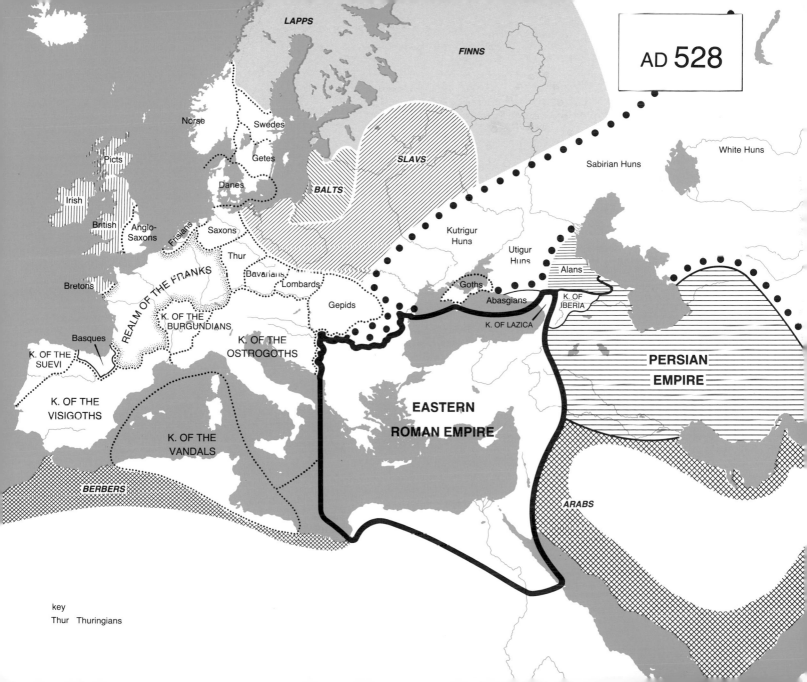

AD **528**

LAPPS

FINNS

White Huns

Norse

Swedes

Sabirian Huns

Getes

Picts

SLAVS

Irish

Danes

BALTS

British

Anglo-Saxons

Frisians

Saxons

Kutrigur Huns

Utigur Huns

Bretons

Thur

Alans

Bavarians

Lombards

Goths

Abasgians

K. OF IBERIA

REALM OF THE FRANKS

Gepids

K. OF LAZICA

Basques

K. OF THE BURGUNDIANS

K. OF THE OSTROGOTHS

PERSIAN EMPIRE

K. OF THE SUEVI

K. OF THE VISIGOTHS

EASTERN ROMAN EMPIRE

K. OF THE VANDALS

BERBERS

ARABS

key
Thur Thuringians

The fourth century saw the triumph of the Christian Church. At the century's start, Christians were still a persecuted minority; by its end, the idea that the Emperor might be other than a Christian had become unthinkable. Church and State had fused to form a new society, Christendom.

The sudden collapse of the old order is not really surprising. Paganism had never been more than a rag-bag of local cults and superstitions: it had few consistencies and no organization at all. By contrast, the Christian Church had a message that many people wanted to hear, and the means of delivering it round the Mediterranean world. In 303 there was a formal confrontation. The Roman authorities, renouncing their traditional tolerance, turned to the wheel and the rack; the Church replied by transforming these instruments of torture into symbols of faith, and the various remains they produced into holy relics. For eight long years the persecution continued: martyrs multiplied, but so did miracles. Finally, in a cloud of special effects, the Church emerged victorious: the Emperor Constantine put his predecessors' policies into reverse and made Christianity the favoured religion of the State.

After that there was only one hiccup, when Constantine's nephew Julian disavowed and disestablished Christianity and attempted to breathe new life into the moribund remains of paganism. But his synthetic neo-Platonism, which borrowed the structure and outbid the superstition of its rival, never acquired any significant following, and on his death his policy was immediately abandoned. Its privileges restored, the Church proceeded to tighten its hold over both rulers and ruled, until, by the age of Justinian, it was the only faith allowed public expression.

A social instrument on this scale required a lot of organizing, and the servants of the Church were as numerous and as carefully ordered as the servants of the State. At the top of the hierarchy was the Pope, the Bishop of Rome and heir of St Peter, acting as a sort of ecclesiastical emperor. Below him were the senior bishops (archbishops, metropolitans), one per province, playing the same role as provincial governors in the civil order. And, as far as the Pope was concerned, that was that. However, as the Empire moved to a more complicated system the Church came under pressure to do the same. If there was an emperor in the East shouldn't there be a quasi-papal ecclesiastic there too? The Emperors thought so and the Pope had to agree to the appointment of a patriarch of Constantinople as his number two (381). And the civil administration now had prefects, ruling blocks of anything up to a dozen provinces. Shouldn't the Church have something similar? The Pope was forced to accept that the patriarchs of Alexandria and Antioch, the equivalents of the prefects of Egypt and the East, had such special rank. But he succeeded in keeping the rest of the Empire – the western half, plus the Balkans – under his direct control. The metropolitans of Carthage and Salonika were allowed some intermediary functions as regards Africa and Macedonia, but the general rule was that western archbishops reported direct to Rome.[1]

Christianity's success was not limited to the area under Roman control. In the east the Armenian and Iberian kingdoms had been converted even earlier than the Empire (in 303 and 318 respectively). In Africa, the sixth century saw the faith spread among the Nubians of the upper Nile and the Abyssinians of Eritrea. The Irish were converted by St Patrick in the fifth century, a gain that was some compensation for the loss of much of Britain to the pagan Anglo-Saxons, and important conversions were made among the German tribes even before they entered the Empire.

Unfortunately, the missionaries who worked among the Germans subscribed to the Arian version of Christianity. Arius was an Alexandrian theologian of the early fourth century. He proposed a slightly different definition of the Trinity from the one that was to be officially adopted, and the Goths, Vandals and Burgundians happened to be converted at a moment when his ideas were in vogue. However, if they acquired their Arianism accidentally, they maintained it tenaciously, perhaps because it suited their image of themselves as a ruling caste. The result was the odd division shown on the map, with much of the area over which the Pope claimed jurisdiction under the rule of a minority that didn't recognize his authority.

The exact nature of the Trinity was the object of much discussion in the early Church. Was God the Father quite separate from God the Son (the Arian view), was one merely an aspect of the other (as held by the Sabellians), or were the two at once distinct and similar? And what about the relation of the human and divine components of Christ: were the two completely fused (the Monophysite position), entirely separate (as the Nestorians said), or separate but commingled? It all sounds unnecessarily hair-splitting nowadays and probably did so to most churchmen at the time – certainly a majority of them always favoured the middle position on both issues – but it took three centuries to make these answers official, and a lot of ink and not a little blood was spilt in the process. And each time a definition was imposed, a group that wanted to emphasize its identity opted for the heretical alternative.

In the case of the Goths this was undoubtedly unwise: their breakaway church was a reminder of the narrow base and foreign nature of their rule. One reason why Clovis was able to run the Goths out of Gaul was his baptism into the Catholic faith, which enabled him to appear as a liberator to the Roman provincials and their priests. The efficacy of this course was shown on the field of Vouillé, in the persistence and vitality of the Frankish state as a whole, and by the imitation of the Burgundians, who transferred from Arianism to Catholicism in 516.

1. A fourth patriarchate was established at Jerusalem in 451, but this didn't really affect the issue of Papal authority because it was carved out of the jurisdiction of Antioch.

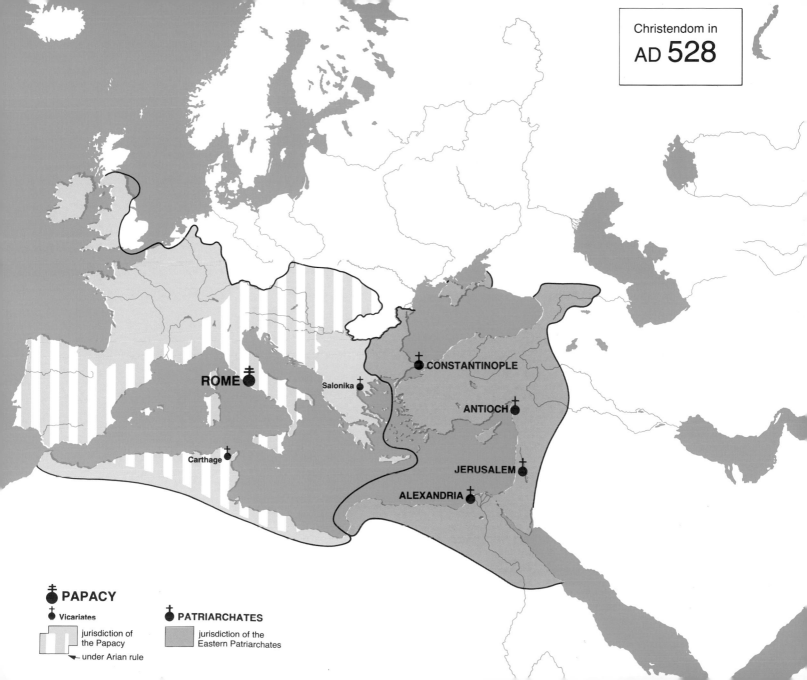

Christendom in
AD **528**

ROME

Salonika

Carthage

CONSTANTINOPLE

ANTIOCH

JERUSALEM

ALEXANDRIA

PAPACY

Vicariates

jurisdiction of
the Papacy

— under Arian rule

PATRIARCHATES

jurisdiction of the
Eastern Patriarchates

This map shows the principal trade routes and towns of the Europe–Near East area in the early sixth century and the commodities that were produced provincially in exportable surplus. The names of commodities that originated outside the area of the map are boxed. These imported items entered the area by two routes, a northern one that crossed the Asian land mass, and a southern one that skirted it. The land route, the famous Silk Road, originated in China, passed north of Tibet and arrived at the north-east frontier of the Persian Empire via Turkestan. Crossing the Iranian plateau on a line that took in Rayy and Hamadan, it reached Mesopotamia and the city of Ctesiphon, the late antique successor to ancient Babylon and Greek Seleucia. From there caravans set out for Roman Syria, either cutting across the desert towards Lebanon and Palestine or moving up the Euphrates to Antioch. The sea route, plied by ships bringing spices from Indonesia and India, branched into two as it entered western waters. One branch passed through the Persian Gulf, where goods were off-loaded for Iraq and Iran, the other rounded Arabia and reached Egypt via the Red Sea.

These long-distance routes carried only low-bulk, high-cost articles. Chinese silk is the perfect example, a luxurious material that shouted status, especially when worked up into designer fabrics. And if the Romans wanted silk they had to import it, for they knew nothing of the silk worm and the technique of cultivating it.

Silk was, of course, the staple of the route named after it. Similarly, the mainstay of the spice trade was the traffic in condiments, notably pepper from India, and cloves and nutmeg from Indonesia. However, the spice trade also concerned itself with a whole host of other commodities, which changed hands in small amounts and at high prices: preservatives, perfumes, dyes and mordants, pigments and gums, incense, and an alarming list of substances that hope rather than experience suggested might be of medical value. Not all came from the Orient: Arabia produced such famous items as frankincense and myrrh. Indeed, the spice trade this side of India was really an Arab enterprise and as such an important source of extra income for the people of the peninsula.

The articles that the Roman Empire imported were distributed round the Mediterranean by a network of sea routes that connected Antioch and Alexandria, the termini of the silk and spice routes, with the cities of the Mediterranean littoral. In this context, however, silks and spices were of relatively minor concern: the Mediterranean trading network was a bulk transport system, measuring its cargoes by the ton. The main commodities were wheat, wine and oil, though timber and metals also figured. Profit, the driving force of the trade in silks and spices, was not a necessary factor: the supply of wheat to Rome and Constantinople, for example, was a state service operated without regard to market forces.

We can get a good idea of how the Roman trading system operated by looking at Egypt, the province that was most important in terms of exports. It produced a reliable surplus of wheat for dispatch to the imperial capitals and a substantial crop of flax that provided the basis for a state-supervised linen industry. It had a monopoly of papyrus, the preferred writing material of the time, and, in the specialist glass manufactories of Alexandria, an industry that produced articles of international repute. Add the transit trade in spices and you have a very considerable volume of exports. However, much of the wheat and at least part of the linen and papyrus were extracted from the country by the imperial authorities without payment of any sort, so the Egyptians weren't all that well off. Indeed they probably found they had to work hard to pay for the timber, iron, wine and oil that they imported.

Until the fourth century, Egypt's wheat went to Rome, where it formed the bulk of the ration issued to the citizens. In 328 Constantine diverted it to his New Rome on the Bosphorus: old Rome had to make do with supplies from Africa and Sicily. In the fifth century the African granary was lost to the Vandals, and subsequently Rome dwindled to a city of the second rank, barely able to maintain the monuments of its victorious past. There is more to its decline, however, than these simple political markers would suggest: the economy of the Empire was in serious trouble, and the West was in worse trouble than the East. Many towns of Gaul had been reduced to fortified posts long before the invasion of 406 that finished them off; much of the agricultural land of Roman Africa had been abandoned before the Vandals ever set foot in the province.

The contraction of the Roman world is clearly visible on this map, which shows Britain, Gaul and Spain without any urban life or trading connections at all. Constantinople, the only city to have gained in numbers in the fifth century, is at the centre of the network that remains and in its continuing prosperity lay the only hope of an imperial *revanche*.

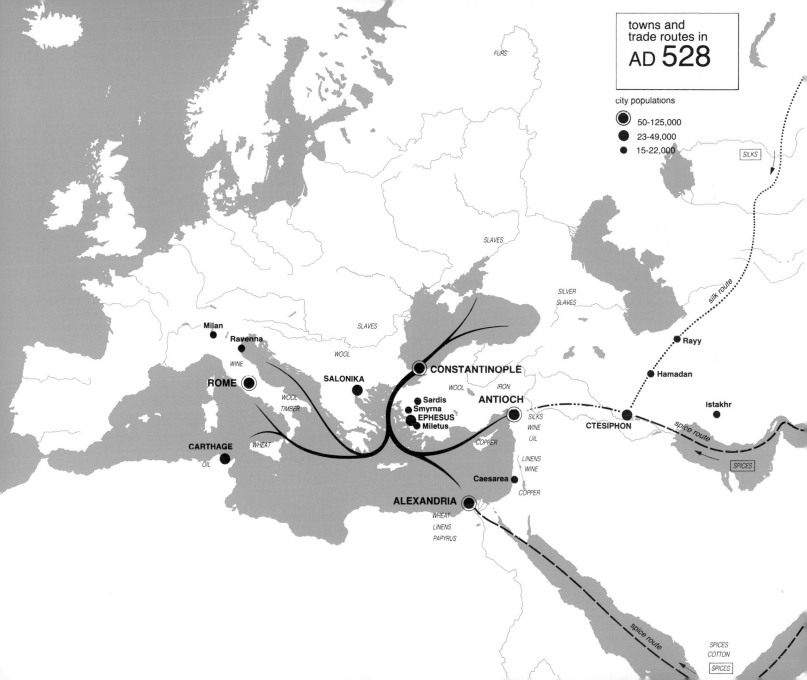

towns and
trade routes in
AD **528**

city populations

- 50-125,000
- 23-49,000
- 15-22,000

FURS

SILKS

SLAVES

SILVER
SLAVES

SLAVES

WOOL

Milan

Ravenna

WINE

ROME

SALONIKA

WOOL

WOOL

CONSTANTINOPLE

Rayy

Hamadan

WOOL

IRON

Sardis
Smyrna
EPHESUS
Miletus

ANTIOCH

Istakhr

silk route

WOOL
TIMBER

SILKS
WINE
OIL

CTESIPHON

spice route

CARTHAGE

WHEAT

COPPER

OIL

LINENS
WINE

SPICES

Caesarea

COPPER

ALEXANDRIA

WHEAT
LINENS
PAPYRUS

spice route

SPICES
COTTON

SPICES

Justinian, who became Emperor in 527, dedicated himself and the Eastern Empire to the reconquest of the west. He began by sending his General Belisarius against the Vandals. Sailing via Sicily with the connivance of the Ostrogoths, the Romans achieved complete surprise. The Vandal king was in Sardinia with half his army. Belisarius beat the half that was guarding Carthage and entered the city (533). When the other half returned he beat that too, captured the king and sent him and his treasure – including the seven-branched candlestick – back to Constantinople. It was a dazzling success which completely confounded the pessimists who constituted a majority of Justinian's cabinet.

Justinian made his next move against the Ostrogoths. He could only spare 9,000 men, little more than half the number sent on the African expedition, so initially all he asked of Belisarius was the recovery of Sicily. However, when this proved an easy task the two of them quickly raised their sights: Belisarius led his little army up the peninsula and occupied Rome (536). The Gothic host duly laid siege to the city, but in the year-long struggle that followed, the Romans, fighting defensively, had the advantage. Gradually the Goths' numerical superiority ebbed away. This so demoralized the Ostrogothic king that when Belisarius went over to the offensive he surrendered his crown and his capital in return for a Roman pension (540).

Belisarius sailed home without quite completing his conquest of Italy: Ostrogothic warlords were still in possession of the area north of the Po. In his absence they made short work of his lieutenants, and when he returned he was unable to stem the German counter-offensive. For ten years the war dragged on, with the Romans clinging to Ravenna but unable to keep much of a grip on anything else. Then Justinian managed to scrape together an adequate army (552). He entrusted it not to Belisarius, whose lustre was now tarnished, but to Narses, an Armenian eunuch who had begun his career as an archivist and developed into a master tactician. Narses took his soldiers through Dalmatia, where he was reinforced by 5,000 Lombards hired for the campaign. At Busta Gallo-

rum, on the road between Ravenna and Rome, he met the main Gothic force and annihilated it. Italy was finally brought back into the Empire. Shortly after, in 554, a civil war in Spain gave the Romans an opportunity to tackle the Visigothic kingdom on favourable terms. They responded with alacrity and managed to make a near bloodless conquest of the southern quarter of the country.

This is a formidable list of victories. Justinian had won back much of the west, and done so while holding off the Persians in the east: the best they could manage was the annexation of Iberia, already their vassal. But whether Justinian had made the Empire any stronger is another matter. The provinces he recovered had proved incapable of defending themselves before and in a military sense were obligations rather than assets. Nor can it be said that he improved the lot of the provincials. In Italy the long war wrecked the cities and reduced the rural population to misery; in North Africa constant efforts failed to prevent the Berbers from infiltrating the areas under Roman control.

None the less, Justinian's reign should not be written off as a fruitless attempt to turn back the clock. He restored, albeit briefly, the dignity and confidence of Mediterranean civilization, and if his conquests proved ephemeral, the mosaics of San Vitale and the dome of Hagia Sophia still testify to the ideals, and greatness, of his age.

In the west, the four sons of Clovis continued their father's aggrandisement of the Frankish realm. Thuringia was annexed (531), Burgundy subjugated (534) and Provence and the central Alps lifted from the failing Ostrogoths (536). In 558, by which time all but one of the sons of Clovis had died, the realm was even reunited. The survivor, however, left the kingdom to his four sons (561), and in their dissensions the first period of Frankish expansion came to an end.

The most important changes elsewhere on the map were precipitated by an event that took place outside it: the destruction of the Mongolian Empire of the Jouan-jouan (552). The vanquished Mongols fled westward to the Caspian, pursued by the Turks who had defeated them. In Transoxiana the Turks came into conflict with the White Huns: they defeated them

too (557), and the White Huns' hegemony over the eastern Iranian lands collapsed. While the Persians, loudly claiming the victory as their own, advanced their frontier to the Oxus, the White Huns joined the remnants of the Jouan-jouan north of the Caspian. A further defeat at the hands of the Turks sent the two of them spinning into Europe, where they were to be known as Avars. Justinian paid this fugitive horde to attack the Huns and Slavs of the Russian steppe who had been raiding into the Balkans. His hope was that the newcomers would keep them too busy to venture abroad. The Avars did better than that: they subjugated all the tribes between the Volga and the lower Danube (559–61). Then they pushed further west and gave the Franks a hard time in Thuringia (562). In the form of the Avar Khan, the shade of Attila had returned to Europe.

On the collapse of the Ostrogothic Kingdom, the Bavarians and Lombards took over the provinces immediately south of the Danube, the Bavarians accepting a measure of Frankish suzerainty as they did so. Some time after 523 the Irish began to colonize western Scotland. The term Scots, originally an alternative to Irish, soon came to be applied exclusively to these settlers, from whom the northern kingdom eventually took its name.

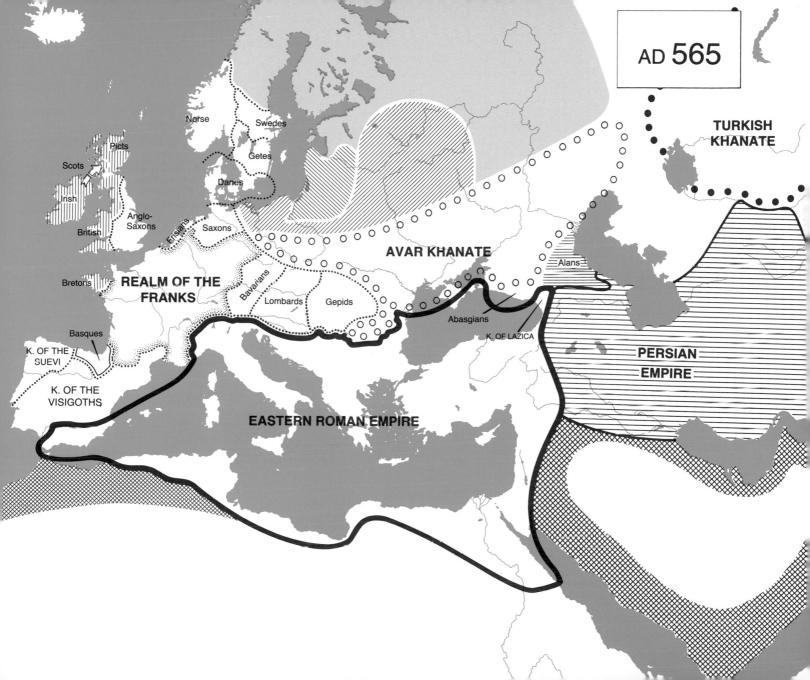

AD 565

TURKISH KHANATE

Norse

Swedes

Getes

Danes

Picts

Scots

Irish

British

Anglo-Saxons

Frisians

Saxons

Bretons

REALM OF THE FRANKS

Bavarians

Lombards

Gepids

AVAR KHANATE

Alans

Abasgians

K. OF LAZICA

PERSIAN EMPIRE

Basques

K. OF THE SUEVI

K. OF THE VISIGOTHS

EASTERN ROMAN EMPIRE

The first Avar thrust into central Europe passed north of the Carpathians. However, the leaders of the horde soon discovered that the area that best suited their needs was the steppe to the south of the mountains, the Great Plain of Hungary, the Alföld, which was currently the object of a war between the Lombards and Gepids. The Avars intervened as allies of the Lombards and helped them to a victory that was so overwhelming that the Gepids ceased to exist as an independent people. The Avars then started making life difficult for the Lombards. Rather than submit to Avar harassment the Lombards preferred to move to Italy, a country many of them knew from the days when they served in Narses' army. In the final migration of the *Völkerwanderung* they crossed the eastern Alps and descended into the Po Valley, leaving the Alföld to become the heartland of the Avar Empire as it had been of Attila's (568).[1]

The Romans had no army in Italy that could face the Lombards in the field: all they could do was lock themselves up in the towns and hope that the invaders would run out of food before they did. On the whole this strategy worked reasonably well on the coast, where the Romans could bring in supplies by ship, but the results in the interior were disastrous: the Lombards took over most of the Po Valley, all Tuscany and much of the mountainous spine of the country. By 600 a temporary balance had been struck. The Romans retained Genoa, Ravenna, Rome, and the provinces immediately dependent on them, as well as Naples and varying amounts of the heel and toe of the peninsula. The rest belonged to the Lombard dukes, of whom the twenty or so in the north fitfully acknowledged the authority of a king ruling from Pavia. The two duchies in the south, Spoleto and Benevento, made no such admission: one of the reasons they were prepared to allow the Romans continuing control of the road between Rome and Ravenna was that it prevented the Lombard king from sticking his nose into their affairs.

The loss of most of Italy was not the only bad news the Romans had to digest at this time. Their Spanish province had been reduced to a coastal strip by the end of the 570s, and the reviving Visigothic monarchy, in control of almost the entire peninsula since its annexation of the Suevic kingdom (584), looked set to eliminate it entirely. The Avars were making threatening gestures in the Balkans, and only payments of Attilan dimensions prevented them from doing worse. And the Persians had been grinding away at the Roman position in the east with considerable success. However, in this area the Romans did have a stroke of luck. Civil strife within Persia led King Chosroes II to flee to the Romans. The Emperor Maurice sent him back with an army that regained him his throne, and in payment Chosroes ceded to his benefactor Iberia and nearly all Armenia (591). After this victorious conclusion, Roman troops could be transferred to Europe to restore the Danube defence line and even advance beyond it to chastise the Avars in their homeland.

While the Avars were consolidating their position in central Europe, their hegemony in the Caucasus was challenged by the Turks. The Avars, mindful of earlier defeats, made no attempt to oppose this intrusion, but the Turks didn't push very hard either. After a campaign which took them as far west as the Crimea, they returned to Transoxiana, leaving the peoples of central and western Caucasia, the Alans and Utigur Huns, to enjoy a liberty they had been unable to win for themselves. Not all the Turks went home: one tribe, the Khazars, remained by the Caspian, a token of continuing Turkish interest in the area. However, the chance of this interest being actively pursued declined with the division of the Turkish khanate into eastern and western halves (582).

1. The Lombards were not the only Germans to pull away from the area of Avar hegemony. The Saxons retreated west of the Elbe, the Franks abandoned east Thuringia and the Bavarians Bohemia. The territories they vacated were immediately occupied by Slav tribes, causing another westward shift in the border between the two peoples. The effect is easier to see on the next map than on this one.

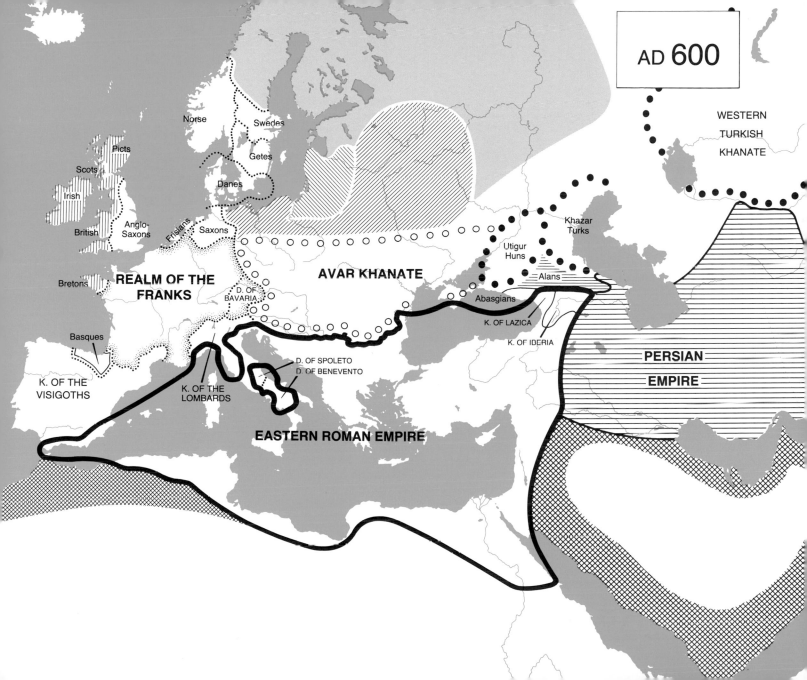

AD **600**

Norse

Swedes

Picts

Scots

Getes

Irish

Danes

British

Anglo-
Saxons

Frisians

Saxons

Bretons

**REALM OF THE
FRANKS**

D. OF
BAVARIA

Basques

K. OF THE
VISIGOTHS

AVAR KHANATE

D. OF SPOLETO

D. OF BENEVENTO

K. OF THE
LOMBARDS

EASTERN ROMAN EMPIRE

WESTERN

TURKISH

KHANATE

Khazar Turks

Utigur
Huns

Alans

Abasgians

K. OF LAZICA

K. OF IBERIA

PERSIAN

EMPIRE

In 602 the Roman soldiers fighting the Avars, provoked by orders to winter on the far side of the Danube, revolted, marched on Constantinople, and murdered the Emperor Maurice. This discreditable act triggered off a series of catastrophes. To no one's surprise, the Avar Khan used the occasion to devastate the Balkans. Less expected was a vast forward movement by the Slavs, who, following in the Avar's wake, settled throughout the peninsula. Within a few years the whole interior was lost to the Empire. At the same time, Chosroes II of Persia, who had learnt from the Romans how to profit from dynastic strife, took the field in the east, ostensibly to avenge his late benefactor, Maurice. Previous wars between the two superpowers had been rather sterile affairs, fought for minor advantages. Chosroes aimed at something far grander, the re-creation of the Empire of the Achaemenids, the Great Kings who, a thousand years earlier, had ruled all the Asian provinces now held by Rome. The first step was to reduce the fortresses of Roman Mesopotamia, a task that required four campaigns (607–10). Then, the job done, the Persians moved forward to conquer Syria (611–13), Palestine (614) and Egypt (616).

By this time the illiterate soldier who had usurped Maurice's throne had been replaced by a more respectable candidate, Heraclius, the son of the governor of Africa (610). Initially he proved no better at stemming the tide of defeat than his predecessor, and at one point he seriously considered returning to his African estates; however, he kept his head and his capital and by 623 had managed to scrape together sufficient troops for a counter-offensive. Refusing to allow this, Rome's last army, to be drawn into attritive attempts to regain the lost provinces, he marched via Armenia to Iberia (where he obtained some useful assistance from the Khazars) and began probing the defences of the Persian homeland. The Persians reacted in kind, advancing against Constantinople in concert with the Avars (626). They had forgotten that the Roman navy still ruled the Bosphorus. Unable to cross to Europe, the Persian host could do no more than watch while the Avars mounted an ineffective demonstration against the land walls of the city.

Meanwhile, Heraclius was gaining the upper hand in the east. A convincing Roman victory at Nineveh the next year was followed by dissension in the Persian ranks and an unexpectedly rapid end to the long war: Chosroes was deposed and murdered by his nobles, who sued for peace while still in possession of half of the east. The Persian forces occupying Egypt, Palestine and Syria were withdrawn, and by 629 the integrity of Rome's eastern frontier was fully restored. Heraclius then embarked on a complete restructuring of the Empire, which recognized, among other things, that its character was now more Greek than Latin. To mark the change, historians have introduced the term Byzantine for the state that Heraclius had saved, Byzantion being the name of the original Greek city underlying Constantinople.[1]

The Avars did no better out of the long war than the Persians. As the Slavs spread out over the Balkans they tended to escape Avar control, and after the Avar failure before Constantinople in 626, most of the tribes between Bohemia and Greece attained complete independence. The Huns also seceded and, Utigurs and Kutrigurs coalescing, formed a united khanate in the Azov region. The name 'Hun' was exchanged for that of Bulgar, and the new nation became known as Great Bulgaria.

In western Europe, events were on a smaller scale. The Frankish kingdom, united again in 613, was finally divided in a manner that is geographically and not merely genealogically valid: the kingdoms of Neustria (the New Land) and Austrasia (the East, the homeland), as defined at their separation in 623, have a continuity that is distinct from the previous disconnected and fluctuating partitions. In Spain, the Visigoths finally eliminated the last Byzantine footholds (621).

The Anglo-Saxon conquest of England was a slow if thorough process, hampered in the south by the number of their petty kings. The north, invaded later, was overrun much more rapidly, and it was here in Northumbria that the first considerable Anglo-Saxon kingdom was established. By extending their control westward, the Northumbrians drove a wedge between the British of the north (Strathclyde) and centre (Wales). The Welsh group had already been separated from their brethren in Cornwall and Devon by a Saxon victory at Dyrham (577).

---

1. It is worth noting that the 'Byzantines' never used the term in this way themselves; right to the end they called themselves and their empire Roman. Westerners agreed about the empire ('Romania') but referred to its inhabitants as Greeks. The Greeks called all westerners Franks.

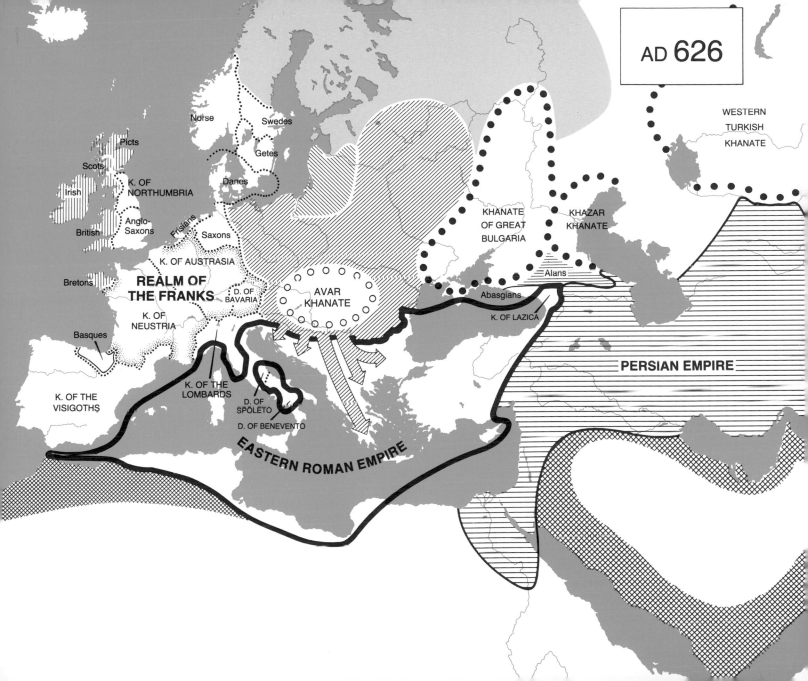

AD 626

WESTERN
TURKISH
KHANATE

Norse

Swedes

Picts

Getes

Scots

Danes

Irish

K. OF
NORTHUMBRIA

Frisians

British

Anglo-
Saxons

Saxons

KHANATE
OF GREAT
BULGARIA

KHAZAR
KHANATE

K. OF AUSTRASIA

Bretons

REALM OF
THE FRANKS

D. OF
BAVARIA

AVAR
KHANATE

Alans

Abasgians

K. OF
NEUSTRIA

K. OF LAZICA

Basques

PERSIAN EMPIRE

K. OF THE
LOMBARDS

D. OF
SPOLETO

K. OF THE
VISIGOTHS

D. OF BENEVENTO

EASTERN ROMAN EMPIRE

While the Byzantine and Persian Empires were engaged in their fruitless and costly war, Arabia experienced a revolution. The Prophet Mohammed, repudiating the patchwork of pagan, Jewish and Christian elements that had previously satisfied the religious impulses of his countrymen, proclaimed a new religion: there was but one God, Allah, and the only hope of salvation lay in Islam, submission to His will. Forced to flee from his home town of Mecca in 622, a date subsequently taken as Year 1 of the Muslim era, Mohammed found security and a following at Medina, the next town to the north. There his fortunes soon improved. In 630 he was able to re-enter Mecca and cast the idols out of the holy Kaaba. By the time of his death two years later, his teaching had been accepted throughout Arabia.

The Romans and Persians probably didn't see the career of Mohammed as posing a significant threat. In military terms the Arabs had never been more than a nuisance: a modest annual subsidy normally persuaded the bigger tribes to keep the smaller ones in order. Islam changed all that. When Mohammed's followers set out from Medina in 634 they may have looked like the usual easily dispersed Arab raiders, but they were nothing of the sort: they were warriors bent on conquest. Within three years they had out-manoeuvred and destroyed the best regiments that the Byzantines and Persians could send against them. At the battle of the Yarmuk, a tributary of the Jordan, they decisively defeated the troops that the Emperor Heraclius had dispatched to eject them from Palestine (636), and at Qadasiya they annihilated the Persian force defending Mesopotamia (637). The Byzantines retreated to Anatolia, allowing the victorious Muslims to overrun Syria and Egypt (640), while the Persians withdrew to the plateau, only to suffer another shattering defeat, at Nehavend (642). After a pause for reorganization, the Arab armies rolled up the rest of Iran, taking Persepolis in 650 and Merv, in the province bordering the Oxus, in 651. Within twenty years of the Prophet's death, the Arabs had created an empire to rival Rome's.

It is difficult not to feel sorry for Heraclius, who had to watch while the provinces so painfully won back from the Persians were lost again to the Arabs. However, it is true to say that he was a lot better off than his rival, the Persian monarch Yezdegerd III, who was murdered by the Satrap of Merv as the Arabs approached the town. By then the only parts of the Persian Empire that remained unoccupied were Tabaristan, between the Elburz mountains and the Caspian shore, and the Transcaucasian dependencies, Iberia and Armenia, where a three-cornered war between Arabs, Byzantines and Khazars remained unresolved. For a few years yet the Iberians and Armenians were able to enjoy the spurious independence of a no-man's land. Cyprus, from which both Arabs and Byzantines exacted tribute, was in a similarly ill-defined and unhappy state.

The Khazars were expanding rapidly at this time: they imposed their authority on the Alans, and they also broke up the Bulgar khanate, driving one of its constituent tribes up the Volga and two others towards the Danube (where a new Bulgar khanate emerged). On the steppe to the east of the Khazars the important event was the break-up of the Western Turkish khanate: this allowed the Arabs an easy run up to the Oxus.

The successors of Mohammed, the Caliphs, combined, as he had, the powers of Emperor and Pope. At first they were chosen from the ranks of the Prophet's companions, but clearly this system had only a limited life. The question that loomed was whether Caliphs should continue to be elected, with personal piety a compelling factor, or whether the office should be hereditary. The third Caliph, Uthman (644–56), of the aristocratic family of the Umayyads, laid the foundations for a hereditary Caliphate by extensive nepotism. However, a majority felt that if there was to be a caliphal dynasty, the preferred candidate was Ali, the son-in-law of the Prophet. The next election went Ali's way, but he was unable to break the grip the Umayyads had established on the empire. They regained the Caliphate on Ali's death (661) and held it for the next century. The matter is of more than dynastic moment, for the feeling, nurtured by the opposition to the Umayyads, that Ali and his descendants were the rightful heirs of the Prophet evolved into a religious dogma of great vitality. The schism between Orthodox (Sunni) and Alid (Shia) Muslims is important today, when the Umayyads are no more than a strain on one's spelling.

In Britain the primacy was taken from Northumbria by the midland Kingdom of Mercia. In Italy the Lombards took Genoa and much of the heel of Italy.

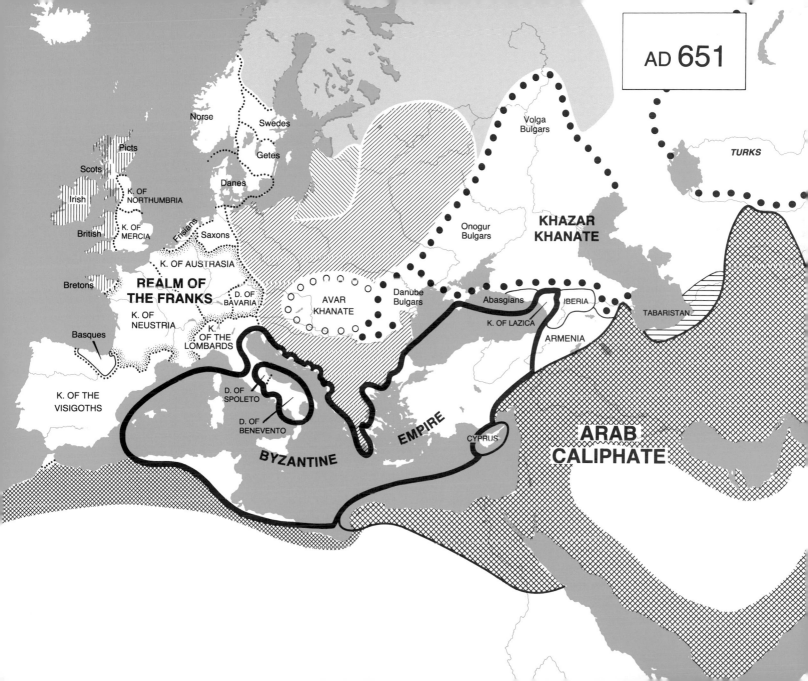

AD 651

Norse
Swedes
Getes
Danes
Picts
Scots
Irish
British
K. OF
NORTHUMBRIA
Bretons
Frisians
Saxons
K. OF MERCIA
K. OF AUSTRASIA
Basques
REALM OF THE FRANKS
K. OF NEUSTRIA
D. OF BAVARIA
K. OF THE LOMBARDS
D. OF SPOLETO
D. OF BENEVENTO
K. OF THE VISIGOTHS
BYZANTINE **EMPIRE**
AVAR KHANATE
Danube Bulgars
Onogur Bulgars
Volga Bulgars
KHAZAR KHANATE
Abasgians
K. OF LAZICA
IBERIA
ARMENIA
TABARISTAN
TURKS
CYPRUS
ARAB CALIPHATE

The first flood of Islam had spent itself by 651 and, although Arab armies continued to probe the borderlands, the next few decades did not bring conquests on the previous epic scale. The Byzantines, holding a shorter line than before, counter-attacked in the Taurus and hung on grimly in Africa. In the east, the Oxus and the mountains of Afghanistan remained the bounds of Arab power. Then, in the years immediately before and after 700, Islam got its second wind, and a series of spectacular campaigns added major new provinces on west and east.

The first breakthrough came in North Africa, where the Arabs had been operating with varying degrees of success from a camp established at Kairouan, in the south of Tunisia, in 670. In 698 they brought these campaigns to a successful conclusion by capturing Carthage, but this event was probably of less importance than the subsequent conquest and conversion of the Berbers of the interior (702). This gave the Arabs the impetus – and the new recruits – necessary to drive across the remainder of North Africa and on into Spain. Crossing at Gibraltar (Jebel al-Tariq, 'Jebel' meaning mountain, Tariq being the Arab commander), the Arabs won a victory over the Visigoths that delivered the entire peninsula, bar a strip in the north, into their hands (711).[1] The invaders then took over the Visigothic corner of Gaul and made it a base for forays into the Realm of the Franks.

At the opposite end of its domain the Caliphate made equally spectacular gains. In the north-east a particularly energetic Emir (provincial governor) managed to conquer both Transoxiana and Khwarizm (the Oxus delta) in 704–15; he also succeeded in occupying Tashkent on the far side of the Jaxartes. In the south-west – off the map – an even more remarkable feat was performed by an expedition that took the coast road to India and subdued the province of Sind in present-day Pakistan (712–13).

On the central front, progress was slower and results less striking. Transcaucasia was gradually reduced (Armenia and Iberia by 653, Lazica in 696, Abasgia in 711 and Shirvan, the province on the Caspian side, in 737). Arab forces then followed up their victories by invading the Khazar's homeland and sacking their capital, the caravan city of Itil on the Volga. This incursion broke the power of the Khazars, who never ventured south of the Caucasus again.[2] However, the Byzantines still held the line of the Taurus and the Arabs' attempts to outflank it by sea were to no avail: major seaborne expeditions launched against Constantinople in 674–80 and again in 717 came to grief despite initial success. The Byzantines still had their navy and they had developed a new weapon for it, a petrol compound that could be projected by a pump to produce what became known as Greek fire. This primitive flame-thrower enabled them to win the sea battles critical for Constantinople's survival.

Elsewhere, the Byzantines were less successful. In peninsular Italy their holdings dwindled to a few coastal enclaves: the villages of the Venetian lagoon, the city of Ravenna, the tip of the heel, rather more of the toe, and a few places on or near the bay of Naples, most notably Naples itself. Rome and its hinterland were no longer under Imperial control; they were ruled by the Pope, who had gradually assumed the authority that the Byzantines had proved unable to sustain.

The Frankish realm was another place where important alterations were taking place behind an unchanging ceremonial façade. By the late seventh century, the kings of the line of Clovis had dwindled into pathetic, short-lived puppets: in both Austrasia and Neustria the man who mattered was not the King but the Mayor of the Palace. As might be expected, this office was usually filled by the biggest and boldest of the local barons. A particularly impressive specimen of the breed was Charles Martel – Charles the Hammer – who fought his way to the top in Austrasia in 717 and subsequently, in 719, took over Neustria too. He earned his nickname in 732, when, in the course of a week-long battle near Poitiers, he pulverized an Arab army that had invaded western France. It was the victory Europe had been looking for, and if it didn't put an end to the Arab threat – there was a second invasion a few years later – it did mark the end of Islam's run of success in western Europe. It also gave Charles the chance to strengthen the Frankish state. As the saviour of Christendom, he was able to force the Church to disgorge some of its vast holdings of land; these lands he gave to his retainers in return for their continuing service as knights. This contract, which transformed what had been a personal following into an instrument of use to his successors, proved to be the starting point for a new way of organizing the military. It was far from perfect, but it was better than the old system of war bands.

In Britain, the Kingdom of Northumbria regained the leadership of the Anglo-Saxons (655) and reduced to vassalage the Welsh (as the British had come to be called) of Strathclyde, the Picts and the Scots. But this revival was brief, and even before the Picts and Scots threw off the Northumbrian yoke (695) the other Anglo-Saxon kingdoms had transferred their allegiance to Mercia (679).

1. This strip contained, besides the inevitably independent Basques, the Kingdom of the Asturias, which had a tenuous claim to be the heir of the Visigoths.
2. The Khazars also lost control of their Bulgarian tributaries on the Russian steppe and upper Volga.

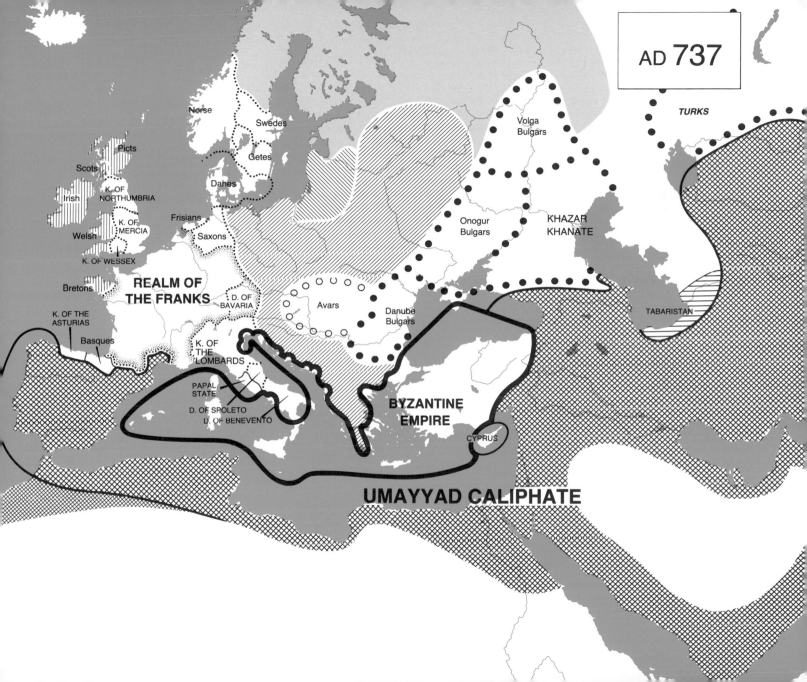

AD **737**

TURKS

Norse

Swedes

Getes

Picts

Scots

Irish

K. OF
NORTHUMBRIA

Danes

Frisians

Welsh

K. OF
MERCIA

Saxons

K. OF WESSEX

Bretons

**REALM OF
THE FRANKS**

D. OF
BAVARIA

Avars

Volga
Bulgars

Onogur
Bulgars

**KHAZAR
KHANATE**

Danube
Bulgars

TABARISTAN

K. OF THE
ASTURIAS

Basques

K. OF
THE
LOMBARDS

PAPAL
STATE

D. OF SPOLETO

D. OF BENEVENTO

**BYZANTINE
EMPIRE**

CYPRUS

UMAYYAD CALIPHATE

The little affection in which Syria, Armenia, and Egypt held the rule of Constantinople was obvious in the ease with which they fell to the Persians. When he had regained them for the Empire, Heraclius attempted to conciliate their Monophysitism by promulgating a compromise doctrine, Monotheletism, which suggested that the union of God and Man in Christ, though not submerging the identity of either component, was sufficiently complete to manifest itself outwardly in one divine-human energy. This creaking form of words did nothing to reconcile the schismatic provinces whose theological waywardness was only a symptom of deeper disaffections; it merely served to irritate the Pope. Eventually, the Arabs disposed of the problem by removing the Monophysite area from the Empire. This deprived Monotheletism of its point and, after some hand-wringing, Constantinople let it drop.

The resolution of this issue didn't put a stop to the quarrels between Constantinople and Rome. The Papacy always insisted on its supremacy as regards matters of doctrine: the emperors were equally firm about their right to have the last word. At first the emperors had the best of the argument. Justinian, for example, simply arrested and deposed a Pope who defied his authority, and Constans II did the same a century later. But by the end of the seventh century the imperial presence in Rome was too weak to sustain such high-handed acts. On one occasion an official sent to arrest the Pope ended up hiding under the Pontiff's bed. The Papacy found that without any very positive action of its own it had achieved political independence.

The situation was now a dangerous one, with both Rome and Constantinople determined to have the ultimate authority but neither able to enforce its will on the other. It was only a matter of time before they found something to fall out over, and in 726 the Emperor Leo III supplied the something in the form of his iconoclastic decrees. Icons – religious pictures and statues – had been multiplying in the east to the point where they rivalled the idols of polytheism. Shamed by the comparison with iconophobic and monotheistic Islam, Leo ordered their wholesale

destruction. Iconodule (pro-icon) priests appealed to the Pope, and he responded by taking all images under his protection.

The Pope went further, excommunicating both Emperor and Patriarch. Leo answered the anathema by transferring Sicily, southern Italy and the Balkans from Papal to patriarchal jurisdiction. The break between the two Churches was now complete. On the one hand there was Eastern (Orthodox or Greek) Christianity, presided over by its ecumenical Patriarch under the protection of the Emperor; on the other, Western (Catholic or Latin) Christianity, ruled by the Pope.

This schism, and the shrinkage of Christendom generally, are the two striking features of this map. There are, however, a few positive items on Christendom's balance sheet. Arianism has been eliminated, either by conquest (as with the Vandals and Ostrogoths) or conversion (as in the case of the Visigoths (589) and Lombards (653)). And the structure of the Church hierarchy has been simplified: the three Patriarchates of Antioch, Jerusalem and Alexandria now lie in the Arab sphere and are no longer contenders for ecclesiastical power. There are also some advances. By Frankish conquest the Christian message has been conveyed to the Thuringians and Bavarians, and by Irish and Roman evangelism to the Picts (sixth century) and the Anglo-Saxons of England (seventh century). Alas, these are small successes to set against the loss of Syria, Egypt, North Africa and Spain.[1]

1. Christendom in this and subsequent maps is defined as the area under Christian rule. In general, the division between East and West is also politically determined, but on this map the situation isn't so straightforward: much as they may have wished to, the Byzantines hadn't the means to impose their ecclesiastical authority anywhere in peninsular Italy north of the heel and toe, or on any of the islands west of Sicily.

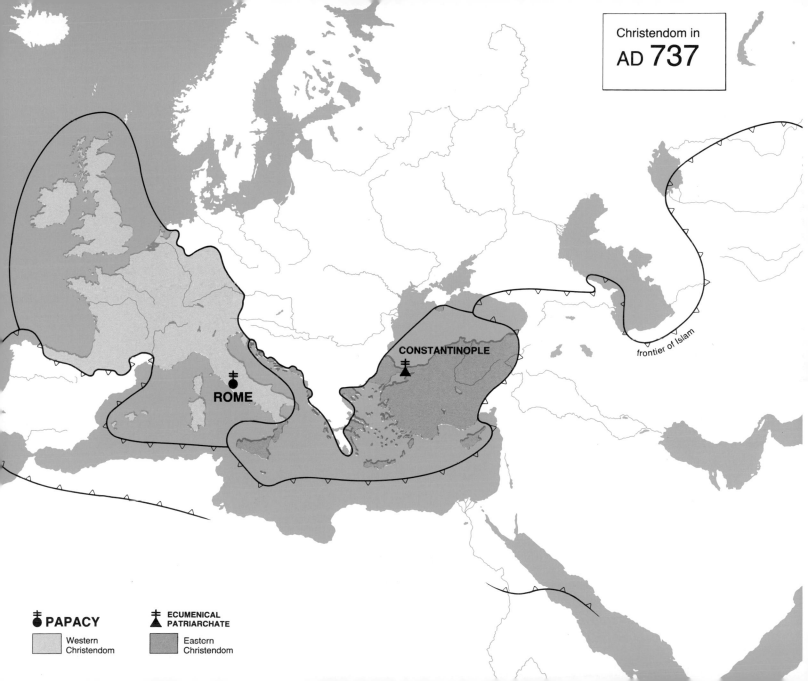

Christendom in
AD **737**

CONSTANTINOPLE

ROME

frontier of Islam

PAPACY

Western
Christendom

**ECUMENICAL
PATRIARCHATE**

Eastern
Christendom

In its heyday, the second century AD, the Roman Empire had a population of about 45 million. Thereafter, a slow decline set in, and on the eve of the Western Empire's collapse the figure was more like 36 million, a drop of a fifth. This fall can hardly have been responsible for the failure of the imperial system, because the Romans still outnumbered their barbarian enemies by better than two to one, but it certainly didn't help. The Empire was essentially an agribusiness, and by the beginning of the fifth century it was operating on a significantly smaller scale than it had been 200 years earlier.

The contraction continued at a similar pace over the next two centuries. At first sight it might appear obvious that the invasions and devastations that brought the Western Empire down and the Eastern Empire to its knees were responsible for the continuing population loss, but as the effect was already established there is no need to look for a supplementary cause. Moreover, communities of the type that made up the Mediterranean polity at this time, which are characterized by high birth-rates and high mortalities at all times, readily make up losses of this sort. Whatever was going on was something more fundamental.

The drop of 20 per cent between 400 and 600 AD brings the total loss up to a third. The Mediterranean world of the seventh century cut a poor figure by comparison with its classical antecedents, and had increasing difficulty defending itself against its enemies.

One aspect of this diminishing competence is the retreat of the boundary between the desert and the sown. In Augustus's day, the nomads had been peripheral in every sense of the word: they were restricted to marginal territories that no one else wanted, and they contributed little or nothing to the history of their times. But as agriculture declined, so the standing of the nomads improved. The hit-and-run methods of fighting that came naturally to them suited a world that had entered the cavalry age, and, by the fourth century, nomad clans that had been content to wait for fields to be abandoned were actively driving the peasantry off fields still under cultivation. Frontiers that the early Roman Emperors had hardly given a thought to turned into problem areas, competing for scarce imperial resources. In North Africa the area controlled by the government was steadily whittled away; in Syria, where the frontier was shorter, the line was held until the seventh century and the final collapse of the old order. Subsequently, the Arabs flooded over the entire east, establishing a new empire that, at least in its initial phase, represented a dramatic triumph for the pastoral way of life.

The Arabs may not have been responsible for the Roman Empire's demographic collapse, but their presence certainly emphasized its extent. Much of the Orient reverted to the lifestyle of a thousand years earlier, and its population settled down at a figure no greater than it had been then. But once again we must distinguish cause and effect. Where the invaders were farming folk, the population dwindled just as much as when they were nomads: German immigration signally failed to stop the Mediterranean world's decline. What had altered was something more fundamental. Life, for some reason, had become more difficult to sustain.[1]

1. It seems a bit cowardly to leave this topic without hazarding a guess as to the mechanism. One obvious candidate is climatic change. If the world got a bit colder at this time, or a bit wetter, if the growing season was a bit shorter or a bit less favourable, then the population that could be maintained by agriculture would diminish. It is attractive to think that a change of this type occurred at the beginning of the Roman Empire's time of troubles, and maybe one day we will be able to analyse past climates with sufficient certainty to prove this was or was not the case. At the moment we cannot: all we can say is that if it is true that climate was at the bottom of it, there are a couple of developments during the period that don't fit too easily into this framework. If any societies were getting the upper hand over their surroundings in the eighth century AD, it wasn't where farming was relatively easy but where it was exceedingly difficult: not in the temperate regions but at the northern periphery of Europe; not in France or Lombardy but in Scandinavia and Russia. For the population nadir coincides with the age of the Vikings and Varangians, and the intense activity in which these people engaged strongly suggests that, whereas there may have been less people in Europe as a whole than there had been 500 years earlier, there were a lot more Scandinavians and Russians.

Another possibility is disease. We know that a series of plague outbreaks could drive the population down by a third, because that is exactly what happened in the fourteenth century. We also know that a plague cycle began in the second century, in the reign of Marcus Aurelius, and another in the sixth century in the reign of Justinian: the two together could have done it. But the time course is troublesome. Europe needed only 150 years to make up the ground lost in the Black Death and subsequent outbreaks: the seven or eight hundred years that it took Europe to get through the Dark Ages seems a bit on the long side for a disease-driven cycle.

population in
AD 737

each symbol represents 1 million people

areas averaging 10 or more persons per km²
left unshaded

Islam, at least at first, brought unity and peace to an area comparable in size to the Roman Empire. Its geography, however, was quite different, for whereas the Roman Empire had been built round the Mediterranean, the Caliphate was centred on the Near Eastern land mass: its lifelines traversed the deserts, not the seas. The earliest network consisted of tracks leading out from Medina, the seat of the Caliph, to the camps in Egypt, Syria and Iraq, where the armies that had conquered these countries were stationed. Later, when the capital was moved north to Damascus, the essential line became the one linking these military bases to the new centre. Of the camps, the two in Iraq (at Kufa and Basra) and the one in Egypt (at Fustat, retrospectively known as Old Cairo) developed into important towns; the Syrian camp was superseded by Damascus and soon forgotten. None of these places was on the sea, and cities that were tended to decline under Arab rule. Some, like Caesarea-in-Palestine, were abandoned altogether.

Arab vessels, of course, continued to sail the Red Sea and Persian Gulf, and there was some expansion of traffic in these areas: Egypt's surplus wheat, for example, was now shipped to Mecca. But, as regards the Mediterranean, the decline in seaborne trade was unmistakable: ships became smaller, sailed at a venture, and rarely went far. By contrast, the overland caravans increased in size and regularity: they traded textiles and metalware, sugar and spices, carpets, jewellery, the manufactures of the towns through which they passed, and products obtained from distant markets. They also traded in people. They escorted pilgrims on their way to the holy cities of Mecca and Medina. And they bought and sold slaves: Abyssinians from Eritrea, blacks from Nubia and the Somali coast, Turks from beyond the Oxus, and Circassians from the Caucasus. A commercial style was established that was to last till the nineteenth century.

The characteristic beast of burden on the Arabs' caravan routes was the camel, the only animal capable of carrying useful loads across long stretches of waterless desert. It faced its greatest challenge in North Africa, where the Sahara had hitherto proved an impassable barrier, restricting communication with the sub-Saharan zone to the Nile valley and the Eritrean and Somali coasts. On the eve of the Arab conquest, this barrier was breached at its western end. Berber camel-drivers, who had been edging further into the desert for a long time, finally reached the far side of the sand sea, the strip of scrub and semi-desert known as the Sahel. There they made contact with the Kingdom of Ghana, whose inhabitants were so eager for salt that they were prepared to buy it with gold dust on a pound-for-pound basis. The Berbers had no difficulty supplying the salt: in the course of their exploration of the desert they had discovered deposits of rock salt which could be mined *en route*. A regular traffic developed: Bilad as-Sudan, 'the land of the Blacks', became Islam's most important source of gold.

If the overall picture of the Arab economy was one of increasing activity, the view from Byzantium was depressing in the extreme. Many cities had gone up in smoke during the war with Persia, and few were rebuilt after it. The Arabs did even more damage, raiding everywhere and lifting whole provinces from the Empire, among them Egypt, the granary of Constantinople. Subsequently, the population of the city fell so fast that New Rome seemed to be going the way of the old. There were a few pluses. One was the development of a native silk industry: it is said that this owed its start to two monks who arrived from China in the sixth century with silkworms concealed in their belongings. Another was a strengthening connection with the Khazars, who were taking steps to develop the commercial potential of south Russia. Furs from the north and slaves from the borderlands were the main articles of trade. Most were shipped to Constantinople, but some went in the opposite direction, to the caravan stations of the silk road in Transoxiana.

Whatever Byzantium's tribulations, it had avoided the complete economic collapse that had overtaken the west. There, the few towns remaining to Christendom were on their last legs. The greatest of them, Imperial Rome, had dwindled into a scattering of villages separated by rubble-strewn fields. Where once Augustus had fed a citizen body 200,000 strong, the Pope was hard put to find rations for a hundred.

city populations

50-125,000

23-49,000

15-22,000

FURS

SILKS
SLAVES

*Khazar
routes*

SLAVES

*SILVER
SLAVES*

SLAVES

Nishapur

● **Rayy**

Mosul

● **Hamadan**

CONSTANTINOPLE

WHEAT

Salonika

SILKS   *WOOL*

SUGAR

Wasit
Ctesiphon   ● **Shiraz**
ANTIOCH   **BASRA**
Kufa

Toledo

*WOOL
WHEAT*

WHEAT

SUGAR

DAMASCUS

SPICES

ALEXANDRIA

Fustat

*WHEAT
LINENS
PAPYRUS
SUGAR*

pilgrim routes to Mecca

*SPICES
COTTON*

GOLD

IVORY   SLAVES   *SPICES*

In 747, discontent with Umayyad rule blazed out into open revolt. The uprising, engineered by the Abbasids, long-standing rivals of the Umayyads, began in the east of Iran: it attracted the support of the local gentry, who wanted a government more responsive to Persian aspirations, and of Shi'ites, who were looking to place an Alid on the caliphal throne. But the Abbasids, descendants of Abbas, an uncle of the Prophet, were interested in neither Ali nor Iran, and as they managed to keep control of the insurrection from start to finish, the end result of the overthrow of the Umayyads was no more than a change of dynasty. After a general massacre of the Umayyad clan – something in which everyone could join with enthusiasm – life went on much as before.

There were peripheral differences. The most important was the failure of the Abbasids to win recognition in Spain. There, one of the few Umayyads to survive founded an independent emirate (756) after a bitter civil war which gave the Christians of Asturias the chance to win back the north west of the peninsula and refound their kingdom on the surer basis that this region, Galicia, provided. Nearer home, the Abbasids lost Abasgia but succeeded in a conquest that had eluded the Umayyads, Tabaristan (759–61). And at the hub, the building of Baghdad (763) marked an eastward shift in the Empire's centre of gravity that was of long-term significance: it made it that much easier for the Iranians to assume the higher profile that they had long been seeking.

In Christendom, the main focus of attention was Italy, where the Lombards took Ravenna in 751. Their next move was clearly going to be against the unintentionally independent and apparently helpless Papal State. The Pope had only one card to play: he appealed to the Franks to protect his temporal domain. The Mayor Pepin III, son of Charles Martel, agreed to help when the Pope sanctioned the deposition of the last of the puppet-kings of the house of Clovis and the elevation of Pepin to the Frankish throne. Pepin then defeated the Lombards and placed under Frankish protection a Papal State that the Pope persuaded him to enlarge to the size of the erstwhile Byzantine province (756–9). During this period Pepin also drove the Arabs from Septimania, the corner of France they had inherited from the Visigoths.

So far, we have had no reason to pay attention to the political set-up in Scandinavia, which is just as well, as we know almost nothing about it. All we have is the names of various peoples, among them two who have disappeared by the date of this map, the Jutes, who were displaced or absorbed by the Danes at an early, though uncertain date (see AD 451, note 1) and the Getes, who succumbed to the Swedes some time between the mid sixth and mid eighth centuries. This leaves Scandinavia divided, much as now, between Norse (Norwegians), Danes (holding southern Sweden) and Swedes. During the eighth century, their history is hardly less blank than before, but it must have been some time during this period that they developed the instrument that was to bring them to the forefront of European history, the northern sailing ship. Remarkable as it may seem, the Teutons of the *Völkerwanderung* era had relied entirely on rowing boats for their maritime expeditions: the vessels that carried the Anglo-Saxons to Britain, for example, were open galleys with thirty to forty oarsmen, but no sails. They served their purpose well enough but, being essentially coastal craft, nobody ever made any discoveries in them. With the appearance of true sailing ships, capable of voyages across the open sea, this situation changed. Scandinavian navigators began to explore the waters around them, looking for new lands and new opportunities. One direction they took was northward along the coast of Norway, where the Lapps had furs and hides to trade and there were walrus and whale to catch. Another was across the Baltic to Kurland, where the Swedes established trading posts around this time.

A minor though significant incident is the establishment by the Bavarian Duchy of a protectorate over the Slavs on its eastern border, the beginning of a movement that was to drive a wedge between the southern Slavs and the main mass of their kin (758).

AD **771**

Norse

Picts

Scots

Irish

Welsh

K. OF
NORTHUMBRIA

K. OF
MERCIA

K. OF
WESSEX

Bretons

K. OF
GALICIA

Basques

**UMAYYAD
EMIRATE**

Swedes

Danes

Frisians

Saxons

**REALM OF
THE FRANKS**

D. OF
BAVARIA

K. OF
THE
LOMBARDS

PAPAL STATE

D. OF SPOLETO

D. OF BENEVENTO

Avars

Danube
Bulgars

Onogur
Bulgars

Volga
Bulgars

**KHAZAR
KHANATE**

Abasgians

TURKS

**BYZANTINE
EMPIRE**

CYPRUS

ABBASID   CALIPHATE

Pepin's son, Charlemagne, who became sole King of the Franks in 771, spent his long reign fighting continual aggressive wars. In the north-east he conquered the remaining fragment of Frisia and, after much hard campaigning, Saxony (782–804). In the south-east he absorbed Bavaria into the Frankish state while pursuing the Bavarian policy of establishing protectorates over the nearer Slavs. This brought him into conflict with the Avars, whose downfall he contrived with the aid of the Bulgars (796). In Italy, Charlemagne annexed the Lombard Kingdom, which had started to nibble at the Pope's estates again, together with the Duchy of Spoleto (774; the Duchy of Benevento later emphasized its continuing independence by promoting itself into a principality). In Spain he was less successful. His first invasion was rebuffed by the Arabs, and as he withdrew, his rearguard was ambushed by the Basques. This incident, suitably glorified, became the central episode in the *Chanson de Roland*, the epic poem that was to become one of the most popular items in the medieval troubadour's repertoire. At the time it must have seemed a lot less glamorous. However, subsequent campaigning did produce a modest Spanish province centred on Barcelona, along with some doubtful promises of obedience from the Basques. Spain apart, the performance was impressive, certainly sufficient to justify Charlemagne's taking the title of Emperor, which he did in Rome in the year 800. Twelve years later the Byzantines gave him official recognition as Roman Emperor of the West, which was praise indeed.

Charlemagne's empire did not, of course, have much to do with the old Roman Empire: it didn't even bear much resemblance to it geographically. However, the order he imposed on western Europe does represent a new base-line, and this is indicated on the map by the introduction of a new set of conventions. The Frankish Empire gets a doubled border, the other kingdoms of western Europe simple linear boundaries. The small dots, once used for all the German peoples, are now reserved for the Scandinavians, the only Teutons still on the boil.

The various Scandinavian enterprises of the period are better documented in the west than the east. The first westward step was the Norse discovery of the crossing to the Shetlands (*c.* 790); from there it was only a short trip to the British mainland, and the first boatloads of Norse were reported off the coast of Northumbria a few years later. At the same time, they were making voyages of reconnaissance to the Faroes, the western isles of Scotland and via the Irish Sea to Ireland, Cornwall and the Atlantic coast of France. Eastward, the Swedes, finding the going hard in Kurland, switched their attention to the Gulf of Finland and Lake Ladoga. From a settlement established on the south side of the lake, probably at the beginning of the ninth century, they made a successful entry into the Russian river system. Their progress must have been rapid, for in 839 one group reached Constantinople via the Black Sea. Up to this point neither the Vikings (the name applied to Scandinavian adventurers in the west) nor the Varangians (the name by which they were known in the east) were sufficiently numerous to pose much of a threat to the peoples through whose lands they were passing. There were, however, plenty more of them at home, eager for a better life than the one they knew. It all spelt trouble.

Towards the end of the eighth century, the Abbasid Caliphate began to lose control of its western provinces. The Shia gained power in Morocco, setting up a line of Caliphs, the Idrisids, who ruled the country from Fez, a city founded by the first of them in 793. Tunisia parted company with Baghdad more gently, the Aghlabid dynasty of emirs becoming less aware of Abbasid suzerainty and more confident in their own sovereignty, until they gradually drifted out of the Abbasid orbit altogether. In Transcaucasia the Abasgians liberated an area corresponding to the old kingdom of Lazica (788). In fact the Abbasids were doing remarkably little to propagate the faith, and the best performances in this department were turned in by groups outside their empire. Spanish Moslems were responsible for the conquests of Ibiza (798) and Crete (823), while the Aghlabids began the reduction of Sicily (827). The interesting thing about these successes is that they were all maritime. Previously the

sea had not been a medium on which the Arabs performed well.

As the Arab Caliphate manifested the first symptoms of decline, Byzantium gave signs of returning vitality. Thrace was recovered from the Slavs in the late eighth century, and, at the beginning of the ninth, the Emperor Nicephorus I brought peninsular Greece under imperial rule again. Nicephorus then turned his attention to the Bulgars. He knew they would be far harder to bring to heel than the Slavs and, mindful of this, raised the best army Byzantium had fielded for many a year. It turned out to be not good enough. The Bulgar Khan Krum trapped the Byzantines in the mountains that marked the border between the two empires and annihilated the entire force. Nicephorus was among the dead; his skull, fashioned into a drinking vessel, subsequently ornamented Krum's dining table.[1]

In England, the event to note is the rise of the Kingdom of Wessex, which overcame the Cornish Welsh and the southern dependencies of Mercia (825) and briefly enforced the submission of both Mercia and Northumbria (829). On the other side of the Channel, the Bretons were forced to recognize the authority of the Franks in 825: this was one of the few achievements of Charlemagne's ineffective son Louis the Pious (814–40).

1. On the Russian steppe the Onogur Bulgars were now overshadowed by the Magyars, a Finnish people originally from the area between the Volga and the southern Urals, who had adopted the Turkish lifestyle and gradually edged westward until, by the date of this map, they had become the dominant people on the grasslands of southern Russia. The Onogurs still counted for something, however, and though the circles that define the Magyars' range are given a grey filling to indicate that the majority of nomads in this area were of Finnish stock, the Onogurs contributed a distinct Turkish strand to the new nation. The point is significant because, although most members of the horde referred to themselves as Magyars, some called themselves Hungarians (an alternative spelling of Onogur), and Hungary was to become the preferred term for the country where the Magyars eventually settled.

AD 830

Faroe Is

Shetland
Is

Norse

Orkney Is

Ladoga

Swedes

Picts

Scots

Danes

Irish

K. OF
NORTHUMBRIA

Welsh

K. OF
MERCIA

K. OF
WESSEX

TURKS

Volga
Bulgars

Magyars

KHAZAR
KHANATE

FRANKISH

EMPIRE

BULGAR
KHANATE

K. OF
ABASGIA

K. OF
GALICIA

BYZANTINE

EMPIRE

ABBASID
CALIPHATE

UMAYYAD
EMIRATE

P. OF
BENEVENTO

CYPRUS

IDRISID
CALIPHATE

AGHLABID
EMIRATE

EMIRATE OF
CRETE

In 843, the Frankish Empire was divided between the three grandsons of Charlemagne, and in the next forty years there was a kaleidoscopic series of partitions and amalgamations reflecting Carolingian reproduction and mortality. Historians describe these divisions as significant when they correspond to modern frontiers, and stigmatize them as typically dynastic when they do not, but by 885 a series of accidents had reunited the Empire, and it was in 887–8 that the definitive disintegration took place. The main successor kingdoms were France, Germany, and Italy; in the gaps between them, ambitious nobles carved out the minor kingdoms of Provence and Burgundy. Frankish authority over outlying areas was allowed to lapse. In Spain, the counties of Barcelona and Aragon became autonomous states; the Basques reverted to their traditional independence. On the eastern border, the Czechs, who had made token submissions to Charlemagne, erected a sovereign state of their own, the Kingdom of Great Moravia. Further south, the Croats, previously members of the Frankish system, recovered their freedom.

During the same period the Abbasid Caliphate continued its own slower devolution. The eastern emirates passed into the possession of dynasties that were of Iranian stock and understandably favoured Iranian traditions, the Saffarids of Herat (from 867) and the Samanids of Bukhara (from 874). The Saffarids, who were sympathetic to the Shia, protected an Alid emirate in Tabaristan that can be regarded as another aspect of the Persian revival. Egypt also became independent at this time under the Tulunid emirs (from 868). The Caliphs were left in direct control of no more than the central tier of provinces, and even there their orders were often ignored by the more powerful emirs. This explains why the Caliph decided to restore the monarchies of two subject Christian states, Armenia (885) and Iberia (888): the Emir of Azerbaijan, the man hitherto responsible for all Transcaucasia, had been getting a bit above himself, and these infidel principalities could provide a useful check on his ambition.

In the central Mediterranean, matters were going better for Islam. The Aghlabids all but completed the conquest of Sicily, and their fleets ranged pretty much at will along the Italian coast. In 846 they sacked Rome; the next year they seized Bari, in the heel of Italy, which became a base for further raids by land and sea. There was no local power capable of stopping them: the Byzantines were down to their last few towns, and the principality of Benevento was breaking up (Salerno split off in 849, and Capua from Salerno in 860). Eventually, papal pleas persuaded the senior Carolingian ruler of the time, Louis II, to intervene, and he succeeded in recovering Bari (871). However, his presence entailed a recognition of Frankish suzerainty, which the Lombards were reluctant to concede, and rather than do so they called in the Byzantines (873). Presented with Bari, the Byzantines used it to rebuild their position in the south. However, they were not strong enough to impose their authority on the area as a whole, which continued to house half a dozen separate sovereignties – the three Lombard principalities, the Byzantine province and the hitherto Byzantine but now effectively independent seaports of Gaeta and Naples.[1]

The storm that had been brewing in Scandinavia since the beginning of the ninth century finally broke in the 840s. Norse raiders mercilessly plundered Scotland and Ireland; Danes looted England and, working from camps that they set up at the mouths of the Somme, Seine and Loire, cut a swathe through much of France. Where possible, the Vikings developed their forays into conquests, a process that brought the northern and western isles of Scotland (the Earldom of Orkney) and the east of England (subsequently known as the Danelaw) under Scandinavian rule. However, the Vikings did not have the numbers needed to eliminate their main opponents in the British Isles, the Kingdom of Scotland (which had absorbed the Kingdom of the Picts in 844) and the Kingdom of Wessex (where Alfred the Great was in the process of establishing England's most effective monarchy yet). The Norse might have done better if they hadn't discovered Iceland (c. 870): the subsequent thirty or forty years in which they were busy colonizing this empty land (as well as Jamtland, in the interior of Norway) are associated with a marked slackening of their efforts elsewhere. The Irish in particular had reason to be thankful for the diversion.

The Scandinavian enterprises in Russia were carried forward with a vigour that fully matched the spirit shown in the west. In the 860s the Varangians founded a triad of fortified towns among the Slav peoples of the north, Izborsk, Beloozero and, most important of the three, Novgorod ('New Town'). These provided a base for a push through to the south and east, where two further sets of strongholds were established in the next decade, one on or near the Dnieper (Smolensk, Polotsk, Kiev) and another on the upper Volga (Rostov, Murom). Piratical expeditions mounted from Kiev were soon rattling the Byzantines, and the potential for even more damaging raids dramatically increased when Prince Oleg of Novgorod began bringing all the Varangian *gorods* under his control. The end result, visible on the next map but already foreshadowed on this, was the creation of a single Russian principality embracing all the Slav tribes between the Pripet Marshes and the upper Volga.

The southern boundary of this Russian state was indefinite, for a new group of Turks, the Patzinaks, had arrived from the east and were contesting control of the steppe with the Magyars and Khazars. The Varangians had to move through these competing nomadic groups to get at Constantinople. Undoubtedly they nursed hopes of bringing the lower reaches of the great Russian rivers under permanent control, but this was a tall order: the Varangians, like the Vikings, were more enterprising than numerous, and they were spreading themselves very thin.[2]

1. Another Italian seaport that drifted out of the Byzantine orbit was Venice. In Charlemagne's day the people of the lagoon were still identifying themselves as Byzantine subjects, but by 886, when a Venetian expedition took out the rival seaport of Commachio, they were clearly acting independently.
2. The nomads extracted regular tribute from the Slav tribes bordering the steppe and continued to do so for many years after the creation of the Varangian state.

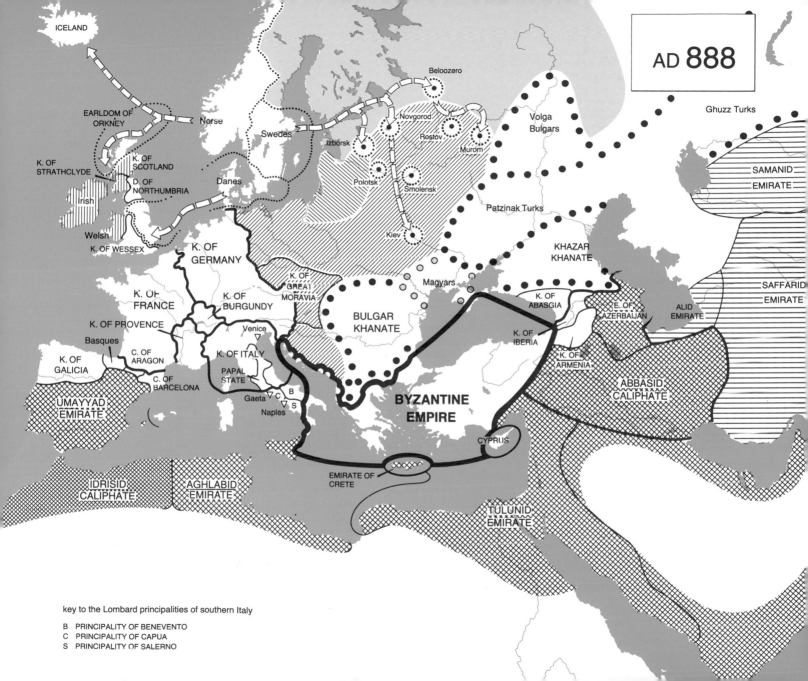

AD **888**

ICELAND

EARLDOM OF ORKNEY

Norse

K. OF STRATHCLYDE

K. OF SCOTLAND

D. OF NORTHUMBRIA

Irish

Danes

Welsh

K. OF WESSEX

Swedes

Beloozero

Novgorod

Izborsk

Rostov

Murom

Polotsk

Smolensk

Kiev

Volga Bulgars

Ghuzz Turks

SAMANID EMIRATE

SAFFARID EMIRATE

Patzinak Turks

KHAZAR KHANATE

K. OF GERMANY

K. OF FRANCE

K. OF BURGUNDY

K. OF PROVENCE

Basques

K. OF GALICIA

C. OF ARAGON

C. OF BARCELONA

UMAYYAD EMIRATE

K. OF GREAT MORAVIA

Venice

K. OF ITALY

PAPAL STATE

Gaeta

C

B

S

Naples

BULGAR KHANATE

Magyars

K. OF ABASGIA

K. OF IBERIA

K. OF ARMENIA

E. OF AZERBAIJAN

ALID EMIRATE

ABBASID CALIPHATE

BYZANTINE EMPIRE

CYPRUS

EMIRATE OF CRETE

IDRISID CALIPHATE

AGHLABID EMIRATE

TULUNID EMIRATE

key to the Lombard principalities of southern Italy

B   PRINCIPALITY OF BENEVENTO
C   PRINCIPALITY OF CAPUA
S   PRINCIPALITY OF SALERNO

By 910 the men of Wessex had the measure of the Danes in England, and over the next decade they conquered all of the Danelaw except the part north of the Humber. The expectation was that the rest would soon be theirs too, but while Wessex had been expanding northward the Norse had been moving south. They established themselves in Ireland, at Dublin and other coastal towns, and in the north of England, at York. The transformation of the Kingdom of Wessex into the Kingdom of England was to be delayed for a few more years.

On the other side of the Channel, the Danes made a better accommodation. In 911 the French King granted the Viking chieftain Rollo extensive lands at the mouth of the Seine, the condition being that he kept his countrymen within these bounds. Presumably he gave satisfaction, for the grant was enlarged in 924. It was to evolve into Normandy, the 'land of the Northmen', a fief that Rollo's descendants were to rule, first as counts, later as dukes, and increasingly as Frenchmen. On the Continent, if not in the British Isles, the Viking age was over.

This didn't mean that Europe's tribulations were at an end. Just as the steam was going out of the Vikings, a new group of marauders arrived on the scene, the Magyars. Defeated by the Patzinaks on the steppe west of the Don (892), the Magyars fled to Hungary, where the Alföld provided the grasslands necessary to their way of life. The Alföld was only lightly held by the Bulgars, whose power lay south of the Danube, and the Magyars soon made it their own. They also made friends with the German King Arnulf, who wanted them to humble his enemy, the Kingdom of Great Moravia. The Magyars did better than that: in a series of campaigns spread over the opening years of the tenth century they destroyed Great Moravia completely. Then their horsemen turned to raiding that was as rapidly conducted, wide-ranging and savage as that of any seaborne pirates. Germany and Italy bore the brunt, but France, Burgundy and Provence all suffered as Magyar bands roamed at will through western Europe. The only person to profit from the situation – apart from the Magyars, of course – was the German King: the Duchy of Bohemia,

which succeeded Great Moravia as the Czech's nation state, acknowledged German suzerainty from the start.

Western Christendom also took some hard knocks from the Muslims, whose fleets continued to dominate the Mediterranean. The Umayyads conquered Majorca and Minorca, the Fatimids ravaged the coast of Italy, and both of them combined to give the inhabitants of Corsica (officially part of the Kingdom of Italy) and Sardinia (technically still Byzantine, but long since left to its own devices) a bad time. The bolder of the pirates set up bases ashore. One on the Italian foot lasted twenty-five years before it was eradicated in a combined operation by the Pope, the Duke of Spoleto and a Byzantine fleet. Another, on the Provençal coast above St Tropez, was to endure for the better part of a century.

Within the Islamic world the most important event was the emergence of the Fatimid Caliphate in North Africa. The Fatimids, who traced their descent from Fatima, the daughter of the Prophet, were, of course, pure Arabs and had most recently been resident in Syria. They were summoned to Africa by Berber supporters of the Shia, who managed to overthrow the Aghlabids of Kairouan. As it was Berbers who had created the new state, it is shaded in this sense on the map. Ironically, this Berber achievement, which soon grew into an empire embracing the entire Maghreb from Fez in the west to Tripoli in the east, was of only limited interest to the Fatimids, whose priority was always to fight their way back to the centre of the Islamic world. Within ten years of his arrival in Kairouan, the first Caliph had launched two major expeditions against Egypt. Both, though initially successful, ultimately failed. It was only then that the Caliph, known to his followers as the Mahdi ('Saviour'), bothered to set up a permanent seat for his North African empire. Situated on the stretch of coast nearest Kairouan, the new town was given the not inappropriate name of Mahdiya, 'City of the Saviour'.

The Fatimids' enemies, the Abbasids, experienced a revival in their fortunes during this period. In the east they profited from the overthrow of the pro-Shia Saffarids by the orthodox and formally obedient Samanids (900). In the west they managed to recover

Egypt from the Tulunids (905) and defend it from the Fatimids (914, 919). Nearer home, the Emir of Azerbaijan continued to go his own way, but, as intended, the Armenians absorbed much of his attention. In 908 he took a leaf out of the Abbasids' book, setting up a second Armenian kingdom, Vaspurakan. The bitter rivalry between the new and old foundations enabled Armenians too to share in the questionable pastime of massacring Armenians.

A few developments that deserve a mention include some changes of nomenclature in the Christian part of Spain, where Galicia became Leon (after its new capital), and the Basques organized into the Kingdom of Navarre. In Italy the Byzantines edged forward on the Adriatic coast, and Capua conquered Benevento (899). In the Balkans, Croatia emerged as a kingdom in 912. In Russia, the enormous Varangian principality created by Oleg passed to his son Igor (912).

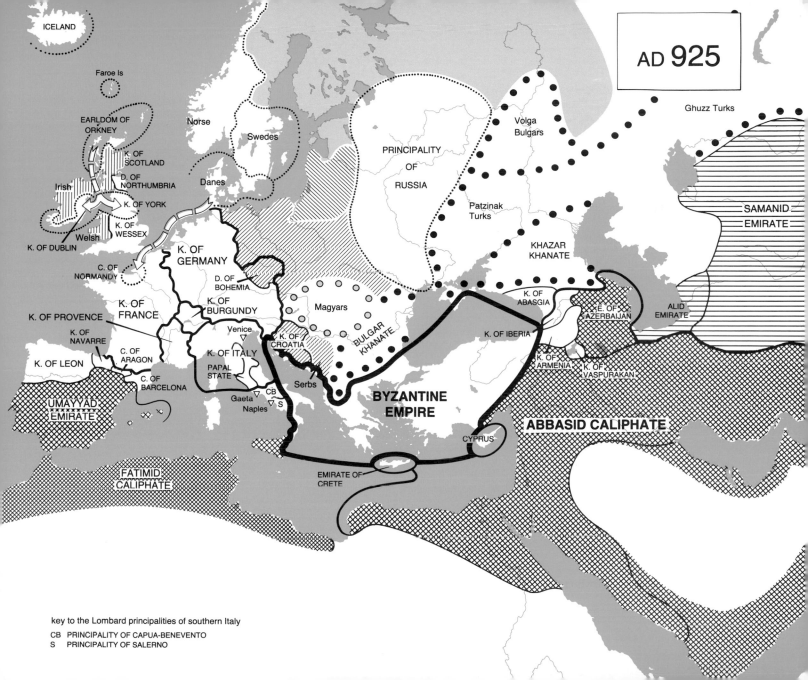

ICELAND

Faroe Is

EARLDOM OF
ORKNEY

Norse

Swedes

AD 925

Volga
Bulgars

Ghuzz Turks

PRINCIPALITY

OF

RUSSIA

K. OF
SCOTLAND

D. OF
NORTHUMBRIA

Danes

Patzinak
Turks

SAMANID
EMIRATE

Irish

K. OF YORK

K. OF
WESSEX

KHAZAR
KHANATE

Welsh

K. OF DUBLIN

C. OF
NORMANDY

K. OF GERMANY

D. OF
BOHEMIA

Magyars

K. OF ABASGIA

E. OF
AZERBAIJAN

ALID
EMIRATE

K. OF PROVENCE

K. OF
FRANCE

K. OF
BURGUNDY

Venice

K. OF IBERIA

K. OF NAVARRE

C. OF
ARAGON

K. OF ITALY

K. OF
CROATIA

BULGAR
KHANATE

K. OF
ARMENIA

K. OF
VASPURAKAN

K. OF LEON

C. OF
BARCELONA

PAPAL
STATE

Gaeta
Naples

CB

S

Serbs

**BYZANTINE
EMPIRE**

UMAYYAD
EMIRATE

ABBASID CALIPHATE

CYPRUS

**FATIMID
CALIPHATE**

EMIRATE OF
CRETE

key to the Lombard principalities of southern Italy

CB PRINCIPALITY OF CAPUA-BENEVENTO
S   PRINCIPALITY OF SALERNO

The tenth century was not one of Christendom's best. What with the Vikings in the north, the Muslims to the south and the Magyars in between, few communities escaped violation of some sort. For many, the idea that the world might end in the year 1000 must have seemed positively appealing. But things got better as the century wore on: Christendom's enemies struck less hard and less often, and life became a little easier, and considerably more secure. When the millennium finally arrived and nothing in particular happened, most people were content to soldier on.

One foe was humbled in a particularly satisfying way. In 955 King Otto I of Germany brought the Magyars to battle by the river Lech, near Augsburg in Bavaria, and inflicted such a crushing defeat on them that they never ventured out of Hungary again. Well, they did mount a few forays eastward, against Byzantium, but they ceased to be a nation that lived by plunder. In the year 1000, when the Magyar Duke Stephen Arpad accepted a gift of coronation regalia from the Pope, the vision of a Christian Kingdom of Hungary was well on the way to being realized.

The victory at the Lechfeld gave Otto the prestige he needed to begin his life-work, the restoration of the empire of Charlemagne. The essential step proved relatively easy: Otto annexed the Kingdom of Italy in 961 and the next year entered Rome and received the imperial crown from the hands of the Pope. There were other successes too, particularly as regards the Slavs. The Bohemians brought Moravia into the imperial system: Lusatia, conquered by Otto's father in 928, was successfully colonized. But an attempt to extend this process up to the Baltic ended in disaster (983), and the homage offered by the emerging Polish state proved purely rhetorical.

The Byzantines did rather well during this period. Though they lost their toehold in Sicily, they more than compensated for this by recovering Crete (961) and Cyprus (965). They also made significant advances on their eastern frontier, taking Antioch in 969 and the nearer parts of Armenia in the closing decades of the century. But the political fragmentation of Islam made the job easy, and even relatively feeble minorities such as the Georgians, Armenians and Kurds were able to establish independent states at this time. The Kurds make their first appearance on this map: their three marcher lordships, Arran, Azerbaijan and Diyarbekr, are given the tighter version of the Iranian shading.

In Russia we have come to a watershed, the reign of Igor's son, Sviatoslav. No doubt of it, Prince Sviatoslav had the roving instinct of an old-time Varangian, leading expeditions against the Khazars (965), the Volga Bulgars (966) and the Bulgar Khanate of the lower Danube (967). But he knew nothing of the sea, and, as his name attests, the nature of the Russian principality was now entirely Slav. This is indicated on the map by the use of a Slav shading, modified to mark the distinction between the Russians and the rest. There is little else to show for Sviatoslav's reign, as most of his acquisitions proved impermanent: the Byzantines forced him out of the Balkans, and it proved impossible to hold on to anything in the steppe zone except the Taman peninsula. Sviatoslav's final end, in a Patzinak ambush (972), was particularly ignominious. He did, however, do significant damage to the Khazars and the Danube Bulgars, neither of whom was of much importance subsequently. The West Bulgarian Empire, which succeeded the original Bulgar state in the Balkans, was more Slav than Bulgar, and, like Russia, is given the shading appropriate to its composition.

The Scandinavian tide was ebbing in the west, too. The English annexed York on the death of its last Norse king (927) and successfully defended it against a counter-offensive by the Scots and the Norse of Dublin (937). In this manner the Kingdom of Wessex became the Kingdom of England. Later, in 945, the English ceded Cumbria to the Scots, who were presumably thought better able to defend it against any further Norse incursions. The precaution was hardly necessary: shortly after, the Irish recovered Dublin, leaving the Earldom of Orkney as the only Norse possession in the British Isles.[1] Within Scandinavia the new era was marked by the appearance of relatively orderly kingdoms for the Norse, Danes and Swedes. They had had kings before, but we know little more of them than their names. Now we have history as well as names, starting with Sveyn Forkbeard in Denmark and an Olaf each for Norway and Sweden.

In 969 the Fatimids achieved their long-time dream, the conquest of Egypt. They immediately moved from Mahdiya to Cairo, the new capital they built to celebrate their victory, and concentrated their attention on extending their empire even further east. Neglected Morocco transferred its allegiance to Spain, whose Umayyad rulers, not to be outdone by the Fatimids, had been calling themselves Caliphs since 929. The Umayyad state never looked stronger than it did in the late tenth century, when the Vizier Almanzor ('the Victorious') was leading the Caliph's armies – now more Berber than Arab – on regular forays through the Christian north.

In eastern Islam this was the era of the Buyids, soldiers of fortune who, starting from a home territory in north-west Iran, gradually won control of much of the plateau; they also dominated Iraq, where they deprived the Abbasid Caliph of his temporal power while respecting his spiritual authority. Further east, the Iranians weren't doing so well. Turks had been playing an increasing role in the Samanid state for some time, and one of them, Alp Tegin, who had been put in charge of Samanid Afghanistan in 961, had already turned this fief into a semi-independent command. In 998 the Samanid Empire collapsed completely: its lands were divided between the Karakhanid Turks, who had delivered the fatal blow, and Alp Tegin's grandson Mahmud of Ghazni.[2]

1. The cession of Cumbria was technically made to Strathclyde, but this once-British kingdom had been an appanage of the Scottish crown since the early tenth century.

2. In the west, Burgundy absorbed Provence (948), Navarre absorbed Aragon (970), Amalfi split off from Naples (c. 950), and Venice annexed the coast of Istria and the nearer of the Dalmatian Islands (1000). In the Caucasus, the retreat of Islam left the Emirate of Tbilisi isolated; Derbent, the guardian of the Caspian Pass, split off from Shirvan.

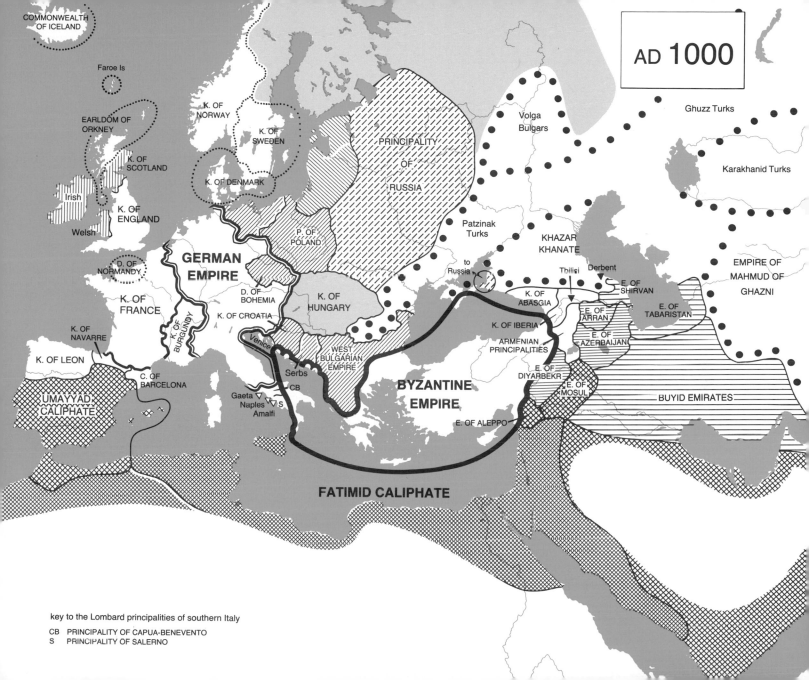

COMMONWEALTH
OF ICELAND

AD **1000**

Faroe Is

EARLDOM OF
ORKNEY

K. OF
NORWAY

K. OF
SWEDEN

Volga
Bulgars

Ghuzz Turks

K. OF
SCOTLAND

K. OF DENMARK

Karakhanid Turks

Irish

K. OF
ENGLAND

PRINCIPALITY
OF
RUSSIA

Welsh

P. OF
POLAND

Patzinak
Turks

KHAZAR
KHANATE

EMPIRE OF
MAHMUD OF
GHAZNI

D. OF
NORMANDY

GERMAN
EMPIRE

to
Russia

Tbilisi

Derbent

E. OF
SHIRVAN

K. OF
FRANCE

D. OF
BOHEMIA

K. OF
HUNGARY

K. OF
ABASGIA

E. OF
ARRAN

E. OF
TABARISTAN

K. OF CROATIA

K. OF IBERIA

E. OF
AZERBAIJAN

K. OF NAVARRE

Venice

ARMENIAN
PRINCIPALITIES

K. OF LEON

C. OF
BARCELONA

Serbs

WEST
BULGARIAN
EMPIRE

BYZANTINE
EMPIRE

E. OF
DIYARBEKR

E. OF
MOSUL

BUYID EMIRATES

UMAYYAD
CALIPHATE

CB

Gaeta ▽
Naples ▽ S
Amalfi

E. OF ALEPPO

FATIMID CALIPHATE

key to the Lombard principalities of southern Italy

CB   PRINCIPALITY OF CAPUA-BENEVENTO
S   PRINCIPALITY OF SALERNO

If the Viking age was over as far as Europe was concerned, the old ways persisted in one corner of the Scandinavian world, Iceland. The Icelanders might have farms to tend, but they were still prepared to make voyages into the unknown, looking for land, loot, or just plain adventure. One such was Eric the Red, who in 982 decided to follow up a story of a large island, far to the west, glimpsed fifty years earlier by a ship's captain who had been blown off course. Eric found it, explored it, and discovered a site at its southern tip where settlement seemed possible. Then he returned home and persuaded a group of Icelanders that Greenland, as he called his discovery, was just the place for a new colony. What they said when they found that 99 per cent of his 'Greenland' was covered by ice is not recorded, but they stayed, and the colony survived. A second settlement was founded on the west coast ten years later.

Eric's son Leif carried on the family tradition. Some time around the year 1000, he set out from Greenland on an epic westward voyage that took him past the forbidding coasts of Helluland ('Land of Stones', probably Baffin Island) and Markland ('Land of Forests', probably Labrador) to a slightly more welcoming shore to which he gave the name Vinland. What he meant by Vinland and where it was situated are questions that remain the subject of much debate: the current consensus is that it means 'Land of Grass' and that it was on or near the northern tip of Newfoundland. Wherever it was, Leif considered that it had possibilities and told the Greenlanders so on his return.

A year or two later, Leif's brother Thorvald found these new lands had a drawback: they were already inhabited. The natives, whom the Norse called Skraelings, were hostile more often than not, and, somewhere in Markland, Thorvald met his death at their hands. Later, when three boatloads of Icelanders tried to colonize Vinland, they too fell foul of the Skraelings – either Algonkians or Inuit, more probably the latter – and after three years the would-be colonists, the first Europeans to attempt a settlement in the New World, gave up and sailed home. Although Greenlanders probably continued to make the occasional voyage to Markland for timber, there were no more ventures westward.

On this rather flat note the Norse Atlantic saga ends. Scandinavian seamanship had added a whole new realm to the European world, but it was a realm of grey seas, ice and emptiness. Nothing really came of it.

The other area opened up to western eyes in the early medieval period was the Sahara, which proved equally empty. However, the far shore of this sand sea, the Sahel, contains features which suggested that a large and more rewarding land mass lay beyond. The kings of Ghana had gold to sell, but they hadn't found it within their own dominion: they got it from somewhere further south. And the river Niger, which traces an arc through the Sahel, obviously flowed on to more interesting regions. Did it continue southward to the Ocean, or turn back up to Lake Chad, or traverse the entire Sahel and join the upper Nile? The caravans brought back no answers to these questions and, disappointingly, knowledge of the sub-Saharan world remained limited to its West African fringe. As for the maritime aspect of the continent, there was no exploration at all. No ships plied between the Maghreb and Bilad as-Sudan, the Land of the Blacks; even the Canaries, well known to classical geographers, went unvisited and unremembered. So once again a very considerable extension to the map of the world, in this case the achievement of Berber camel drivers, petered out just at the moment when it might have generated further advance.

In fact this map is very little better than the one for the fourth century A D in the introduction. The Norse have completed the outline of the Scandinavian peninsula, added Iceland, the southern half of Greenland and, less certainly, Baffin Island and Labrador. Much more of the Atlantic coast of Africa is visible, but only as viewed from the landward side: the more significant advance is in the interior, where the Berbers have conquered the western Sahara and penetrated a little way into the Sahel. As for Asia, Ptolemy's synthesis still rules, with everything beyond the eastern edge of the base map used in this atlas – everything, that is, beyond the realms of the Karakhanid Turks and Mahmud of Ghazni – perceived only darkly in the West.[1]

1. Although this passage gives credit for the exploration of Iceland to the Norse, it is generally conceded that the Irish were the first to set foot on the island, some time in the eighth century. They didn't make much of their discovery, however, and the population was limited to half a dozen hermits when the Norse arrived.

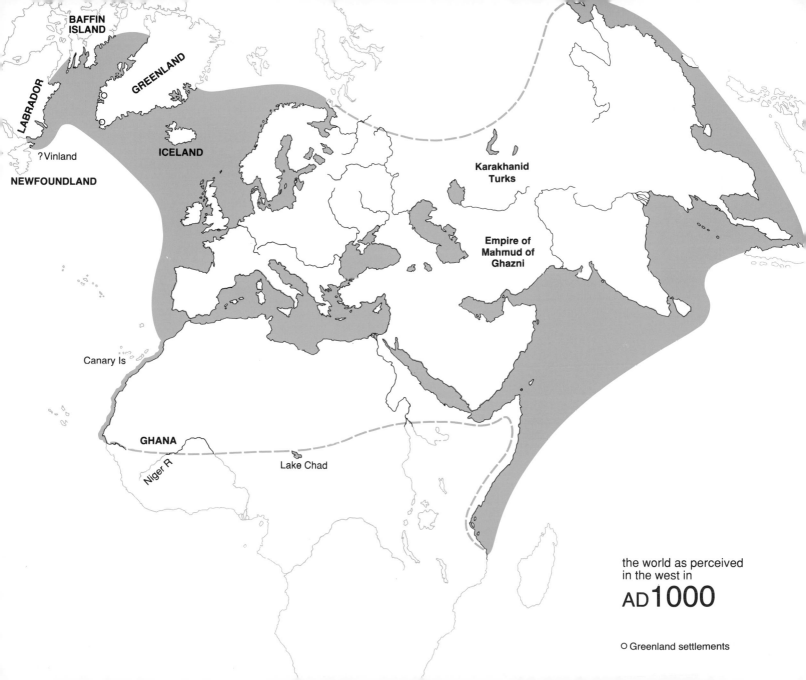

BAFFIN
ISLAND

LABRADOR

GREENLAND

○

○

?Vinland

NEWFOUNDLAND

ICELAND

Karakhanid
Turks

Empire of
Mahmud of
Ghazni

Canary Is

GHANA

Niger R

Lake Chad

the world as perceived
in the west in

AD1000

○ Greenland settlements

The main business of the Papacy in the eighth century was to stop the Lombards taking over Rome. This was achieved by calling in the Franks. The Papacy had to pay a price: Charles Martel refused to move when offered the title of Patrician, and Pepin only did so after the Pope had told him that he could, he should, he must, assume the crown of Clovis. Even then the initial blessing, by post, was not enough (750): Pope Stephen II had to cross the Alps and annoint Pepin with his own hand (751).

This makes it sound as if the Franks were calling the shots, but in fact by accepting the papal seal of approval, Pepin was more than halfway towards admitting a need for it. And this interpretation was strengthened when Charlemagne was crowned Emperor in Rome (800): the title of Emperor, it appeared, was something that only a Pope could bestow. So who stood at the head of Christendom, the Emperor or the Pope?

This was just the sort of question to agitate the medieval mind, and in due course it was to set Emperor and Pope at each other's throats. But this was only hinted at in the ninth century, for both Empire and Papacy collapsed before they could really get into the argument. The successors of Charlemagne weren't able to keep his Empire in order, and the Papacy proved incapable of running Rome, let alone the Papal State. Instead of acting as a seat of power, the throne of St Peter became the plaything of local mafiosi, who often deposed and not infrequently murdered Pontiffs of whom they disapproved. It was only with the help of the revived Empire of the early eleventh century that the Papacy managed to extricate itself from the clutches of the city's political bosses and resume a dignity appropriate to its ecumenical claims.

Despite the lack of leadership, the Catholic Church prospered. Most of the pagan peoples of north and central Europe were brought within the faith, starting with the Saxons whom Charlemagne converted at the point of his very effective sword. Gentler missionary activities subsequently converted the Bohemians and Croats (by the end of the ninth century) and the Scandinavians, Poles and Hungarians (at the end of the tenth). Clerical quality also improved, slowly at first, then more rapidly as the tenth century progressed. The acceleration is associated with the Cluniac monastic reform, which makes this an appropriate moment for an aside on monasticism in general.

The monastic way of life, like Christianity itself, had its roots in the east, where hermits were always admired and often emulated. From the single hermit to the hermit colony, to the monastery with established rules, was a natural progression. St Simeon Stylites sat atop his column, his disciples collected at its foot, and after his death it became the centrepiece of a famous monastic community. The same sort of thing happened in the west, though the element of asceticism, which in the east became almost an end in itself, was never so extreme. In fact, as time passed it sometimes ebbed away altogether. There was an upside to this. Monasteries tended to be good landlords, taking a long-term view of their properties: they saw to it that fields were drained, wells dug and mills built. The downside was diminished respect for monks who rollicked too loud and too often. Hence the need for rules and regulations.

The most important western rule was established by St Benedict in the sixth century. By the tenth century its enforcement had lapsed, and many Benedictine monasteries were more of an obstacle than a credit to the faith. At this point Odo, Abbot of Cluny in present-day Burgundy, tackled the problem. Cluny was new and successful, Odo influential and energetic. Reform on Cluniac lines became the fashion and, gaining momentum from the economic upsurge of the late tenth century, catalysed a surge of lay donation and ecclesiastical construction that led to Latin Christendom, in the picturesque expression of one chronicler, 'shrugging off the burden of the past and dressing itself in a white cloak of churches'. The secular consequences were important too, the reform movement encouraging the aspirations to better order that heralded the opening of Christianity's second millennium.

The Eastern Church also found calmer waters during this period. Iconoclasm was abandoned, which led to improved, though never really cordial, relations with the Western Church. And, in the competition for converts, the east kept its end up remarkably well. The one failure was in Bohemia, which eventually went over to the Catholic Church, but even there the effort wasn't entirely wasted: the mission's leader, St Cyril, devised the 'Cyrillic' alphabet that subsequently became standard for Slavonic languages. And generally the Slavs proved more receptive to orthodoxy than catholicism. Bulgaria was won in 879, when the Patriarch of Constantinople topped the papal offer of an archbishopric by allowing the Bulgarian Church its own patriarch. The concession cost little, as Constantinople's supremacy within the Eastern Church as a whole – in ecclesiastical terms, its ecumenical status – was generally recognized by this time. The Serbs also adopted the eastern rite in the 870s. But the culminating success for orthodoxy came a century later, in Russia. Prince Vladimir of Kiev sent an embassy westward to see which of the two forms of Christianity would best suit his people. The envoys were not impressed by western ceremonial, finding 'no glory there'. But when they visited Constantinople and were taken to Hagia Sophia, their jaws dropped. As they said to Vladimir on their return, 'We knew not whether we were in heaven or on earth. We can never forget that beauty.' Russia had found its faith.

One feature of this map that requires special mention is the appearance of the Armenian Church, headed by its Catholicos. The Armenians subscribed to the monophysite theology that had been in fashion at the time the country was overrun by the Arabs; this distinction, which the rest of Christendom had largely forgotten about, helped the Armenian Church resist reabsorption into orthodoxy when the area was recovered by Byzantium.

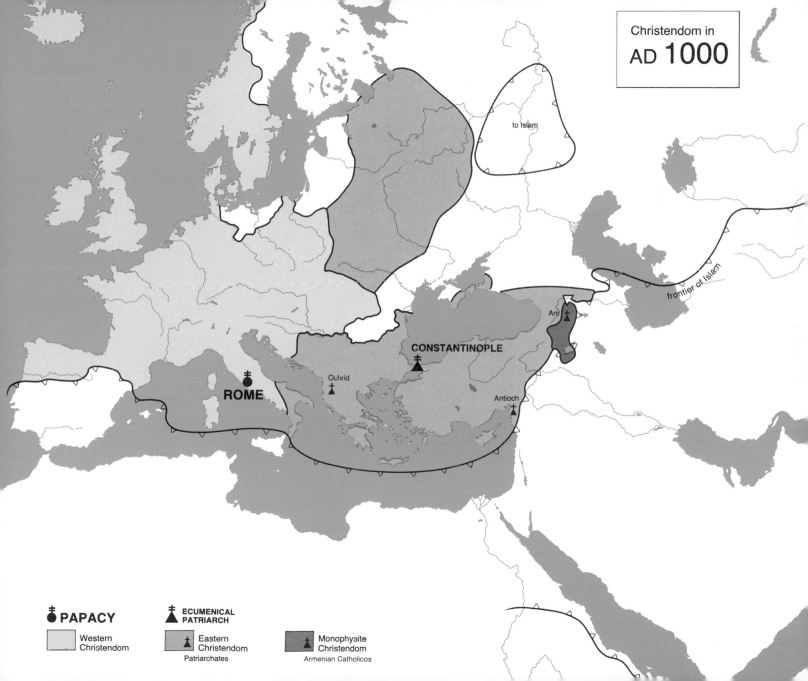

Christendom in
AD **1000**

to Islam

frontier of Islam

Ani ☦

CONSTANTINOPLE ▲

Ochrid ☦

ROME ☦

Antioch ☦

⚲ **PAPACY**

Western
Christendom

☦ **ECUMENICAL**
PATRIARCH

☦ Eastern
Christendom
Patriarchates

☦ Monophysite
Christendom
Armenian Catholicos

The new feature of this map is the network of sea and river routes opened up by the Vikings and Varangians. The most dramatic but not the most important of them led across the north Atlantic to Iceland, Greenland and tentatively North America. Another route followed the Scandinavian peninsula northward, rounded North Cape (off the map) and entered the White Sea (just visible). The third, mainly frequented by the Danes, skirted the coast of Germany and reached the Atlantic via the English Channel. The long reach of these sea lanes was matched by the range of the fresh-water routes opened up in the east. There the Varangians used the rivers and lakes of Russia as stages on the journey to the Black Sea and Caspian. The Neva provided an entry to Lake Ladoga, and the Volkhov took them on to Lake Ilmen. From there they passed along the Lovat and upper Dvina to the Dnieper, and from the middle Dnieper, whose navigation is interrupted by rapids, to the Donetz, the Sea of Azov and the Taman peninsula. The overall span, western and eastern routes together, is an astonishing 100° of longitude, and if it is unlikely that any single individual ever travelled from one end to the other of this network, it was by no means unusual for a Northman who had sailed into the British Isles one year to be mooring his boat in the Golden Horn the next.

The Scandinavians used these routes for trading and raiding, with raiding as the preferred activity. The first step was to size up the opposition. Was there merchandise that could be got to the ships without the question of payment coming up at all? Only if the answer was no, only if the locals looked capable of defending themselves and ready to do so, did the Viking captain deign to display his wares. Slaves were his stock in trade, picked up in sudden swoops and unloaded as opportunity offered. Next to slaves came furs. These were taken as tribute from the peoples of the sub-Arctic, the Lapps and Finns of north Scandinavia and the Finns and Russians of the northern parts of European Russia. Then there were agricultural products of the more readily transportable sort: honey, beeswax, tallow and hides; manufactures such as textiles, tableware and weaponry; and finally the beads and bangles, gems and jewels that formed part of every medieval trader's luggage. In return they sought things they could hoard: gold, silver and silk.

To judge by the vast number of foreign coins found in Scandinavia, the Northmen made a good deal of money out of their ventures abroad. It is difficult to say how much of it was ill-gotten. The sums extorted from England as ransom must have far outweighed anything earned by trade; on the other hand, Islamic coins (40 per cent of the total recovered in Gotland) were presumably acquired peaceably, because the Varangians weren't strong enough to raid the Islamic lands successfully. But even the profits made in the east depended on the sale of goods that had been forcibly extorted from the peoples along the way, Lapps, Finns and Russians. The Scandinavians produced nothing except the routes themselves.[1]

The limited role of trade in Scandinavian affairs is matched by the absence of trading towns in the north. Places like Hedeby (at the root of the Danish peninsula) and Birka (near Stockholm) are often described as such but were really no more than villages: Hedeby covered 24 hectares and may have had 2,000 inhabitants; Birka was only half the size. Not that the other parts of western Europe could boast anything better. There was still not a single place anywhere in the west with the 15,000 inhabitants necessary to qualify for a place on the map. The biggest was probably Venice, which did have some long-distance trade with Constantinople (where its merchants were accorded special privileges in 992) and Alexandria (from where, so the story goes, two enterprising Venetians stole the body of St Mark in 888). But even so, it is unlikely to have had more than 8–9,000 people at this time, and most of these will never have left the lagoon.

If this picture seems disappointing, it nevertheless represents a considerable advance on the situation a hundred years earlier. The little towns of Italy may have had only a few thousand inhabitants apiece, but in most cases this was probably twice as many as they had had in the early part of the tenth century. And in the north the records show that the seeds of future urban growth had already been planted. Baldwin Iron-arm, Count of Flanders, had built castles at Bruges and Ghent in the 860s, and by this date there were regular fairs being held under their walls. In 886 King Alfred of England reoccupied the Roman city of London, deserted since the fifth century: by 1000 it was once again the premier place in the kingdom, contributing 12 per cent of the Danegeld raised in 1018. The towns of France and Germany, which for centuries had consisted of no more than a few hovels clustered round decaying church halls, tell the same story. Communal life was quickening again, albeit on a purely local scale. The Dark Ages were drawing to an end.

1. The import of Islamic silver into Scandinavia suddenly stopped in the 970s. This could be due to the nomads of the steppe getting the upper hand and cutting the caravan route, in which case the route shown in south Russia had ceased to exist by the date of this map. However, it could also be that the Varangians were trading for silk rather than silver, and we know that the terms of trade as regards silver did alter pretty abruptly at this time. As the mines in the Pamirs that supplied the Samanid mints became worked out, silver became scarce in the Orient; at the same time, as a result of the opening up of new mines in Saxony, it became relatively abundant in Europe.

towns and trade routes in AD 1000

city populations

- ◉ 50-125,000
- ● 23-49,000
- • 15-22,000

FURS

FURS

Bulgar routes

SILKS
SLAVES

Viking routes

Varangian routes

SLAVES

Nishapur

SILVER

TIN

SLAVES

Rayy

IRON

Mosul

Hamadan

Isfahan

TIMBER

CONSTANTINOPLE

SILKS

WOOL

BAGHDAD

PAPER

Wasit

SILKS
SUGAR

Shiraz

Toledo

WOOL
WHEAT

ANTIOCH

BASRA

SILK

Seville

CORDOBA

Palermo

SUGAR

Damascus

SUGAR

SPICES

WOOL
WHEAT

WHEAT
SUGAR

SUGAR

Fez

SUGAR

Kairouan

ALEXANDRIA

CAIRO

pilgrim routes to Mecca

WHEAT
LINENS
PAPER
SUGAR

Mecca

GOLD

COTTON
SPICES

IVORY SLAVES

SPICES

From a position that, in the year 1000, seemed unassailable, the Umayyad Caliphate of Cordoba made a remarkably rapid descent into impotence and oblivion. By the date of this map it was simply one of twenty petty governments fighting for a share of Muslim Spain; the next year it was abolished altogether. The Christian kings of the north began to stir again, though they were still happier fighting each other than the common enemy: the only border change to note here is Navarre's advance at the expense of Leon.[1]

The collapse of the Umayyads and the move of the Fatimids to Egypt left the Maghreb free to work out its own destiny. The result was the appearance of Berber dynasties in Kairouan (where the governors of the Zirid line, appointed by the Fatimids, became effectively independent), Qalat (an offshoot of the Zirid lineage) and Fez (seat of the Maghrawanids, originally protégés of the Umayyads). This is an interesting first appearance of the tripartite division obtaining in recent times. At the opposite end of Islam, the Turkish armies of Mahmud of Ghazni were continuing their westward advance, though their main thrust now was eastward into the Punjab.

In northern Europe, King Sveyn Forkbeard realized the Viking dream of conquering England (1012); his son Canute proved statesman enough to retain this prize and subdue Norway as well (1028). Elsewhere in the British Isles, the Viking tide continued to ebb: the Earl of Orkney failed miserably in an attempted coup against Dublin (1014) and was subsequently eased out of his fiefs on the Scottish mainland. Shortly afterwards, the Scots advanced their southern frontier to the Tweed (1018). On the Continent the man of the moment was Boleslav the Brave of Poland, whose policy of all-round aggression added Lusatia (lifted from Germany in 1002) and Galicia (lifted from Russia in 1018) to the nascent Polish state.

Russia plunged into civil war on the death of Prince Vladimir (1015), who had too many sons and left something to each of them. By 1030 only three were left, one of whom ruled the backwater principality of Polotsk, while the other two, ruling from Novgorod and Chernigov, divided the rest of the country between them. To the south, in the Caucasus, the national state of Georgia was formed by the union of Abasgia and Iberia (1008).

During this period the Byzantines eliminated the West Bulgarian Empire (1018) and reduced the Serbs to vassalage. They also annexed the Armenian Kingdom of Vaspurakan (1022). All in all, a pretty good performance from a state whose arteries were a good deal harder than those of its rivals.

1. The area acquired by Navarre, the County of Castile, was made into a separate kingdom for Sancho of Navarre's son Ferdinand.

The petty states of Muslim Spain are indicated by their capitals, numbered as follows: 1 Badajoz; 2 Mertola; 3 Santa Maria del Algarbe; 4 Huelva; 5 Seville; 6 Carmona; 7 Niebla; 8 Arcos; 9 Moron; 10 Malaga (with Ceuta and Tangier as dependencies); 11 Granada; 12 Almeria; 13 Denia (ruling the Balearics); 14 Valencia; 15 Tortosa; 16 Zaragoza; 17 Albarracin; 18 Alpuente; 19 Toledo; 20 Cordoba.

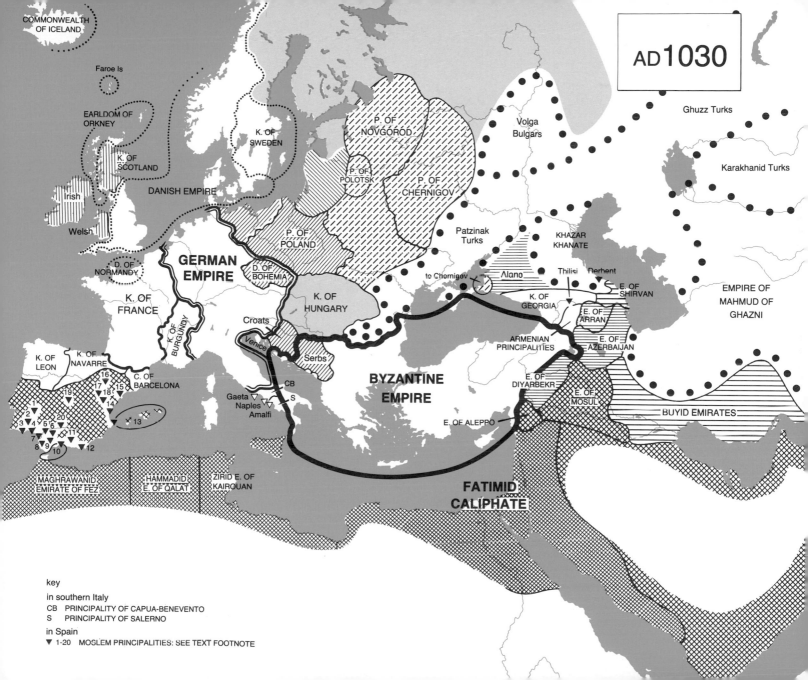

COMMONWEALTH
OF ICELAND

AD**1030**

Faroe Is

EARLDOM OF
ORKNEY

K. OF
SWEDEN

K. OF
SCOTLAND

Ghuzz Turks

DANISH EMPIRE

P. OF
NOVGOROD

Volga
Bulgars

Karakhanid Turks

Irish

Welsh

P. OF
POLOTSK

P. OF
CHERNIGOV

D. OF
NORMANDY

GERMAN
EMPIRE

D. OF
BOHEMIA

P. OF
POLAND

Patzinak
Turks

KHAZAR
KHANATE

to Chernigov

Alano

Thilisi Derbent

EMPIRE OF
MAHMUD OF
GHAZNI

K. OF
FRANCE

K. OF HUNGARY

Croats

K. OF
GEORGIA

E. OF
SHIRVAN

K. OF
BURGUNDY

Venice

Serbs

BYZANTINE
EMPIRE

ARMENIAN
PRINCIPALITIES

E. OF
ARRAN

K. OF
LEON

K. OF
NAVARRE

16

C. OF
BARCELONA

CB

E. OF
AZERBAIJAN

E. OF
DIYARBEKR

E. OF
MOSUL

19 17 18 15

20 14

Gaeta
Naples
Amalfi

S

E. OF ALEPPO

BUYID EMIRATES

1
2 19 20 11
3 4 5 6
7 8 9 10 12

13

MAGHRAWANID
EMIRATE OF FEZ

HAMMADID
E. OF QALAT

ZIRID E. OF
KAIROUAN

FATIMID
CALIPHATE

key

in southern Italy
CB   PRINCIPALITY OF CAPUA-BENEVENTO
S   PRINCIPALITY OF SALERNO

in Spain
▼ 1-20   MOSLEM PRINCIPALITIES: SEE TEXT FOOTNOTE

The middle decades of the eleventh century saw major upheavals in the Muslim world. Everywhere people were on the move: Berbers in the Sahara, Arabs on the North African littoral and, most important of all, Turks in the east. The Turks belonged to the Nine Tribes of western Turkestan (the Toghuz Oghuz, or Ghuzz for short). For their migration they divided into two streams, one moving westward into Russia, one south-west into Iran. The groups that invaded Russia became known as Cumans; by and large they stayed within the steppe zone, and their political impact was correspondingly limited. The influx into Iran spilled over much of the Near East: politically it is memorable because it created the Seljuk Sultanate, the first in the sequence of nomad empires that were to dominate the region for the remainder of the medieval period.[1]

The Seljuks are first heard of at the beginning of the eleventh century, when they were simply one of the many Ghuzz clans living to the north and east of the Aral Sea. Moving south they entered the service of Mahmud of Ghazni, who allotted them lands in the neighbourhood of Merv. On Mahmud's death the Seljuks set up on their own account, and when his son Masud tried to bring them back into line they inflicted such a crushing defeat on his forces that the Ghaznavid Empire in Iran collapsed (1040). This success attracted other Ghuzz tribes to the Seljuk banner: as the Ghaznavids drew back into Afghanistan, the Seljuks proceeded to a piecemeal conquest of Iran and Iraq that brought them to Baghdad by 1055. The Muslim half of Transcaucasia came under their control in the 1060s, northern Syria and the Hejaz in 1070. By then the Seljuk Sultan Alp Arslan was master of the most extensive empire Islam had known since the noontide of the Abbasids.

The Arab movement was on a smaller scale, involving only two tribes, the Beni Sulaym and the Beni Hilal. The official story has the Fatimids pulling the strings. In the late tenth century they had forcibly transferred the Sulaym and Hilali from Arabia, where they had been making a nuisance of themselves, to Upper Egypt. In the mid eleventh century they put these unruly clients to use, dispatching them westward against the Zirids of Kairouan. The provocation was said to be a declaration by the Zirid Emir that he no longer considered himself either a vassal of the Fatimid Caliph or – and this was the real insult – a member of the Shia faith (1049). Whatever the merit of this explanation – and the movement has a surging quality which makes it difficult to believe it could be controlled so precisely – the result was a migration that gave the Libyan provinces of Cyrenaica and Tripolitania a predominantly Arab population, and the Zirids an unpleasant surprise. Defeated in the field, the Zirids retreated to the coast, where the old Fatimid capital of Mahdiya proved a safe haven. The Hammadids of Qalat, who had initially welcomed the Hilali, were subsequently forced to make a similar retreat, from Qalat to Bougie.

The last of these migratory movements is the most exotic. Deep in the Sahara lived the Sanhaja, Berbers of a sterner cast from their brethren in the Maghreb. Proud, fearless and inured to privation, these 'men of the veil' – the ancestors of today's Tuareg – were recent converts to Islam. Their particular inspiration was a puritanical monastic community, a *ribat*, established on an island site somewhere in the Sahel. Its graduates were known as al-Murabitun, 'Men of the *Ribat*', a term traditionally anglicized as Almoravids. The Almoravids proved doughty soldiers. In 1056 they seized control of the Sijilmasa oasis on the southern side of the Atlas, and in 1060 they established an armed camp at Marrakesh, which became the base for further advances. Over the next ten years they conquered all Morocco, a country to which they had given both a new capital and, Marrakesh and Morocco being variants of the same word, the name by which it has been known ever since.

In Christendom, these same decades belonged to the Normans. The blend of Viking and Frank in the Duchy of Normandy produced men of extraordinary vigour, valiant in the field and tenacious in the counting house. Among the first to make their mark were the ten sons of a minor Norman noble called Tancred d'Hauteville. Facing limited prospects at home, they journeyed to Italy, where the constant skirmishing between Lombard and Byzantine offered enterprising mercenaries the chance to make their fortunes. In 1040 the eldest son seized the castle of Melfi in the no man's land between the two; twenty years later, the sixth son Robert Guiscard ('Robert the Cunning') began the reduction of the Byzantine province. By 1071 Robert had mastered the area, which was subsequently known as the Duchy of Apulia; he also won a foothold in Sicily and pressed hard on the Lombard principality of Salerno. Gaeta and the principality of Capua had meanwhile fallen to another Norman adventurer.

Back home the Duke of Normandy, William the Bastard, had been making news too. William inherited a claim to the crown of England, which was in play again following the death of Canute and the break-up of the Danish Empire. The English, however, preferred one of their own barons, Harold Godwinson (1066). Undeterred, William put together a formidable expeditionary force and led it across the Channel. At the Battle of Hastings, the English (fighting on foot, like Vikings) were decisively defeated by the Normans (fighting on horseback, like Frenchmen): Harold perished, along with the old order. But the battle was only the beginning. Over the next twenty years William – no longer the Bastard but the Conqueror – changed England from a laggard to a front-runner among European kingdoms. Enshrined in the mystique of 1066 is the seed of the national, secular state.[2]

Russia went through an interesting devolution at this time. Yaroslav of Novgorod, who had become ruler of all Russia bar Polotsk when his brother the Prince of Chernigov died, followed his father's example and left each of his sons a separate principality (1054). The principalities were ranked in order,

(continued over)

---

1. The title of Sultan, the Islamic equivalent of Emperor or Khan, indicates complete secular sovereignty. Its use by Sunni Muslims – which is what the Seljuks became – emphasizes the restriction of the Caliph's authority to spiritual matters.

2. As William was sovereign in England but only a fief-holder in France, the map shows Normandy as an English possession. The special border round it – two dots for each dash – indicates that it wasn't an outright

(footnote continued on p. 106)

COMMONWEALTH
OF ICELAND

AD 1071

to Norway

EARLDOM OF
ORKNEY

K. OF
NORWAY

K. OF
SWEDEN

Ghuzz Turks

Volga
Bulgars

Karakhanid
Turks

K. OF
SCOTLAND

K. OF
DENMARK

to Kiev   to
Pereyaslavl

Irish

P. OF
SMOLENSK

NORMAN
K. OF
ENGLAND

P. OF
POLOTSK

P. OF
CHERNIGOV

Welsh

Cumans

to
Chernigov

GERMAN

to
England

D. OF
BOHEMIA

P. OF
PEREYASLAVL

Alans

EMPIRE

GREAT
P. OF KIEV

K. OF
FRANCE

P. OF
POLAND

P. OF
GALICIA

K. OF
CASTILE

K. OF
HUNGARY

Patzinaks

K. OF
GEORGIA

K. OF NAVARRE

Croats

K. OF
LEON

K. OF
ARAGON

Pisa

SELJUK
SULTANATE

K. OF
GALICIA

VENICE

Serbs

Zaragoza

C. OF BARCELONA

NORMAN
C. OF CAPUA

BYZANTINE
EMPIRE

Badajoz

Toledo

Albarracin

to
Pisa

Naples

Alpuente

Amalfi

Seville

Denia

Salerno

NORMAN
D. OF APULIA

Granada

Murcia

Almería

arrakesh
60

Fez 1069

ZIRID
EMIRATE OF
MAHDIYA

HAMMADID EMIRATE
OF BOUGIE

Beni Sulaym 1050

FATIMID
CALIPHATE

Sijilmasa 1055

Beni Hilal
1051

Beni Sulaym
Beni Hilal

Almoravids

with the Great Principality of Kiev taking precedence and, in theory at least, exercising a degree of control over the others. What was odd was the system of succession, which was 'lateral', not 'vertical': when Prince A died, his younger brother B took his place, leaving principality B vacant for Prince C, and so on down the line. The next generation joined the queue at the far end.

Ferdinand of Castile was another monarch to leave a divided estate, splitting the two kingdoms he had acquired (Leon and Castile) three ways at his death (1065; the third kingdom, Galicia, was carved out of Leon). This didn't help the Christian counter-offensive, which Ferdinand himself had begun with some useful advances on the Atlantic coast. The Muslims had meanwhile sorted themselves out into ten emirates (down from twenty in 1030). In the Mediterranean, Pisa was emerging as a significant sea power. Her exertions had saved Sardinia from the attentions of the Emir of Denia, and in 1050 Pope and Emperor agreed to entrust the island to her protection. In Germany, there are a couple of changes to note: the recovery of Lusatia (1031) and the acquisition of Burgundy (1032).

The Byzantines recorded their final advances during this period: Edessa, annexed in 1032, and Ani, the capital of Armenia, annexed in 1045. Then the tide began to turn. Southern Italy, as we have seen, was lost to the Normans in the 1060s; at the same time Armenia came under attack from the Turks. Alp Arslan seems to have had no interest in acquiring the country: he was simply protecting his flank before moving against the Fatimids. But whereas the Byzantines could afford to let Italy go, they had to defend Armenia: it was the key to the Anatolian heart of the Empire.

The Byzantine Emperor Romanus took the job seriously. He mustered the main force of the Empire and began a drive through the eastern provinces. News of his advance reached Syria, and Alp Arslan, fearing for his communications, turned back towards Armenia. The two armies met at Manzikert, by Lake Van. The Turks employed their usual tactics, their mounted bowmen retiring before each Byzantine advance, then wheeling round and pouring in volleys of arrows whenever the pursuit slackened. Frustrated, exhausted, and suffering a steady trickle of casualties for no advantage, the Byzantine army began to come apart. It contained too many mercenaries for good discipline. Some of them were Turks able to find refuge with their compatriots, while others, including a Norman contingent, are said to have held back from the battle. The remaining regiments struggled on, lost contact with each other and, sooner or later, found themselves surrounded by superior Turkish forces. By the time the Emperor was brought to the Sultan's tent that evening, the army that he had led out from Constantinople had ceased to exist.

The battle of Manzikert is unimpeachably one of the decisive battles of history. Whereas Adrianople, an equally crushing defeat from the strictly military point of view, had few immediate consequences, Manzikert cost the Byzantine Empire half its territory. All the Anatolian provinces were lost to the Turk; only the Bosphorus saved the remainder.

Alp Arslan himself did not follow up his victory: he had to leave for the east, where trouble was brewing with the Karakhanids. But the conquest of Anatolia went forward no less rapidly for that: Turkish clans moved on to the central Anatolian plateau, driving their flocks before them and turning the peasantry off the land. Powered by the same migratory force, the Seljuk Empire expanded equally dramatically in other directions. By the date of this map it included Syria and Palestine (bar the coastal towns, which the Fatimids' sea power enabled them to retain), most of Arabia, all of Transoxiana and all but the extreme west of Transcaucasia.[1]

The conquest of Byzantine Asia was a major triumph for Islam. Christendom couldn't match it but at the other end of the Mediterranean did have one important success to record, the capture of Toledo in 1085. The Christians of Spain were now beginning to get their act together: the number of kingdoms dropped from six to three, as Aragon absorbed Navarre and, more importantly, Alfonso VI of Leon acquired Castile and Galicia (1072–5). The Muslims, by contrast, were losing confidence. Doubtful of their ability to stem the Christian tides, they called on the Almoravids of Morocco for aid. This was to summon King Stork: in 1090–92 the Almoravids gobbled up most of the Spanish emirates and of the five surviving in 1092 the largest, Badajoz, succumbed three years later. But from a military point of view the remedy was effective: the arrival of the Almoravids stabilized the frontier for a generation.

Another significant Christian advance was made in the central Mediterranean, where the youngest of the d'Hauteville brothers, Roger, completed the conquest of Sicily (1091; Malta was included in the surrender). This rounded off the Norman hegemony over the south of Italy, of which the overall suzerain was the Duke of Apulia. Other changes are relatively minor. Pisa, having made a success of its Sardinian fief, was encouraged to take over Corsica by the Pope (1077). The Duchy of Normandy and the Norman Kingdom of England parted company on the death of the Conqueror (1087), with the result that the Duchy, as a purely French fief, disappears from the map. The Anglo-Scottish border assumed its final form when the Conqueror's son William Rufus annexed Cumbria (1092). The Hungarians absorbed Croatia in 1091. In the same decade the Cumans forced the Russians to abandon their positions on the Taman peninsula and all but annihilated the Patzinaks.

1. Within the boundary of the Seljuk Empire, but outside its control, was the fortress of Alamut, where, in 1090, the Grand Master of the Shia sect of Assassins set up his headquarters. The Assassins exerted an influence out of proportion to their number by the unsparing use of the political technique to which they have given their name. This in turn derives from the word 'hashish', the effect of which was interpreted as a glimpse of the paradise to come and made the initiates of the sect impatient of this world and oblivious of the personal consequences of their actions.

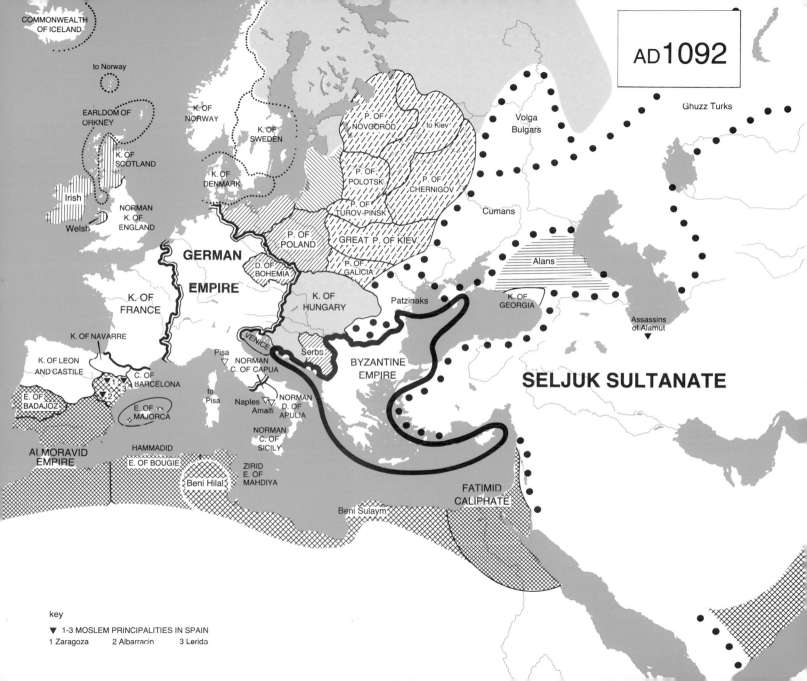

AD **1092**

COMMONWEALTH
OF ICELAND

to Norway

EARLDOM OF
ORKNEY

K. OF
SCOTLAND

K. OF
NORWAY

K. OF
SWEDEN

Irish

Welsh

NORMAN
K. OF
ENGLAND

K. OF
DENMARK

GERMAN

EMPIRE

K. OF
FRANCE

D. OF
BOHEMIA

P. OF
POLAND

P. OF
NOVGOROD

to Kiev

P. OF
POLOTSK

P. OF
CHERNIGOV

P. OF
TUROV-PINSK

GREAT P. OF KIEV

P. OF
GALICIA

K. OF
HUNGARY

Patzinaks

Volga
Bulgars

Ghuzz Turks

Cumans

Alans

K. OF
GEORGIA

Assassins
of Alamut

SELJUK SULTANATE

K. OF NAVARRE

K. OF LEON
AND CASTILE

▼ 1
▼ 3

C. OF
BARCELONA

E. OF
BADAJOZ

▼ 2

E. OF
MAJORCA

Pisa

to
Pisa

VENICE

NORMAN
C. OF CAPUA

Naples
Amalfi

NORMAN
D. OF
APULIA

Serbs

**BYZANTINE
EMPIRE**

NORMAN
C. OF
SICILY

ALMORAVID
EMPIRE

HAMMADID
E. OF BOUGIE

Beni Hilal

ZIRID
E. OF
MAHDIYA

Beni Sulaym

**FATIMID
CALIPHATE**

key

▼ 1-3 MOSLEM PRINCIPALITIES IN SPAIN
1 Zaragoza   2 Albarracin   3 Lerida

Among the embassies received by Pope Urban II in 1095 was one from the hard-pressed Byzantines, who wanted his help in raising a volunteer force to fight the Turks. The Pope thought about it and decided to go one better. Eastern Christendom might be floundering, but the West was riding high. The Muslims had been evicted from Sardinia and Sicily and put on the defensive in Spain. There was no reason why an army, raised under papal auspices, couldn't save the East and, for that matter, fight its way through to the Holy Land and liberate Jerusalem itself. Later that year, in a ceremony that was none the less moving for being carefully rehearsed, Pope Urban preached the Crusade.

The Crusade was a very different proposition from the limited aid the Byzantines had been seeking. What the Pope was calling for was an all-out effort by Latin Christendom to drive the Muslims out of Anatolia, Syria and Palestine. Itinerant preachers spread the Pope's message through the villages of France and Germany, arousing the enthusiasm of men who had neither experience of war nor arms with which to wage it. In the summer of 1096 this excited rabble arrived at Constantinople, eager to begin the great work. The first enemy they had to overcome was the Seljuk Sultan of Rum (meaning Rome-in-Asia, i.e. Anatolia), an enterprising prince who had managed to turn his fief into an independent kingdom. He didn't hang back, and the two sides clashed on the Byzantine–Turkish frontier. The battle was a massacre. At the end of the day nearly all the 20,000 poor souls involved in the People's Crusade were dead, dying or *en route* for the slave market. The Turks had hardly lost a man.

This was not, however, the end of the Crusade. The Pope's appeal had stirred some harder hearts to make more deliberate preparations. Among the names now making their way east were Raymond of Toulouse, a veteran of the Spanish wars, Robert of Normandy, the son of the Conqueror, Godfrey of Lorraine and Stephen of Blois. Each brought with him a small army of retainers. At Constantinople they were joined by Bohemond, Robert Guiscard's eldest son, who, only a few years earlier, had been fighting the Byzantines in the Balkans. After some prickly negotiations, the Emperor Alexius and the western barons agreed a plan of campaign.

The crusaders, supported by a small Byzantine force, crossed to Asia in the spring of 1097. They marched straight for Nicaea, the capital of the Sultanate of Rum, and laid siege to it. The Sultan was on his eastern border at the time, having written off the whole crusading movement as a farce; he hurried back only to find that his men could make no headway against the carefully ordered lines of the besieging army. Reluctantly he withdrew, promising himself revenge if the Christians ever ventured into the interior.

The crusaders came on immediately after the surrender of Nicaea. They marched in two divisions, Bohemond leading the van, Raymond of Toulouse the rear. Bohemond had advanced as far as Dorylaeum, where he was about to break camp, when the Turks appeared in full strength, circling his surprised forces and pouring in volley after volley of arrows. Bohemond made his knights dismount and put their horses out of arrowshot in the centre of the camp. There were to be no sorties, just an unyielding defence. The sun rose high in the sky; hope ebbed, but the perimeter held. Then Raymond's division came in view, and it was the Turks' turn to be surprised: they thought they had trapped the whole Christian army, and now it turned out that they had been fighting only half of it. They sensed that they had been too prodigal with their arrows and too demanding of their horses. As Bohemond's men joined the long line of mailed knights that fronted the crusader order of battle, the Turks kept the field, but they gave a backward look to the hills on the east which marked their line of retreat. When they saw a third Christian army advancing from this direction – a detachment of Raymond's force that had deliberately taken this route to the battlefield – they broke and fled. The crusaders had an easy pursuit, the plunder of the Turkish camp and, at day's end, a famous victory.

After Dorylaeum, the crusaders were able to advance unchecked across Anatolia, through the Taurus Mountains to Cilicia and the gates of Antioch. By October they had begun the siege of the city, which was to hold out for eighteen months and bring the besieging force to desperate straits on several occasions. If the Emirs of Mosul, Aleppo and Damascus had acted together, they could certainly have crushed the rapidly weakening Christian force, but they never made a common plan. By a hair's breadth the Christians won the victories they needed. By some timely treachery Bohemond got his men into the city, and with Antioch safe in Christian hands the crusaders were free to move against Jerusalem. They arrived there in June 1099.

The crusading army had now been fighting for more than three years; it could hardly maintain itself for much longer, and if it was to take Jerusalem at all it would have to be soon, by assault. After an unsuccessful attempt to rush the walls, the crusaders put their remaining energies into the construction of three movable towers, which took a month. Then they dragged them forward. By 14 July, Raymond of Toulouse had his tower up against the south-west wall, and the next day Godfrey of Lorraine's tower was in position on the north side. It was Godfrey's men who worked to best effect. While crossbowmen kept the parapet clear of defenders, engineers bridged the gap between tower and wall, and at midday two knights led the Lorrainers across. From there they fought their way to the gate-towers on either side. Their capture sealed the fate of the city. The gates were thrown open, the crusaders poured through, and there was nothing for the Muslims to do but try to make their surrenders individually. Few had their offers accepted, and fewer still had them honoured. It was a bloodstained banner that the exultant victors unfurled over Jerusalem.[1]

1. The defence of Jerusalem was conducted by the Fatimids, who had moved back into the city while the Turks' attention was concentrated on Antioch. More permanent advances of this sort were made by the Byzantines, who recovered – and retained – the west of Anatolia and much of its seaboard. Also worth a mention is the placing of a crusader force in the city of Edessa. The only changes to note elsewhere on the map are the capture of Valencia by the Castilian soldier of fortune El Cid (1094; it was recovered by the Almoravids eight years later) and Norway's imposition of overlordship on Orkney and Man (1098; the Faroes had submitted earlier, in 1035).

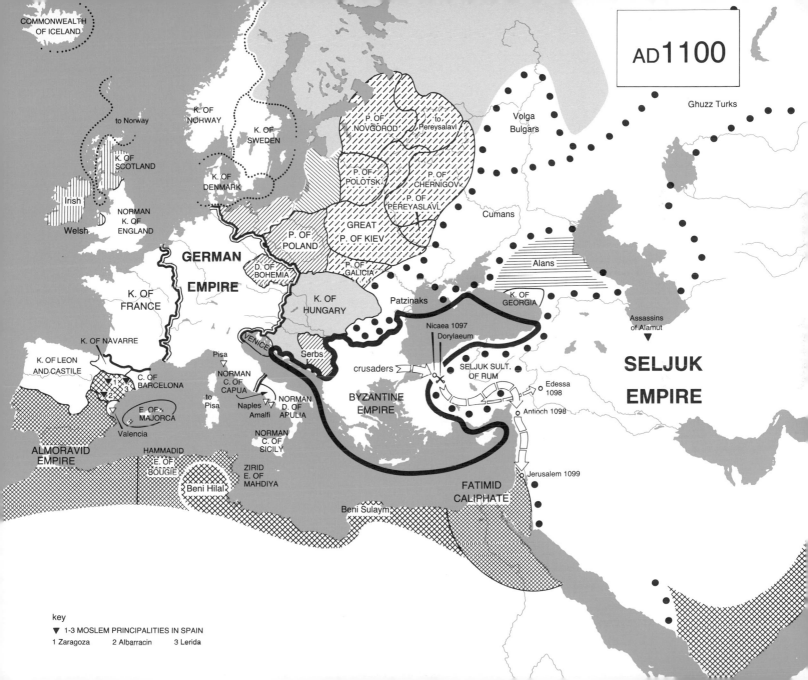

COMMONWEALTH OF ICELAND

AD1100

Ghuzz Turks

to Norway

K. OF NORWAY

K. OF SWEDEN

K. OF SCOTLAND

K. OF DENMARK

Irish

Welsh

NORMAN K. OF ENGLAND

P. OF NOVGOROD

to Pereysalavi

Volga Bulgars

P. OF POLOTSK

P. OF CHERNIGOV

P. OF PEREYASLAVL

GREAT P. OF KIEV

Cumans

GERMAN EMPIRE

P. OF POLAND

D. OF BOHEMIA

P. OF GALICIA

Alans

K. OF FRANCE

K. OF HUNGARY

Patzinaks

K. OF GEORGIA

Assassins of Alamut

K. OF NAVARRE

Pisa

VENICE

Serbs

crusaders

Nicaea 1097
Dorylaeum

SELJUK SULT. OF RUM

SELJUK EMPIRE

K. OF LEON AND CASTILE

1
2 3

C. OF BARCELONA

NORMAN C. OF CAPUA

to Pisa

Naples
Amalfi

NORMAN D. OF APULIA

BYZANTINE EMPIRE

Edessa 1098

E. OF MAJORCA

Valencia

NORMAN C. OF SICILY

Antioch 1098

ALMORAVID EMPIRE

HAMMADID E. OF BOUGIE

ZIRID E. OF MAHDIYA

Beni Hilal

Beni Sulaym

FATIMID CALIPHATE

Jerusalem 1099

key

▼ 1-3 MOSLEM PRINCIPALITIES IN SPAIN

1 Zaragoza   2 Albarracin   3 Lerida

The First Crusade was a great success, but it left the Near East deplorably congested with petty states. Both the success and the congestion reflect the decline of Seljuk authority, and all three combine to make the map more difficult to read than usual. Start with the Seljuks: there are now three Seljuk sultanates, one covering Rum (Anatolia), one the central provinces, and one the east. Each of these sultanates has the usual Turkish marking, a border of black circles. Each also has, at its seat of government (respectively Konya, Hamadan and Merv), a flagged and outlined circle. The other flagged (but not outlined) circles represent provincial governments that have escaped central control. This devolution is most marked in the west of the Empire. In Rum, for example, the Danishmend Emir of Sivas, the first Muslim leader to inflict a significant defeat on the Crusaders, was fully the equal of the Sultan. The Sultanate of Hamadan held up better, but this was because the Sultan proved adept at playing his unruly vassals off against each other; aside from this he took few initiatives and never appeared in his western borderlands at all. But the most successful of the Seljuk monarchs, at least at this stage, was Sultan Sanjar of Merv. All the eastern provinces accepted his rule, and many of the princes of further Turkestan and Afghanistan offered their homage. What Sanjar couldn't control was the continuing movement of Turkish tribes through his dominions. This migration, which had built the Seljuk Empire in the first place, was constantly remodelling it, sometimes underpinning, sometimes undermining, the existing provincial governments.[1]

While the Sultan of Hamadan was preoccupied with his balancing act, the crusader barons were able to complete their conquest of the Levantine coast (bar Ascalon, which didn't fall till 1153) and organize their holdings into a modest-sized kingdom with its capital at Jerusalem, plus three dependent mini-states: the Principality of Antioch, the County of Edessa and the County of Tripoli. Seljuk decline also enabled the Georgians to make a comeback: in 1121 they recovered their ancient capital, Tbilisi, and from there they went on to liberate most of the lands inhabited by people of Georgian stock.

The Norman conquests in southern Italy were consolidated by Roger of Sicily. He acquired the Duchy of Apulia on the death of a cousin in 1127; three years later he took the title of King. He ruled from Palermo, where his court, with its black servants, its Saracen guards, its harem and its pleasure-domes became the scandal and the envy of Christendom. Normandy itself, pawned by its Duke to raise money for the First Crusade, passed to his fraternal creditor, the King of England, when the Duke on his return proved incapable of redeeming it (1106).

In Spain, the Almoravids completed their conquest of the Muslim sector (1110–15) but then lost Zaragoza to Navarre (1118). Barcelona and Provence were united (1112). Poland subdued the Pomeranians (1102–24); the Cumans absorbed the remnants of the Patzinaks. In Russia there are several changes worth noting. A new principality, Suzdal, emerged in the north-east of the country, where population was growing faster than elsewhere. And Novgorod is to be termed a republic rather than a principality after 1126, the date when the city fathers started electing their mayor instead of accepting the Prince's nominees. Novgorod still had its princes, but their job was to defend the city, not rule it. Elsewhere the tendency was for the principalities to become hereditary in a single lineage: lateral succession was practised within the principalities, but not between them.[2]

1. The nomenclature of these local governments – the flagged circles on the map – is complicated. Some were run by Seljuk princes, who usually bore the title of King. Others were in the hands of emirs (governors) who, though Turks, were not of Seljuk stock. A third variety consisted of a Turkish nobleman ruling on behalf of an infant Seljuk prince: these officials were termed atabegs (guardians). Needless to say, the inability of the atabegs to keep their charges alive soon outpaced the fertility of the Seljuk house, and the atabegs, like the emirs, quickly evolved into hereditary fief-holders, impossible to dislodge.

2. The term republic doesn't imply any tendency to democracy: medieval republics were always oligarchic and had constitutions that were intended to keep them that way. In Novgorod's case, the assembly that elected the mayor had about 300 members, each representing an important land-owning family. No one else had any say at all in the way the city was run.

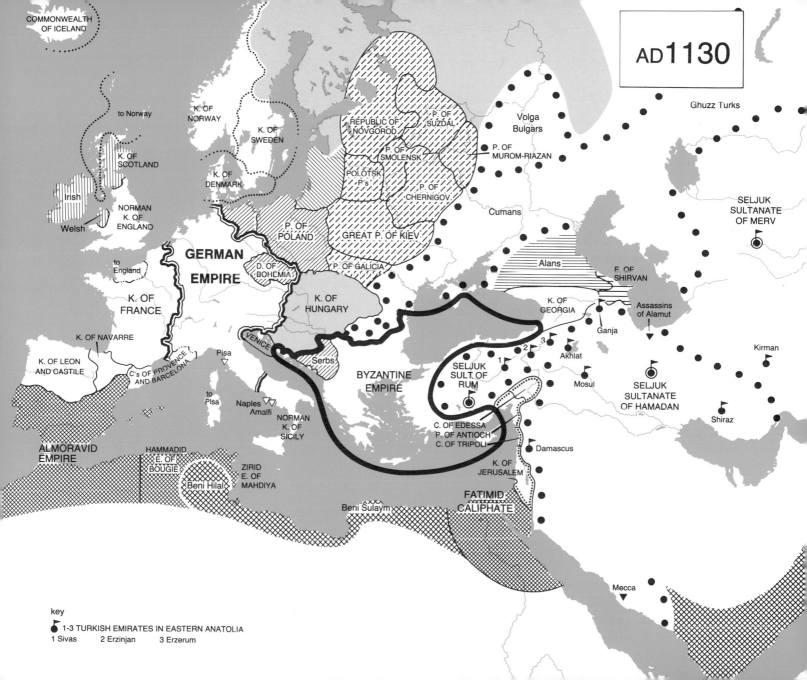

AD 1130

COMMONWEALTH OF ICELAND

to Norway

K. OF NORWAY

K. OF SCOTLAND

Irish

Welsh

NORMAN K. OF ENGLAND

to England

K. OF FRANCE

K. OF NAVARRE

K. OF LEON AND CASTILE

ALMORAVID EMPIRE

HAMMADID E. OF BOUGIE

Beni Hilal

ZIRID E. OF MAHDIYA

K. OF SWEDEN

K. OF DENMARK

GERMAN EMPIRE

D. OF BOHEMIA

P. OF POLAND

C's OF PROVENCE AND BARCELONA

Pisa

to Pisa

Naples
Amalfi

NORMAN K. OF SICILY

Beni Sulaym

REPUBLIC OF NOVGOROD

P. OF SUZDAL

P. OF SMOLENSK

P. OF MUROM-RIAZAN

POLOTSK 'P's'

P. OF CHERNIGOV

GREAT P. OF KIEV

P. OF GALICIA

K. OF HUNGARY

VENICE

Serbs

BYZANTINE EMPIRE

Volga Bulgars

Cumans

Alans

K. OF GEORGIA

Ganja

SELJUK SULT OF RUM

1   2 3

Akhlat

Mosul

C. OF EDESSA
P. OF ANTIOCH
C. OF TRIPOLI

Damascus

K. OF JERUSALEM

FATIMID CALIPHATE

Ghuzz Turks

SELJUK SULTANATE OF MERV

E. OF SHIRVAN

Assassins of Alamut

Kirman

SELJUK SULTANATE OF HAMADAN

Shiraz

Mecca

key

● 1-3 TURKISH EMIRATES IN EASTERN ANATOLIA
1 Sivas   2 Erzinjan   3 Erzerum

As it turned out, the most imposing of the Seljuk successor states, the Sultanate of Merv, was the first to fall. Defeated by the Qarakhitai Mongols in Transoxiana, Sultan Sanjar retreated south of the Oxus (1141).[1] There, twelve years later, what was left of his dominion was destroyed in an uprising of newly arrived Ghuzz tribes. It was an ending that perfectly mirrored the dynasty's beginning, but, alas for symmetry, the other two Seljuk sultanates were far from done. The Sultan of Hamadan had lost lands all round: in the west where the Zangid Atabegs of Mosul developed a powerful kingdom, in the south, where the Abbasid Caliph resumed his secular power, and in the north, where the native princes of Shirvan and Mazandaran recovered their independence. However, thanks to a powerful Atabeg of his own, the Sultan still remained a significant potentate. The same could be said of the Sultan of Rum, who would certainly have unified all Turkish Anatolia if the Byzantines and Zangids hadn't made it their business to stop him.

As far as the crusader states were concerned, the varying fortunes of the Seljuk Sultanates were of little import: the Turks that mattered to them were Zangi, Atabeg of Mosul, and his son and successor, Nureddin. Zangi opened the Muslim counter-offensive by capturing Edessa (1143), and Nureddin easily rode out the pitiful Second Crusade, which was Christendom's response (1147–8). Not long after, Nureddin was able to unify Muslim Syria by annexing Damascus (1154). The struggle then moved to Egypt, fat with wealth and convulsed by the death throes of the Fatimid Caliphate. Each side realized the importance of this country, whose resources would decide the outcome of the struggle between Cross and Crescent in the Levant, but the Christians could not prevent victory and Egypt going to Nureddin (1169).

Though the Christians were in trouble in the Levant, they still held the initiative in Spain. The separation of Navarre from Aragon (1134) was balanced by the union of Aragon and Barcelona (1137); a decade later, the King of Aragon was able to clear the lands along the lower Ebro (1148–9). On the Atlantic coast, Portugal, which had started off the century as a mere county, proclaimed itself a kingdom in 1139; its southern frontier was advanced significantly by the capture of Lisbon (1147). In the centre, the advance went more slowly, impeded by the division of Leon and Castile (1157) and the arrival of the Almohads. The Almohads (properly al-Muwayidun, 'Devotees of the One God') were Shi'ite sectaries, similar in many ways to the Fatimids. They replaced the Almoravids in Morocco in the 1140s, conquered the rest of the Maghreb and Tripolitania in 1152–60 and took over Muslim Spain in 1150–72.

If the Second Crusade was a fiasco as regards the Holy Land, it achieved some useful results elsewhere. The English shared in an important success when their fleet stopped off at Lisbon and helped the Portuguese take the town. The north Germans and the Danes got permission to discharge their obligations even closer to home: an attack on the pagan Slavs in the Elbe–Oder region was given the status of a crusade and, perhaps because of this, was eventually pushed through to a successful conclusion (1147–68).

England acquired a rather odd empire at this time. After the extinction of the house of William the Conqueror, the crown passed to Henry Plantagenet, Count of Anjou, the territory immediately to the south of Normandy (1154). Two years earlier, Henry had married Eleanor, Duchess of Aquitaine, whose lands covered the entire area between Anjou and the Spanish frontier. The result was that, by the time he mounted the English throne, Henry held a solid block of territory extending from the Channel to the Pyrenees. This made him the richest monarch in Europe, for, leaving aside the revenues of the English crown, he actually owned more of France than the French king. Henry added to his dominions by sanctioning an invasion of Ireland, which got off to a misleadingly easy start.

The shifting pattern of the Russian principalities received a fundamentally new cast when the forces of Suzdal put Kiev to the sack (1169). The title of Great Prince was henceforth borne by the ruler of Suzdal, usually in the style of Great Prince of Vladimir, this being Suzdal's capital city. The Byzantines built up a commanding position in the Balkans, recovering control of the Adriatic coast and gaining recognition of their suzerainty from the Serbs and Bosnians; they also exacted similar homage from the Principality of Antioch (as was their due: it lay within the pre-Manzikert frontier of the Empire). In Germany, where Frederick Barbarossa was making heroic efforts to breathe new life into the Empire's fading institutions, the Duke of Bohemia was promoted to King. Poland disintegrated.

1. The Qarakhitai were Buddhists: Islam, which had made great strides in Central Asia in the days of the Karakhanids, now entered a period of retreat.

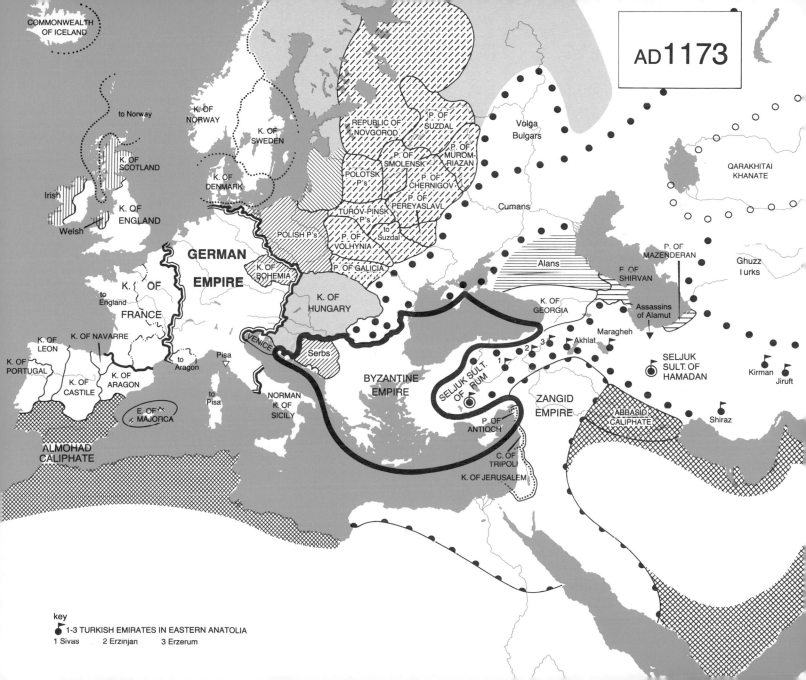

AD 1173

COMMONWEALTH OF ICELAND

to Norway

K. OF NORWAY

K. OF SWEDEN

REPUBLIC OF NOVGOROD

P. OF SUZDAL

Volga Bulgars

QARAKHITAI KHANATE

K. OF SCOTLAND

K. OF DENMARK

P. OF SMOLENSK

P. OF MUROM-RIAZAN

Cumans

Irish

POLOTSK P's

P. OF CHERNIGOV

K. OF ENGLAND

Welsh

P. OF PEREYASLAVL

Alans

P. OF MAZENDERAN

Ghuzz Turks

GERMAN EMPIRE

TURÓV-PINSK P's

to Suzdal

P. OF VOLHYNIA

K. OF BOHEMIA

P. OF GALICIA

E. OF SHIRVAN

to England

K. OF FRANCE

K. OF HUNGARY

K. OF GEORGIA

Assassins of Alamut

P. OF MAZENDERAN

K. OF LEON

K. OF NAVARRE

Akhlat

Maragheh

VENICE

Pisa

Serbs

SELJUK SULT. OF HAMADAN

to Aragon

2 3

1

K. OF PORTUGAL

K. OF CASTILE

K. OF ARAGON

to Pisa

BYZANTINE EMPIRE

SELJUK SULT. OF RUM

ZANGID EMPIRE

Kirman

Jiruft

E. OF MAJORCA

NORMAN K. OF SICILY

P. OF ANTIOCH

ABBASID CALIPHATE

Shiraz

ALMOHAD CALIPHATE

C. OF TRIPOLI

K. OF JERUSALEM

key

1-3 TURKISH EMIRATES IN EASTERN ANATOLIA

1 Sivas   2 Erzinjan   3 Erzerum

Nureddin continued to reside at Mosul after the conquest of Egypt, which was ruled in his name by a Kurdish general, Saladin. This was a mistake, for the new tail was quite capable of wagging the dog, and as soon as Nureddin was dead, Saladin moved to take over the sultanate (1174). The success of his regime and of the Ayyubid Dynasty he founded was assured by the victory of Hattin (1187), which brought the Muslim counter-offensive against the Latins of the Levant to a triumphant culmination. The army of the Kingdom of Jerusalem was all but annihilated and the Kingdom itself reduced to a single town, the seaport of Tyre.

The Pope immediately called for a Third Crusade to restore the Christian position. His appeal was royally answered: by 1190 the German Emperor Frederick Barbarossa and the kings of England and France were all *en route* for the Holy Land. Frederick marched across Anatolia, captured Konya, the capital of Turkish Rum, but then dropped dead. Germany's contribution subsequently faded out. Richard of England arrived by sea, covered his expenses by taking Cyprus from the Byzantines (1190), then wrested Acre and a useful strip of Levantine coast from Saladin (1191). But the army he captained was never strong enough to move inland, and Jerusalem remained in Muslim hands. Philip of France, who had only joined the Crusade for appearance's sake, did little and went home as soon as he decently could. Saladin had small cause for discontent. The new Kingdom of Acre was only a minor blemish on his Empire.

The disappointing results of the Third Crusade explain the strategy planned for the Fourth, an amphibious assault on Egypt, the key to the Levant. This would exploit the one advantage remaining to the Christians, their increasing command of the sea. The Venetians were particularly keen to help. Perhaps because of their pre-existing connections with Byzantium, they had been a bit slow to exploit the opportunities offered by the crusading movement: the Fourth Crusade was their opportunity to catch up.

The crusaders assembled at Venice in 1204. Unfortunately, they brought with them little more than half the price agreed for their passage to the Levant. The Venetians suggested that they make up the difference by taking Zara, an Adriatic seaport that the Hungarians had recently lifted from the Byzantines and which Venice had long coveted. This done, another diversion presented itself in the form of a fugitive Byzantine prince who offered total support for the Crusade provided the crusaders installed him in Constantinople first. With varying degrees of reluctance – in the case of the Venetians, almost none at all – the leaders of the Crusade succumbed. The armaments intended for the discomfort of the Turks were used to replace one Byzantine Emperor with another.

The Byzantines had been fading for a generation, ever since an ill-advised offensive against the Seljuks of Rum had come to grief at the battle of Myriocephalum (1176). Many of the peripheral provinces had been lost: Croatia and Dalmatia to the Hungarians, Serbia and Bulgaria to independence movements and Cilicia to the Armenians.[1] The treasury was empty. It soon became apparent that the payments promised by the new Emperor would never be made. Infuriated, the crusaders put Constantinople to the sack, placed one of their own number on the imperial throne, and, in the name of this Latin Emperor, proceeded to take over as much of the Empire as they could lay hands on. This amounted to most of the European provinces. Meanwhile, the Venetians, operating on their own account, conquered Crete and such other islands and headland strongpoints as the geography of their sea routes suggested might be useful. All that remained to the Greeks were five provincial governments: the 'Empires' of Nicaea and Trebizond, the Despotates of Epirus and Rhodes, and Monemvasia, a fortress in the Peloponnese, which held out till 1248.

As he would have been the first to admit, Philip of France hurried home from the Third Crusade to steal a march on Richard, who, in Philip's view, held far too many French fiefs. Luck was on his side. Crossing Germany, Richard was seized and held to ransom by the ignoble Emperor Henry VI: it took him fifteen months and £100,000 to obtain his freedom, and by then Philip had made significant progress. However, Richard soon recovered the lost positions, and it was not until the English crown passed to his lacklustre brother John that the tide set in Philip's favour. The key to Normandy was Château Gaillard, the great castle Richard had built overlooking the Seine. In 1203–4 Philip took Château Gaillard, then Normandy, and finally all the English possessions north of the Loire. Men may have sung the deeds of Richard Lionheart, the valiant knight of the Third Crusade, but history remembers Philip Augustus, whose single-mindedness made France the foremost state in Europe.

France's rising star shone the brighter for Germany's decline. The elective nature of the German monarchy was one source of weakness, the quarrel with the Papacy, of which more overleaf, another. But the main problem was that the Empire was too big and too polyglot. The gap between its power and its pretensions was starkly revealed on the battlefield of Legnano, where Frederick Barbarossa, a better than average emperor, was defeated by the forces of the Lombard League (1176). As far as Italy was concerned, the Empire was an empire in name only. Yet, to contemporaries this was not so obvious as it is to us: Barbarossa's son Henry VI married the heiress to the Kingdom of Sicily and his son was to possess both Empire and Kingdom. It looked an impressive combination.[2]

In the Baltic the Northern Crusade was now getting its second wind. The Swedes got a foothold in Finland; a German crusading order, the Knights of the Sword, established itself in Livonia. On the already pacified southern shore, the Danes extracted homage from the various German and Polish baronies.

---

1. The Armenians had moved into Cilicia after the Byzantine reconquest of the region in the tenth century. There was plenty of room for them because the Muslim population had either fled or been expelled, and the Byzantines made no objection to a movement that strengthened the Christian element. After Manzikert and the collapse of the Byzantine administration of the region, the Armenians submitted to the Turks, before finally emerging as players in their own right in the wake of the First Crusade.

2. Henry VI's expedition to enforce his son's claim on Sicily was financed out of Richard Lionheart's ransom, a *(footnote continued on p. 106)*

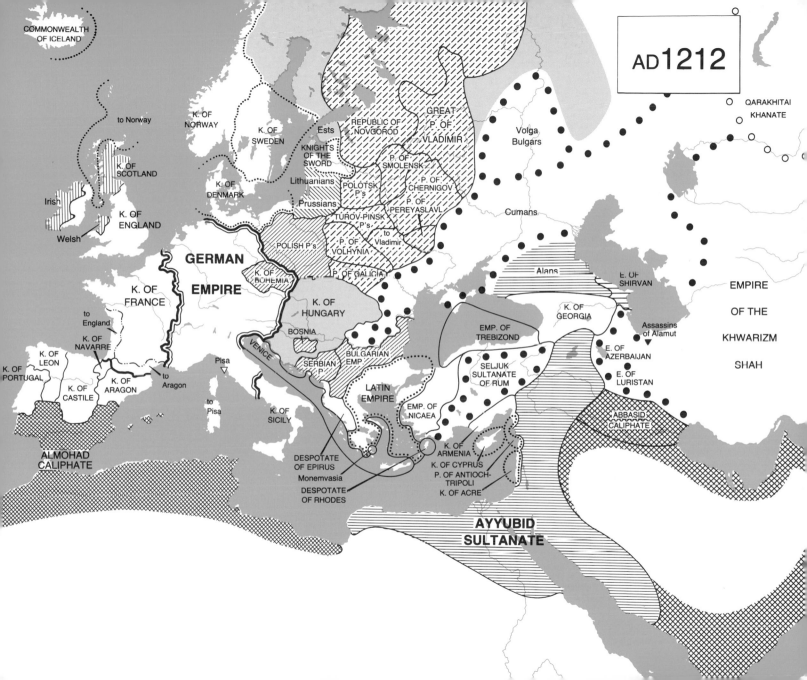

AD **1212**

COMMONWEALTH OF ICELAND

to Norway

K. OF NORWAY

K. OF SWEDEN

Ests

Lithuanians

Prussians

KNIGHTS OF THE SWORD

REPUBLIC OF NOVGOROD

GREAT P. OF VLADIMIR

Volga Bulgars

QARAKHITAI KHANATE

K. OF SCOTLAND

Irish

Welsh

K. OF DENMARK

K. OF ENGLAND

P. OF SMOLENSK

POLÓTSK P's

P. OF CHERNIGOV

P. OF PEREYASLAVL

TÚROV-PINSK P's

to Vladimir

Cumans

to England

GERMAN EMPIRE

POLISH P's

K. OF BOHEMIA

P. OF VOLHYNIA

P. OF GALICIA

K. OF FRANCE

K. OF HUNGARY

BOSNIA

Alans

E. OF SHIRVAN

EMPIRE OF THE KHWARIZM SHAH

K. OF NAVARRE

to Aragon

Pisa

VENICE

SERBIAN P.

BULGARIAN EMP.

K. OF GEORGIA

EMP. OF TREBIZOND

Assassins of Alamut

E. OF AZERBAIJAN

K. OF LEON

K. OF PORTUGAL

K. OF CASTILE

K. OF ARAGON

to Pisa

K. OF SICILY

LATIN EMPIRE

EMP. OF NICAEA

SELJUK SULTANATE OF RUM

E. OF LURISTAN

ABBASID CALIPHATE

DESPOTATE OF EPIRUS

Monemvasia

DESPOTATE OF RHODES

K. OF ARMENIA

K. OF CYPRUS

P. OF ANTIOCH-TRIPOLI

K. OF ACRE

ALMOHAD CALIPHATE

AYYUBID SULTANATE

The rapidity with which the Carolingian Empire disintegrated was a lesson in the impermanence of barbarian success that was not lost on the German emperors: to stop the same thing happening to their Empire they borrowed administrators from the German Church. This was standard practice in medieval kingdoms, but the German emperors took it further than most: clerics acted not just as bureaucrats but as barons. When Emperor Otto II led his army into Italy in 981, 70 per cent of the troops were supplied by ecclesiastical vassals. Church and State acted as one.

The next step was to refurbish the Papacy and get equally good value out of that. A succession of German incumbents breathed new life into the decayed office (1047–57), and in return the Papacy fully endorsed the Emperor's position. Alas, the partnership between Emperor and Pope didn't last long. The Empire, for all its international aspirations, never succeeded in being much more than a state run for Germans by Germans. And the Church, as a supranational organization, could never tie itself to any particular secular authority.

The first stage on the Papacy's road to freedom was a decree placing responsibility for papal elections with the college of cardinals (1059). Ostensibly, this was to prevent elections being hijacked by the Roman mob, but the new rules also had the effect of excluding the Emperor from any say in the matter. The architect of the decree, the Tuscan prelate Hildebrand, got away with it because the Emperor of the day was an infant and the regency weak. His success encouraged him to proceed to a more daring formulation: not just a Church free of state control but a Church that controlled the state. When Hildebrand became Pope (as Gregory VII, in 1073), this became the official position. For a moment it worked. One of the enduring images of medieval history is the Emperor Henry IV standing in the snow at Canossa, dressed in the shift of a penitent, waiting for the Pope's forgiveness. But once Henry had his absolution he soon crushed the rebellion in Germany that had forced him to this humiliation. Then he denounced the tyrannical Pope, marched on Rome and installed a new Pope of his own (1084). Hilde-

brand's lonely death at Salerno ('I have loved justice and hated iniquity, so I die in exile') is the necessary counter-image to Canossa.

So began a famous controversy, centred on the question as to whether Emperor or Pope had the final say in the world in general and the appointment of bishops in particular. The emperors couldn't afford to give way because the German bishops were the pillars of the Empire. The Popes, swept up in Hildebrand's intoxicating theory, found it difficult to compromise even as regards the bishops' secular responsibilities. The quarrel shook Christendom. The emperors regularly invaded Italy and placed their candidates on the throne of St Peter: just as regularly, the Romans threw them out as soon as the emperors had gone home. The rival emperors raised up by the Popes to oppose their imperial enemy didn't last much longer than his 'anti-Popes', but they caused even more confusion. Eventually, frightened by the growing lawlessness, the two sides agreed to a compromise: both Emperor and Pope would have a role in ecclesiastical appointments (1122). But the quarrel went deeper than its cause. As leaders of the Church, as Princes in their own right, as (usually) Italians, the Popes were reflexly opposed to a power that was secular, imperial and alien to the peninsula. Few of them, given the opportunity, could resist rocking the Empire's creaking structure. And there was an additional attraction in doing so: the Empire was slowly weakening. At a simple military level it was losing control of Lombardy, and even north of the Alps it was having increasing difficulty maintaining its authority. War against such a groggy opponent could only make the Papacy look good.

In fact, by the early thirteenth century the Papacy was looking very good indeed. Latin Christianity was expanding at the expense of pagans (in the Baltic), infidels (in Spain) and schismatics (meaning Greeks). It had been a little difficult to bless the Fourth Crusade, but Pope Innocent had managed it. As a result, there was now a Latin Patriarch in Constantinople to match the Latin incumbents installed in Antioch and Jerusalem at the time of the First Crusade. The Bulgars had agreed to transfer their allegiance to the western Church in return for a Patriarch of their own:

the Armenians of Cilicia had come over too. The Crusades, it could be said, had confirmed to the Papacy the leadership of Christendom that had originally been sought by the emperors.

There were, indeed, some signs of over-confidence. When the Count of Toulouse failed to act against heretics with the vigour the Papacy required, Innocent III called for a crusade to do the job properly (1208). This Albigensian Crusade (named for Albi, one of the schismatics' strongholds) certainly extirpated the heretics but also did other, less laudable, things. The Pope had shown he could unleash the dogs of war: what he failed to demonstrate was any ability to control them.

Christendom in
AD **1212**

to Islam

frontier of Islam

Trnovo ⊕✝

Constantinople ⊕✝

NICAEA ▲✝

ROME ⬤⚇

Antioch ✝

Acre ✝

⬤⚇ **PAPACY**

✝⬤ Western
Christendom
Patriarchates

▲ **ECUMENICAL
PATRIARCH**

Eastern
Christendom

In the eleventh century the weavers of Flanders started producing a moderately priced woollen cloth that was far superior to the usual homespun. It had increasing success, first at home, then abroad. The looms began to clatter away to such effect that the local sheep farmers could no longer meet the demand for wool: the weavers had to look around for new sources of supply. They found the answer in England, long renowned for the quality of its wool, and both willing and able to reorganize its farmlands to produce the quantities required. By the date of this map England was the primary producer and the southern Netherlands the manufacturing centre of a truly international industry. Flemish cloth was selling as well in Italy as it did in the north.

The cloth towns boomed. Ghent, the largest producer, and Bruges, the main entrepöt, rivalled London and Paris, the emerging political centres of the region. And the industry benefited Europe generally, not just England and the Netherlands. The Genoese, Pisans and Venetians trading in the east found Flemish woollens to be the most popular and profitable of their wares: it became a powerful instrument in their own expansion.

These Italian cities, and their neighbours in the interior of the peninsula, had experienced an economic miracle every bit as remarkable as the awakening of the Low Countries. In the year 1000 their profile had been so low as to be almost imperceptible. Hardly any of them had as many as 5,000 inhabitants. The ones on the coast lived in dread of Muslim pirates and the ones inland in total obscurity. Yet two centuries later they counted among their number a dozen major cities, including the two largest in western Europe, Milan and Venice. The phenomenon is so general, taking in the entire northern half of the peninsula, that it is impossible to give much credit to the specific factors involved in the rise of an individual town: powering the boom is surely a population explosion of such vigour that it funnelled people into the towns whether they were needed or not.

The first use the Italians made of their extra muscle was to gain control of their home waters: this they achieved in the course of the eleventh century. Then the seamen of Pisa, Genoa and Venice turned east to exploit the opportunities created by the First Crusade. By the mid twelfth century, the Genoese had more money invested in trade with the Levant than in all their other trading connections put together. The Venetians were to become even more heavily involved. Their masterly perversion of the Fourth Crusade brought them a useful slice of the Byzantine Empire ('a quarter and a half of a quarter'), which they wisely took in the form of islands. Thereafter, the galleys plying to Constantinople, Antioch or Alexandria could make use of a string of bases that took them more than half way to their destinations.

Nothing comparable happened in the North Sea, where everyone concerned, English, Flemish, French and German, seems to have had a share in the carrying trade. The Scandinavians' role was declining: they still maintained their hold on the fishing industry, marketing cod from Iceland and the Lofotens and, more important, herring from the Baltic. But for the Danes the important opportunities lay on the Baltic littoral, where new routes and new markets were being opened up by the Northern Crusade. The enterprise was largely German, but by seizing political leadership of the movement the Danes hoped to reap much of the profit.

The Islamic countries didn't show the revolutionary increase in commercial activity that characterized the west during these centuries, but they were starting from a much higher base-line and they did well enough. To judge by the growth in the number and size of their cities, they seemed to have added around 50 per cent to their GNPs: certainly they had no difficulty at all in balancing their trade with the west. The Levantine countries had their traditional monopoly of the traffic in oriental spices and could set prices pretty much as they pleased; they also had in cotton a textile fibre that was as much in demand as wool. Cotton cultivation, which originated in India, had reached Arabia by the sixth century and subsequently spread round the Mediterranean along with Islam. By the thirteenth century, Syria and Egypt had become major producers.[1] In fact, the Levantine countries were always in surplus as regards the trade in goods, and the west depended on exports of silver to cover the gap. Luckily, the new mines opened up in Saxony, Carinthia and Sardinia in the course of the twelfth century proved equal to the need.

1. Egyptian weavers were especially famous for their 'fustians', cotton-linen mixtures produced in Fustat (Old Cairo). Analogous etymologies apply to muslin (fine cotton, from Mosul) and damask (cloth with a pattern in the weave, from Damascus).

COD

FURS

**towns and
trade routes in
AD 1212**

city populations

⬤ 50–125,000

● 23–49,000

• 15–22,000

SILKS

SLAVES

SAMARKAND

Bukhara

Novgorod

COAL

HERRING

WOOL

WHEAT

HERRING

COPPER

SILVER

London

TIN

Bruges

Ghent

WOOLLENS

WINE

Paris

WINE

SLAVES

Nishapur

Herat

SLAVES

Tabriz

Rayy

Brescia   **Verona**

Milan   **Padua**

SILKS

Venice

SILVER

Mosul

Hamadan

Isfahan

Pavia

WOOLLENS

Genoa

Florence

Pisa

Rome

IRON

TIMBER

IRON

Venetian routes

CONSTANTINOPLE

SILKS

COTTONS

SUGAR

BAGHDAD

Wasit

BASRA

SHIRAZ

SUGAR

SILKS

WOOL

WHEAT

Konya

ANTIOCH

Aleppo

Naples

Toledo

SILVER

SILK

COTTONS

DAMASCUS

COTTONS

SUGAR

Cordoba

Seville

PAPER

SUGAR

Palermo

Genoese routes

SUGAR

WHEAT

COTTON

TUNIS

Kairouan

WINE

SPICES

Rabat-Salé

Fez

Marrakesh

SUGAR

ALEXANDRIA

COTTONS

Mahalla

CAIRO

WHEAT

LINENS

PAPER

SUGAR

ALUM

Qus

Mecca

GOLD   *IVORY*

SLAVES

IVORY   *SLAVES*

SPICES

Sana

In the early medieval period the nomads who gave the west a hard time were migrants. Whether they travelled in a single body, far and fast, like the Avars, or a clan at a time in a movement spread over centuries, as was the case with the Turks, they took their flocks and families along with them, and the centre of whatever political power they wielded moved as they did. In 1206 a *kuriltai* (grand council) held in Outer Mongolia celebrated the creation of a new type of nomad empire, one which could dispatch armies east or west without shifting its centre. This empire was the achievement of the Mongol chieftain Temujin who, in twenty years of continuous warfare, brought all the tribes of the grasslands north of the Gobi under his personal rule. At the *kuriltai*, Temujin also announced the second stage of his programme, the conquest of the world beyond the Gobi. In anticipation of a successful outcome he took the title of Genghiz Khan, 'Lord of the Earth'.

By any standards except his own, Genghiz Khan can be called a successful man, for in the last twenty years of his life he made a good start towards the conquest of China, annexed the remnant of the Qarakhitai Khanate and, in two merciless campaigns (1220–21), smashed the empire of the Khwarizm Shah. The lands further west were probed by a corps originally detached in pursuit of the unfortunate Shah: this force delivered a series of crushing defeats to the Georgians, Alans, Cumans, and south Russian Princes (1221–2). Death came to the Khan (1227) before he could exploit the weaknesses this victorious raid disclosed. The Empire he had created, which continued undivided, stretched from Persia to Korea; its incomparable pagan armies remained a threat to each and all of its neighbours.[1]

Only eastern Iran was incorporated into the Mongol dominions at this stage: in the western provinces Khwarizmenian rule was revived by an energetic young Shah who to some degree recouped himself for his father's losses by conquering Azerbaijan and Georgia. Seljuk and Ayyubid combined, however, to oppose his further advance, and he fell back defeated to rest against the teeth of the Mongolian dragon. The Ayyubids let the Christians have Jerusalem and a corridor to the coast to forestall any pin-pricking crusades while these important events marched in the east, a true if insulting assessment of the crusaders' residual potential.

The Latin Empire began to fail as soon as its first impetus was spent. All its Asian territory was lost to the Nicaeans (who also absorbed the Despotate of Rhodes); in Europe it was pressed hard by the Epirotes, who took Salonika (1223) and made it the capital of a rival empire. But the Epirotes then blew their chance of winning the race to Constantinople by making an unnecessary and totally disastrous foray against the Bulgars (1230). The Latins, to their surprise, found themselves able to cling on to their capital and a higgledy-piggledy collection of fiefs in Greece and the islands. The third Greek Empire, Trebizond, never sought a role in the main drama and, after the Seljuks occupied Sinope in 1214, tended to look to Georgia for comfort.

Sixteen years after their defeat at Los Navos de Tolosa, the Almohads decided to abandon Spain and let the Muslims there fend for themselves (1228–9). Of the local leaders who emerged, only one, the Sultan of Granada, proved to be of any importance, and even he was unable to slow the Christian advance. Aragon conquered Majorca, while Castile, with which Leon was now permanently united, closed in on Seville.

In the Baltic the main event was the collapse of the Danish hegemony (1227). The Knights of the Sword conquered Estonia; a rival outfit, the Teutonic Knights, began operations at Torun, in south-west Prussia.

1. Many people have speculated on the nature of the mechanism driving the 'nomad cycle'. Were the outpourings of Huns, Turks and Mongols triggered by population increase, or by desiccation of the grasslands or by improvements in the equipment of the nomad warrior? Or were they purely political events in which a successful Khan simply extended his campaigns beyond the usual horizon? And why did Genghiz do so much better than any of his predecessors or successors?

It seems unlikely that we will ever have the data we need to test the over-population hypothesis but the cyclical desiccation idea, much touted at one time as the 'Pulse of Asia', should be testable once the palaeoclimatologists have got their act together. Technical advance doesn't seem a runner: the only revolutionary innovation on the steppe was the stirrup, which was brought west by the Avars and may well have helped them win their battles there. However, it doesn't help us to distinguish the Avar Empire from that of the Huns before it or the Mongols after it. In fact, it is arguable that the stirrup's most important influence was not on the steppe, where existing modes of warfare seem to have been little affected, but within Christendom, where it permitted the Frankish cavalry to develop the sort of shock tactics – charging with a couched lance – that ultimately became the hallmark of feudal chivalry.

What does seem likely is that the dynamics of the steppe were, in the mathematical sense, chaotic. There is a resonance between the big sweeps of the empire-builders and the small-scale movements of individual clans which is like the recurrently emerging patterns of fractal sets. My guess is that, much as you have to admire Genghiz, his empire fell within the statistical range of such creations: he just happened to be riding a particularly big whirlwind.

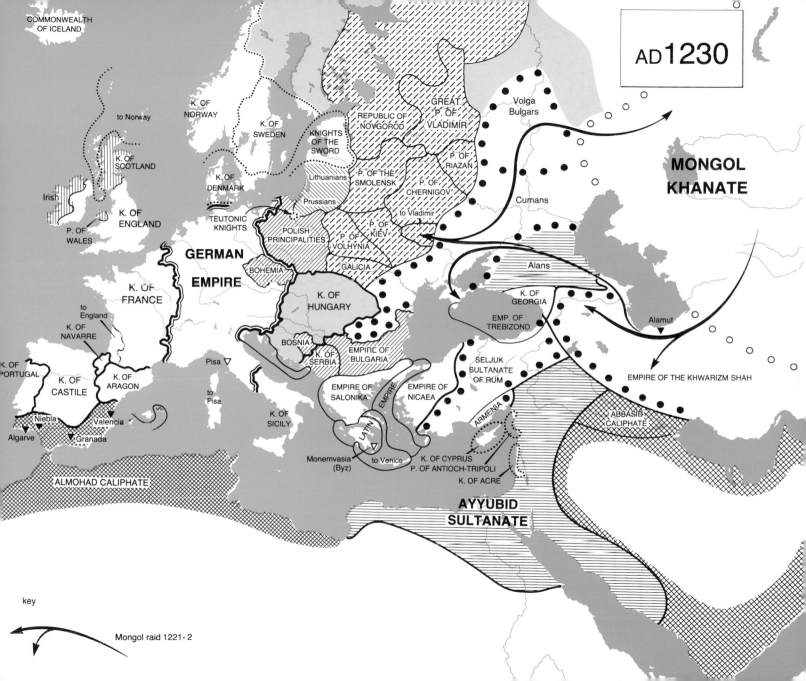

COMMONWEALTH OF ICELAND

to Norway

K. OF NORWAY

K. OF SWEDEN

KNIGHTS OF THE SWORD

REPUBLIC OF NOVGOROD

GREAT P. OF VLADIMIR

Volga Bulgars

MONGOL KHANATE

AD 1230

K. OF SCOTLAND

Irish

K. OF DENMARK

Lithuanians

P. OF THE SMOLENSK

P. OF RIAZAN

P. OF ENGLAND

Prussians

P. OF CHERNIGOV

Cumans

P. OF WALES

TEUTONIC KNIGHTS

POLISH PRINCIPALITIES

to Vladimir

P. OF KIEV

GERMAN EMPIRE

BOHEMIA

P. OF VOLHYNIA

GALICIA

Alans

K. OF FRANCE

K. OF HUNGARY

K. OF GEORGIA

EMP. OF TREBIZOND

Alamut

to England

K. OF NAVARRE

BOSNIA

EMPIRE OF THE KHWARIZM SHAH

K. OF PORTUGAL

K. OF CASTILE

K. OF ARAGON

Pisa

K. OF SERBIA

EMPIRE OF BULGARIA

SELJUK SULTANATE OF RUM

to Pisa

K. OF SICILY

EMPIRE OF SALONIKA

LATIN EMPIRE

EMPIRE OF NICAEA

ARMENIA

ABBASID CALIPHATE

Niebla

Valencia

Algarve

Granada

Monemvasia (Byz)

to Venice

K. OF CYPRUS

P. OF ANTIOCH-TRIPOLI

K. OF ACRE

ALMOHAD CALIPHATE

AYYUBID SULTANATE

key

Mongol raid 1221- 2

No one in the west made any use of the fourteen-year interval between the Mongols' first appearance on the Russian steppe and their return in 1236: the Mongol generals were able to pick their enemies off one by one, just as they had the first time. They started with the Volga Bulgars, moved on – via Riazan – to Vladimir, then turned south and cowed the Cumans and Alans. After wintering in the Don region they struck west, sacking first Pereyaslavl, then Kiev. Finally they divided their army in two and thrust deep into Europe. The northern force beat the Poles and the Teutonic Knights, while the southern force defeated the Hungarians. The intention seems to have been to make Hungary the centre from which the new extension of the Empire would be ruled. But in 1242 news came that the Great Khan Ogedei, Genghiz Khan's son and successor, had died and the army commanders decided they ought to position themselves nearer the centre of the Empire. They withdrew via Bulgaria, which was to remain within the Mongol orbit; Poland and Hungary did not.

The Mongols conquered the Near East in a more piecemeal fashion. In 1231 the Empire of the Khwarizm Shah Jalal ad-Din was eliminated by a Mongol corps, which subsequently based itself on the grasslands of Azerbaijan. Eleven years later, this force defeated the Seljuks of Rum, reducing them to tributary status. (The Empire of Trebizond and the Kingdom of Armenia, Seljuk vassals for a decade past, consequently changed masters.) Finally, in 1256, the Mongol Prince Hulagu arrived with major reinforcements and instructions to bring the entire Near East under Mongol control. Hulagu started by extirpating the Assassins of Alamut, an operation that brought the history of the sect to a suitably lethal end. Then he moved against the Abbasid Caliphate. Baghdad fell after a brief resistance: its inhabitants were massacred and the Caliph trampled to death beneath the hooves of the Mongol cavalry. The news sent a wave of panic through Syria and Palestine, where Hulagu's subsequent advance was barely resisted. But the intended invasion of Egypt never took place. Once again a Khan had died, and this time there was civil war at the heart of the Mongol Empire. Hulagu turned back, leaving only a few regiments to watch the Egyptian frontier.

Egypt had a new line of Sultans, the Mamluks, drawn from the Turkish Guard of the last Ayyubids. The Mamluks took the offensive and, at the battle of Ain Jalut ('Goliath's spring') annihilated the Mongol force defending Palestine. There was now nothing to stop them liberating Syria and making the Euphrates their frontier. And this they did, and on the Euphrates the frontier remained. The Ilkhanate (subordinate khanate) established by Hulagu, began quarrelling with the Khanate established to oversee Russia (known in the west as the Khanate of the Golden Horde), and as Kublai Khan of China, the nominal overlord of both, had neither the will nor the means to make them desist, their dispute gradually consumed the resources needed to renew the westward advance. Both in Europe and in the Near East the Mongol Empire had found its final limit.[1]

The Christians in the east had hoped the Mongols would deliver them from the Islamic *revanche* that was gradually squeezing them out of existence. In the case of Georgia, the Mongol rescue was real enough: the little kingdom regained its territory and prosperity during its spell as a Mongol protectorate. But the crusader states lay on the wrong side of the line and gained no such respite. Jerusalem had already fallen to a horde of Khwarizmenians fleeing from the first Mongol offensive (1244). The Mamluks eliminated Antioch in 1263 and, not long after the date of this map, Tripoli (1289) and Acre (1291).

The Papacy had spent the second quarter of the thirteenth century locked in a vicious quarrel with Frederick II Hohenstaufen, Emperor of Germany, and, just as important from the Pope's point of view, King of Sicily. It was the Papacy's recurring nightmare that it would be ground into submission between the upper and nether millstones of Frederick's two dominions, and though with Frederick's death (1250) the immediate danger passed, who would say it could never be revived? The only answer was the complete eradication of the Hohenstaufen line. The Papacy got its chance to achieve this when Conradin, Frederick's infant grandson and the legitimate heir to Sicily, was elbowed off his throne by his uncle Manfred. The Pope denounced the usurpation, declared the crown forfeit and offered it to Louis IX of France. Louis passed the offer on to his brother Charles of Anjou. Charles duly invaded Italy, defeated and killed Manfred at the Battle of Benevento (1266) and made himself master of the south Italian kingdom. Two years later when Conradin came of age and tried to claim his inheritance, Charles disposed of him too. The connection between Sicily and Germany was severed.

Given Charles's support, the Papacy now had the chance to obtain effective control of the central Italian principality that had, in theory, belonged to the Church since Charlemagne's day. Their joint efforts were successful, and the new Papal State even won diplomatic recognition from the next German Emperor, Rudolph of Habsburg, who might have been expected to insist that it was no more than an imperial fief. But Rudolph was only interested in Germany: the Italian communes, the Papal State and the Kingdom of Sicily were free to go their own various ways.[2]

Charles's ways were various indeed. He was interested in reviving old Norman projects for expanding the kingdom both in Africa and the Balkans. As regards Africa, he persuaded his brother, a keen if

(continued over)

1. With Kublai's accession (1260), the Mongol Empire effectively broke up into four separate khanates: the Golden Horde, the Ilkhanate, Kublai's China, and a Central Asian Khanate, of which a corner is visible on the map. This is usually referred to as the Jagatai Khanate, as it was the appanage of Genghiz Khan's second son, Jagatai, but at the date of this map the overlord of the region was Qaydu, a grandson of Ogedei: the Jagatai line only took over in 1309.
2. The map only shows two of the fifty or more communities that divided the north of Italy between them: Pisa (because of its possession of Corsica and Sardinia) and Venice (because it lay outside the Empire). To get an idea of the political situation you have to look ten pages further on, where the map of towns and trade routes gives an idea of the relative importance of the top twenty. All of them, big and small, quarrelled like rats in a basket, and for many years to come they used the labels adopted when the issue was between Papacy and Empire: Guelf (pro-Papal, after the House of Welf, opponents of the Hohenstaufen) and Ghibelline (pro-imperial, after Waiblingen, a Hohenstaufen castle).

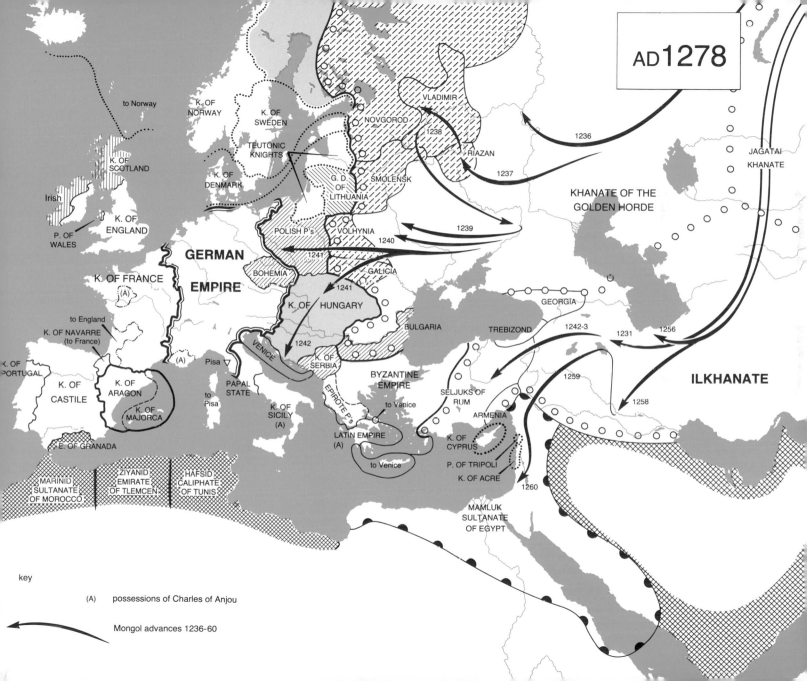

AD 1278

to Norway

K. OF
NORWAY

K. OF
SWEDEN

TEUTONIC
KNIGHTS

K. OF
SCOTLAND

K. OF
DENMARK

Irish

P. OF
WALES

K. OF
ENGLAND

GERMAN

EMPIRE

BOHEMIA

POLISH P's

G. D.
OF
LITHUANIA

SMOLENSK

NOVGOROD

VLADIMIR

1238

RIAZAN

1236

1237

VOLHYNIA

GALICIA

1239

1240

1241

1241

K. OF FRANCE

(A)

to England

K. OF NAVARRE
(to France)

K. OF
PORTUGAL

K. OF
CASTILE

K. OF
ARAGON

K. OF
MAJORCA

(A)

Pisa

to
Pisa

PAPAL
STATE

VENICE

K. OF HUNGARY

1242

K. OF
SERBIA

EPIROTE P's

K. OF
SICILY
(A)

to Venice

LATIN EMPIRE
(A)

to Venice

BULGARIA

BYZANTINE
EMPIRE

TREBIZOND

GEORGIA

1242-3

SELJUKS OF
RUM

1259

ARMENIA

K. OF
CYPRUS

P. OF TRIPOLI

K. OF ACRE

1260

E. OF GRANADA

MARINID
SULTANATE
OF MOROCCO

ZIYANID
EMIRATE
OF TLEMCEN

HAFSID
CALIPHATE
OF TUNIS

MAMLUK
SULTANATE
OF EGYPT

JAGATAI
KHANATE

KHANATE OF THE
GOLDEN HORDE

1231

1256

1258

ILKHANATE

key

(A)   possessions of Charles of Anjou

          Mongol advances 1236-60

incompetent crusader, to make his next venture against Tunis. The results were disappointing: Louis died of dysentery and nothing was gained except a promise of tribute, soon revoked. In the Balkans, Charles did better, but then the Latin fiefs there were looking for a protector following the Byzantine recovery of Constantinople (1261). He was able to gather up the remnants of the Latin Empire and assume the title of Prince of Achaea (1278). His extraordinary collection of territories now stretched from Anjou (inherited) via Provence (acquired by marriage) and Sicily (by conquest) to outposts in Albania, a kingdom in Corfu and the Latin fiefs in the Balkans (acquired by a mixture of all three). What it was all worth is another matter: when Sicily revolted, in the rising known as the Sicilian Vespers (because its start was signalled by the tolling of the evensong bell), Charles immediately found himself in deep trouble.

These were good years for the Byzantines. The Nicaeans moved into Europe as the Epirote Empire of Salonika collapsed. In 1259 they won an important victory over the Latins of Greece, gaining a quarter of the Peloponnese as a result. Two years later they made an unopposed re-entry into Constantinople. Subsequently the Epirotes submitted (1264), and a naval expedition recovered many of the Aegean islands. Byzantium had been reconstituted, and if the success was partial and the achievement precarious, it was still a moment to savour.

In the Baltic the front runners were the Teutonic Knights, who conquered their allotted sphere, Prussia, and then absorbed the Knights of the Sword and their territory, Livonia. Estonia fell to a reviving Denmark; Sweden enlarged its foothold in Finland. Only the Lithuanians and, in the far north, the Finns and Lapps remained as legitimate targets for the Northern Crusade. But the Lithuanians had turned out to be unexpectedly doughty fighters, and the Finns and Lapps were too thin on the ground to be worth attacking. Novgorod looked a better bet. It was wealthy, it had a reputation for pusillanimity – it had submitted to the Mongols without ever being invaded – and it was by Russian standards relatively easy to get at. Novgorod entrusted its defence to one of the princes of Suzdal, Alexander Nevsky. The critical

battle, fought on the frozen surface of Lake Peipus in 1242, was a triumph for Alexander, who was subsequently to be remembered as the saviour of the Russian state in its darkest hour.[3]

In Spain, Portugal and Aragon completed the conquest of the sectors allocated to them, while Castile reduced the sole surviving Muslim state, the Emirate of Granada, to provincial dimensions. The Balearics were made a separate kingdom for a cadet line of the Aragonese house; Navarre passed under French rule. In Morocco, the Almohads were overthrown by the Marinids of Fez (1269): they had already been driven from the eastern Maghreb by the Ziyanids of Tlemcen and the Hafsids of Tunis (in the 1230s). In the Atlantic, the Norwegians obtained the submission of the Icelanders (1248) but agreed to surrender the western isles to Scotland (1266). The English continued to bear down on the Welsh but didn't finally annex the principality till 1282.

3. One part of the legend has Alexander turning back a Swedish invasion in a battle by the Neva (1240): hence the epithet Nevsky. Modern scholarship is a bit dubious about this: the battle is only mentioned in one very late and very pro-Alexander source, and the title was never used in his lifetime. What is certainly true is that Alexander hitched his wagon firmly to the Mongol star. He faithfully executed all the Khan's orders, and when the Novgorodians attempted to get an adjustment of their tribute it was Alexander, by this time Great Prince of Vladimir, who fell on them like a thunderbolt and extracted the full amount (1260).

The most striking event of the early fourteenth century was the collapse of the Mongol Ilkhanate. The last effective Ilkhan, Abu Said, died in 1335, and subsequently various Mongol factions fought each other for control of the central provinces, with the Cubanids of Tabriz coming out ahead but not on top. At the periphery the tendency was for the provincial governments to evolve into hereditary fiefs: in western Anatolia there was a particularly interesting development that led to the creation of a raft of new political units, the *ghazi* emirates. *Ghazi*, meaning a warrior dedicated to the struggle against the infidel, was a title adopted by many of the Turkish chieftains on the Byzantine border: these marcher lords went on the offensive in a big way in the late thirteenth century, and by the middle of the fourteenth they had succeeded in driving the Byzantines out of Asia altogether. Of the emirates founded by *ghazis*, the most important was the Ottoman (2 on the map). It is named for its founder, Osman, who between 1280 and 1324 transformed what started out as a minor Seljuk barony into a principality covering most of the north-west of Anatolia. Osman was a faithful vassal, first of the Seljuks, then, when the Seljuk dynasty petered out in the early 1300s, of the Mongol governors who replaced them. But with the Ilkhanate falling apart, the governor had more important things on his mind than the affairs of the princelings of the far west, and by the date of this map the *ghazi* emirates had drifted out of the Mongol orbit.[1]

The Golden Horde lasted better than the Ilkhanate. The Khan's grip on the north Russian princes never slackened: they came to his tent to have their titles confirmed and marched their armies when and where he told them to. But on the central and southern sectors of the Mongol frontier, the Khan's authority no longer reached out quite as far as it had. On the lower Danube, both the Bulgars on the right bank and, more surprisingly, the Vlachs on the left bank were able to slip the Mongol yoke. In the centre, the Horde actually yielded some of its vassals to the Lithuanians, who annexed Volhynia, established a protectorate over Smolensk and advanced their south-eastern border as far as Kiev. Between Wallachia and Lithuania lay Galicia, which still paid the Mongol tax. But then it also paid tribute to anyone else who asked: Lithuania, Hungary, even Poland.

It is surprising to find Poland on this list, because the Poles had been cutting an increasingly poor figure of late. In the opening years of the fourteenth century they lost east Pomerania and the last of their Baltic seaboard to the Teutonic Knights and, in 1327, Silesia to Bohemia. But at least they re-established their monarchy: by 1346 all Poland bar the Principality of Mazovia in the north-east recognized the rule of King Casimir III, and he was determined to prevent any further whittling down of his kingdom.

The Sicilian Vespers, the revolt that, in 1282, swept over the island half of Charles of Anjou's Italian kingdom, proved impossible to suppress. Charles might have managed it if the islanders hadn't had the support of Aragon, but he couldn't match Aragonese sea power. Eventually, in 1302, long after Charles's death, a treaty was signed that recognized two kingdoms of Sicily: one, consisting of the island, ruled by a junior branch of the Aragonese House, the other, comprising the mainland territory, under Angevin control. The second, better named the Kingdom of Naples, became the core Angevin possession. The connection with Anjou had been lost in 1290 when the county became a daughter's dowry; the remnants of the Latin Empire were entrusted to a cadet line in 1307.

The technical justification for Aragon's intervention in Sicily was a claim on the throne via Manfred's daughter, who had married King Peter III of Aragon. But the kingdom's maritime role was expanding anyway, thanks to the enterprise displayed by the inhabitants of its main seaport, the Catalonian capital, Barcelona. The Catalan Grand Company could have gone home when the war in Sicily ended: instead it hired itself out to the Byzantines (1302) and ended up taking the Duchy of Athens from its Duke and turning it into an Aragonese fief (1311). In 1322, when the Pope persuaded the Venetians and Genoese to observe an embargo on trade with the Mamluks, the Catalans simply used the opportunity to strengthen their presence at Alexandria. In 1323 they took over Sardinia in a move that emphasized Pisa's

eclipse and Barcelona's assumption of third place in the Mediterranean trading hierarchy.

If Pisa had moved down, Genoa had moved up and was now level-pegging Venice. Byzantium's recovery resulted in Genoa, not Venice, becoming the most favoured nation trading at Constantinople, and if the Venetians' position in the Aegean was too well established to be easily overturned, the Black Sea trade was in Constantinople's gift. In the 1270s the Genoese set up trading posts in the Crimea and at Trebizond, which gave them access to the Russian and Iranian markets. Gradually, an empire comparable to the Venetian emerged. In the Crimea, Caffa became an outright possession in 1343, when a Mongol attempt to seize the city was rebuffed; Samsun, on the western border of Trebizond, was garrisoned too. In the Aegean, Chios was taken from the Byzantines in 1346. Nearer home, a crushing victory over Pisa (at Meloria, off Leghorn, in 1284) was followed by the acquisition of Corsica. But, if a single victory was enough to decide the issue between Genoa and Pisa, the many battles between Genoa and Venice rarely resulted in any permanent advantage to either. One of them did have consequences of a different sort, though. In 1298 a Genoese fleet penetrated the Adriatic and administered a sound thrashing to a superior Venetian force off Curzola, modern Kerkula. Among the 5,000 Venetian prisoners was Marco Polo, recently returned from China, and it is to his subsequent spell in captivity that we owe the book that made him famous.[2]

As the fourteenth century progressed, the Byzantines began to fade again. Their last success was the absorption of the Epirote principalities; thereafter they came under increasing pressure from the Serbs.

(continued over)

1. The *ghazi* states shown on the map overleaf are (capitals in brackets): 1 Jandar (Kastamonu); 2 Ottoman (Bursa); 3 Sarukhan (Manisa); 4 Aydin (Birgi); 5 Menteshe (Milas); 6 Germiyan (Kutahya); 7 Hamid (Egridir); 8 Tekke (Antalya); 9 Karaman (Laranda).
2. This isn't called *The Travels of Marco Polo* and it isn't a narrative of his twenty-five years in the east: it is called *A Description of the World* and is an almost useless mishmash of bits and pieces put together by Marco's

(footnote continued on p. 106)

The Serbian Prince Stefan Dushan had won an important victory over the Bulgars before he came to the throne: in the 1330s he broke the Byzantine defence line across peninsular Greece and annexed Albania and all of Macedonia bar Salonika. In 1346 Stefan laid claim to what was left of the Byzantine heritage by having himself crowned 'Emperor of the Serbs and Greeks'; it seemed only a matter of time before he scooped up the remaining European provinces.

In Scandinavia the Danish monarchy entered another period of eclipse, during which the provinces in southern Sweden had to be made over to the Swedish Crown as security for a loan. However, a process of recovery began in 1346 with the sale of Estonia to the Teutonic Knights. Norway and Sweden, which temporarily shared the same king, were now probing the lands of the far north. The Swedes established control over both sides of the Gulf of Bothnia (the upper Baltic) and forced Novgorod to recognize their rule over western Finland (1323). Further north (and off the map), the Norwegians mounted a series of expeditions around the North Cape to the Kola peninsula, areas to which Novgorod also had claims. The result was an extraordinary war of raid and counter-raid fought entirely within the Arctic Circle, which eventually left the Norse in effective possession of the Cape (Finnmark), but not the peninsula.

The Scandinavians were not the only enemy Novgorod had to face at this time. The Great Princes of Vladimir, who had had their eyes on Novgorod's fur trade for a long time, annexed many of the posts in the far north-east during the 1330s. The title of Great Prince of Vladimir, incidentally, no longer implied residence at Vladimir. The town had never recovered from the Mongol sack of 1238, and it was princes from other places in Suzdal who competed for the senior title. The most important princely seats in the early fourteenth century were Moscow and Tver: the Muscovite line was generally more successful in winning the Khan's approval, and after 1331 the title remained with Moscow permanently.

The German Emperors had now given up trying to control Germany, let alone Italy, and were concentrating instead on feathering their nests. Rudolph of Habsburg, owner of a modest estate in Switzerland, used his spell as Emperor to gain control of Austria (1282); Henry of Luxemburg, Emperor from 1308 to 1314, made his son King of Bohemia, a much more imposing possession than the county of Luxemburg. The self-interest was a little alarming, but attempts by earlier emperors to buy the loyalty of their peers with gifts of land had never really worked: it seemed more sensible to keep windfalls in the family. It was even arguable that what was good for the Habsburgs and Luxemburgs (who after this provided most of the emperors) was good for the German Reich: there were enough weak principalities already.

Finally, some minor points should be made regarding this period: the Venetians took their first significant step on to the Italian mainland when they annexed Treviso in 1339, while in the Aegean they recovered control of the island of Euboea. The Knights of St John, evicted from the Holy Land, established a new headquarters on the island of Rhodes (1309). In the Maghreb, the Moroccans won control of Tlemcen. In Central Asia, the Jagatai Khanate divided into eastern and western halves. English rule in Ireland, shaken by a Scots invasion in 1315–18, was now only effective in the east and south, and not always there.

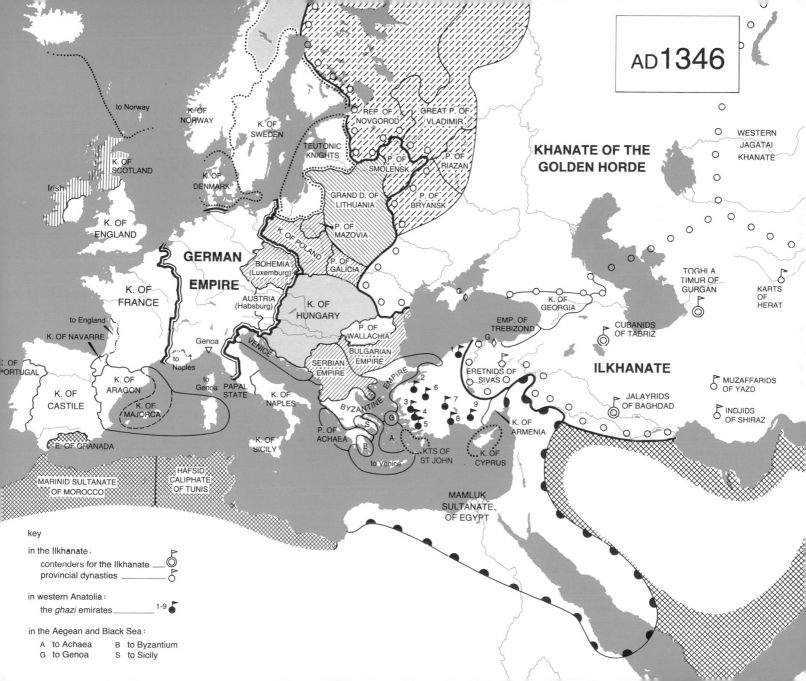

AD **1346**

WESTERN JAGATAI KHANATE

KHANATE OF THE GOLDEN HORDE

to Norway

K. OF NORWAY

K. OF SWEDEN

K. OF SCOTLAND

Irish

K. OF ENGLAND

TEUTONIC KNIGHTS

REP. OF NOVGOROD

GREAT P. OF VLADIMIR

P. OF SMOLENSK

P. OF RIAZAN

K. OF DENMARK

GRAND D. OF LITHUANIA

P. OF BRYANSK

P. OF MAZOVIA

TOGHI A TIMUR OF GURGAN

KARTS OF HERAT

GERMAN EMPIRE

K. OF FRANCE

K. OF POLAND

BOHEMIA (Luxemburg)

P. OF GALICIA

AUSTRIA (Habsburg)

K. OF HUNGARY

P. OF WALLACHIA

G

K. OF GEORGIA

EMP. OF TREBIZOND

CUBANIDS OF TABRIZ

ILKHANATE

to England

K. OF NAVARRE

Genoa

to Naples

to Genoa

VENICE

SERBIAN EMPIRE

BULGARIAN EMPIRE

BYZANTINE EMPIRE

ERETNIDS OF SIVAS

MUZAFFARIDS OF YAZD

K. OF PORTUGAL

K. OF CASTILE

K. OF ARAGON

K. OF MAJORCA

PAPAL STATE

K. OF NAPLES

K. OF SICILY

P. OF ACHAEA

1

2

3

4

5

6

7

8

9

G

G

S

B

A

KTS OF ST JOHN

to Venice

K. OF CYPRUS

K. OF ARMENIA

JALAYRIDS OF BAGHDAD

INDJIDS OF SHIRAZ

E. OF GRANADA

MARINID SULTANATE OF MOROCCO

HAFSID CALIPHATE OF TUNIS

MAMLUK SULTANATE OF EGYPT

key

in the Ilkhanate :

contenders for the Ilkhanate

provincial dynasties

in western Anatolia :

the *ghazi* emirates ——— 1-9

in the Aegean and Black Sea :

A to Achaea   B to Byzantium
G to Genoa   S to Sicily

The association between Charles of Anjou and the Papacy was fateful for both. At first everything went well. Charles got his kingdom, the hegemony of Italy and the beginnings of an empire in the east. The Papacy had its rule over central Italy confirmed. Then the Sicilian Vespers broke the spell. Both the Angevin dynasty and the Papacy committed themselves to the recovery of the island, and both were dragged down by the long, unsuccessful struggle that ensued. By 1294 the Pope of the day had dwindled into an Angevin puppet, resident at Naples.

Escaping from the Angevin embrace required a strong Pontiff. Boniface VIII, the next Pope, proved to be just that. After forcing the resignation of his unfortunate predecessor, he moved the papal court back to Rome. There he ruled autocratically, excommunicating anyone, king or cardinal, who disputed his pronouncements. The Jubilee year of 1300 found him on top form. Thousands of pilgrims converged on the Holy City, delighting the Pope, who had thought up the idea, and his minions, who found themselves literally raking in the money. But next year Boniface went over the top. He denounced the French King, Philip the Fair, for taxing the clergy, reminding him that like all secular rulers he was bound to obey his spiritual father. Philip's reply was an equally uncompromising counterblast, and by 1303 Boniface was ready to use his ultimate weapon, a bull of excommunication. Before he could publish it, Philip struck. One of his henchmen recruited a band of ruffians in Rome, marched to Anagni, the Pope's summer residence, and took him captive. Boniface found himself threatened with a trial for lese-majesty, and though the locals rallied to his aid and quickly forced his release, the experience knocked the puff out of the Pontiff. A month later he was dead, his bull of excommunication still unpublished.

The subsequent surrender to the French interest was rapid and complete. In 1305 the cardinals picked the Archbishop of Bordeaux as the next Pope. He chose to be crowned at Lyon and made no attempt to go to Italy: in fact he never got any closer to Rome than Avignon. And Avignon remained the seat of the Papacy under the next half dozen Popes, all of whom were Frenchmen. Boniface's captivity at Anagni had lasted barely 24 hours; the 'Babylonian captivity' at Avignon was to continue for seventy years.[1]

These were not very stirring years for the Church at large. There were some small but useful gains in Spain and the Baltic lands, but in the east the story was one of retreat. The Greek Church was re-established at Constantinople, extinguishing the Latin Patriarchate (1261). The Bulgar Patriarchate had reverted to Orthodoxy even before that (1235), and there was never any question of the Serbian Patriarchate, which Dushan created expressly for his coronation (1346), being anything else. Only the Armenian Patriarch (resident at Sis since 1294) remained faithful to the Papacy. Not that the Orthodox Church had very much to be pleased about either: the Greeks had recovered much of the Balkans, but they had lost all bar a few isolated towns in Anatolia, and both the Russian and Georgian Churches regularly paid tribute to Muslim overlords. None the less, Christendom had not had to suffer the extreme vicissitudes experienced by Islam, which had seen the Near East overrun and its culture ransacked by the pagan Mongols, then converted its conquerors – the Ilkhans in the 1290s, the Golden Horde *c*. 1340 – and made, in territorial terms, a net gain. Even the reinforcement of the nomad element in Near Eastern society could be read two ways. It undoubtedly weakened traditional Islamic society, but it also brought renewed impetus to the Holy War as waged by the *ghazis*.

1. Babylon, of course, is a metaphor for France, but it is perhaps worth noting that the Pope's residence was technically outside the French kingdom: Avignon lay in the county of Provence, which was a fief of the German Empire. And after 1348, when the Papacy purchased Avignon town from the Queen of Naples (who was also Countess of Provence), the Popes could claim to be as sovereign in Avignon as they were in Rome. The reality, of course, was very different: Avignon was both geographically and socially an adjunct of France, and during the period when the Popes resided there they were subservient to French interests.

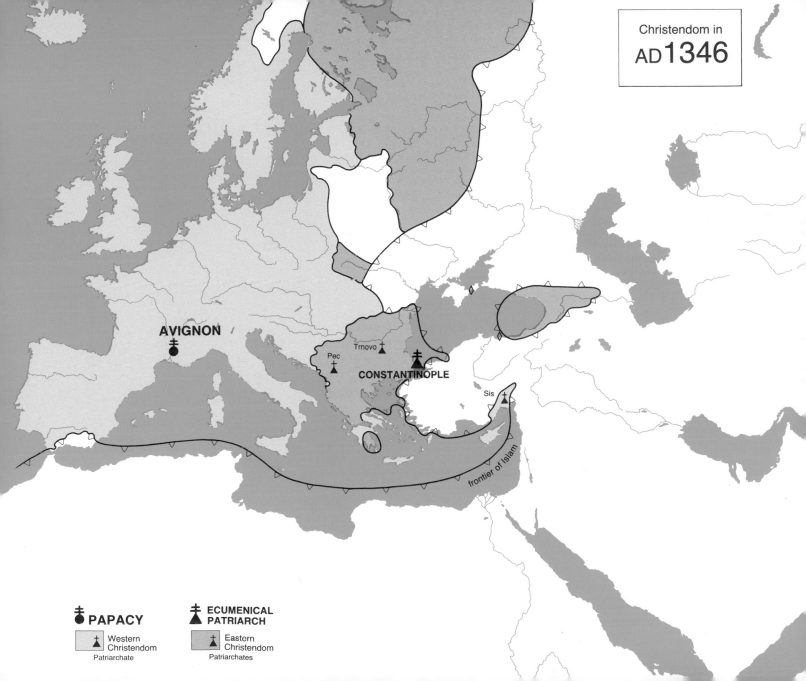

Christendom in
AD **1346**

AVIGNON

Pec

Trnovo

CONSTANTINOPLE

Sis

frontier of Islam

♆ **PAPACY**

♱ **ECUMENICAL
PATRIARCH**

Western
Christendom
Patriarchate

Eastern
Christendom
Patriarchates

The upturn in Europe's population that became apparent around the year 1000 had been building for some centuries previously. From the Dark Age nadir of the seventh century numbers edged up at a slow but increasing rate: on the set of figures adopted here, from 7.5 per cent in the eighth century to 10 per cent in the ninth and 12.5 per cent in the tenth. This brought the European total up from its low point of 27 million to a level that equalled the best figure achieved in the classical period, 36 million. It was at this point that the real push began. In the eleventh century the pace more than doubled, with the growth rate rising above 20 per cent for the first time. In the twelfth century it went up again, to better than 30 per cent. And in the thirteenth century it reached 36 per cent. In these three centuries the number of people living in Europe more than doubled, reaching the unprecedented total of 80 million.

There may have been a bit of good luck to this. Plague disappeared from Europe in the eighth century, and that must have helped. And maybe the climate played a part: summer temperatures were on average slightly higher than normal in the period 875–1100 and no worse than average thereafter. But good management was certainly the major factor, and, in a society as overwhelmingly agricultural as medieval Europe, that means better procedures down on the farm. There is ample evidence for improvements of this sort. Perhaps the most important is the spread of the three-field system, which cut the proportion of land lying fallow at any one time from a half to a third. But there are many other ways in which medieval husbandry demonstrated its superiority over classical practice. One is the use of horses for farm work, because, properly shod and harnessed, the horse is a much better worker than the ox. Another is the proliferation of water mills (known, but little used, in antiquity) and windmills (a medieval invention). Better axes made forest clearance easier; better ploughs drained the heavier, more fertile soils.

The result of this more intensive exploitation of the environment was an improved standard of living for a larger number of people. But, this being said, it remains true that there was never enough land for all the extra people and that many of them were forced to seek their subsistence away from home. Some migrated to the relatively empty regions east of the Elbe. Others moved less far but changed their lifestyle more radically: they became the working class in the new cities. Flanders, it is clear, had a surplus of labour over land as early as the eleventh century: it solved its problem by urbanizing and by making an unusually large contribution to the First Crusade.

In contrast to Europe, the Near East marked time, its population in the fourteenth century being no greater than it had been in the eighth. There had probably been some increase in the ninth and tenth centuries, for the Byzantine recovery of this period suggests that, in Anatolia at least, the peasantry was enjoying a modest revival, but whatever gains were made during this period were lost in the nomad incursions that began in the eleventh century. The Turks and Mongols used terror as a method of political control and were happy to see the towns they ruined standing empty. They were also quite prepared to depopulate the countryside to get the pasture they needed for their flocks. In Iran, Iraq and Anatolia, numbers fell every time a new group of nomads moved in.

In North Africa the situation was slightly better. A balance was struck between the agricultural and pastoral ways of life that allowed for a relatively comfortable coexistence, and if Tunisia and Egypt seem to have made few advances on their traditional positions, there were significant developments in Morocco. Of little importance in Roman times, Morocco emerged as the strongest component of the medieval Maghreb: it was Moroccan manpower that time and again deprived the Christians of final victory in Spain.

So far we have taken the story up to the year 1300. What happened between 1300 and 1346? Given the uncertainties of the data, it is difficult to be sure, but it seems likely that Europe's demographic boom ran out of steam and that growth fell off to near enough zero. There were widespread crop failures in 1315 and 1316, and subsequently the climate deteriorated – not by much, but perhaps enough to put the brakes on a population that must have been near its Malthusian limit. Whether or not this is true, one thing is certain: by 1346 the medieval cycle had run its course.

population in
AD **1346**

each symbol represents 1 million people

areas averaging 10 or more persons per km²
left unshaded

When Denmark's Baltic hegemony collapsed in the 1220s, the main beneficiary was Lubeck, the German seaport at the base of the Danish peninsula. With the cooperation of the other German cities of the region, the Lubeckers transformed the relatively insignificant 'association of German merchants trading with Novgorod' into the Hansa, an urban cartel with monopoly power in the Baltic and a powerful influence in the North Sea. In its heyday, around the date of this map, the Hansa included all the German towns of the Baltic littoral and most of the inland cities north of a line joining Cologne and Magdeburg (both Hansa members). Lubeck's leadership of this league was confirmed in 1293 when – shades of Athens and Delos – the treasury was transferred to the city from Visby, the original meeting place of the association.

One reason for the Hansa's success was the size of its ships. The Danes clung too long to the Viking tradition of small, open craft, able to put ashore anywhere. The Hansa introduced the cog, a round-bellied, fully decked vessel capable of carrying ten times as much cargo as a Viking boat while costing little more to run. The results were soon visible in the fisheries. The herring of the Baltic and the cod of the North Atlantic were still cropped and salted by Scandinavian fishermen, but they were barrelled and marketed by the Hansa. When it came to shifting cargo, neither Danes nor Norwegians could compete.

Fish, an obligatory article of diet for the medieval Christian, was an important component in the Baltic economy. So was Russian wax, much in demand for liturgical candles. Furs, of course, were still the prime export, just as woollens remained the premier import. The carrying capacity of the cog, however, made it possible to add new cargoes: Swedish copper and iron, Prussian wheat and barley. The grain came from estates belonging to the Teutonic Knights, and in the fourteenth century its sale became an important source of revenue for the Order. The Grand Master was enrolled in the Hansa, which recognized his right to reserve to himself the trade in amber, the most ancient of all Baltic commodities.

The Hanseatic trading network is an impressive testimonial to the energy of medieval Germany. However, it has to be said that by Italian standards the Hansa was a modest outfit. Genoa had ten times the trade of Lubeck, and it was only one of four Italian cities operating at this level. The Italian economy had moved ahead just as fast as the German and, starting from a higher base, reached a much higher volume.

One area with which Italy ran a consistent trade surplus was North Africa. The bill was settled in gold, which enabled the north Italian cities to issue a gold coinage, the first to be seen in the west for 500 years. The coins, known as genovinos, florins or ducats depending on whether they were minted at Genoa, Florence or Venice (which was classed as a ducate, or duchy), were all of the same weight (3.5 grammes) and fineness (100 per cent); they quickly became a European standard, enhancing Italy's role as the Continent's banker.

This role dated back to the beginnings of the medieval revival, for the Papacy, the only international organization to have come through the Dark Ages, naturally favoured Italian employees. But collecting Peter's pence, the tithe that the Western Church paid to Rome, was only a first step: the real expansion followed the growth of the Flemish textile industry, which came to rely heavily on Italian buyers. By the beginning of the fourteenth century, the banking network that supported the textile trade stretched from London to Tabriz. There were sizeable colonies of Italians both Oltramonte (over the Alps) and Oltramare (overseas), and banking houses like the Bardi and Peruzzi of Florence had incomes beyond those of most monarchs.

The Italians had also moved into the textile trade as producers. Until the early thirteenth century, the best they could manage was run-of-the-mill cloth for local sale. In the 1220s they began to turn out cloth that was good enough to export, and by the 1320s they were producing fabrics that would stand comparison with the best products of Flanders and the Levant. The raw materials had to be imported. Wool was brought from England, at first overland then, thanks to a Genoese initiative of the 1270s, by sea. Egypt supplied cotton, Persia provided silk. But the exports of high-value cloths, of Florentine woollens, Milanese fustians and Lucchese silks, more than covered the cost.

With more and bigger towns linked by trading connections of greater strength and complexity, the impression given by this map is of a Europe experiencing unrivalled prosperity. By comparison with earlier eras this is certainly true, but the economy was not without serious blemishes. The creation of the Italian textile industry was achieved at the expense of the Flemish weavers, whose output declined after 1320. The collapse of the Ilkhanate disrupted the silk trade: the Venetians and Genoese, who withdrew their agents from Tabriz in 1338 and 1340 respectively, lost an important source of supply and a useful market. And the repudiation by the English King Edward III of the mountainous debt he had built up during the opening phase of his war with France resulted in the bankruptcy of his main creditors, the Bardi and Peruzzi (1343). This was a bitter blow for Florence, the pace-setter of the Italian Renaissance. But worse was to come.

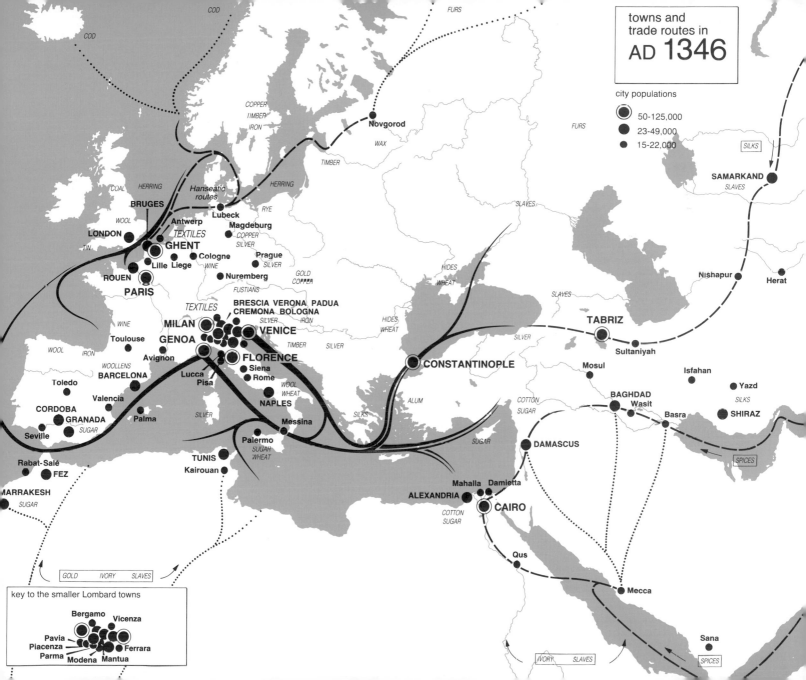

COD

COD

FURS

COPPER
TIMBER
IRON

WAX

TIMBER

FURS

SILKS

city populations

● 50–125,000

● 23–49,000

● 15–22,000

SAMARKAND

SLAVES

*Hanseatic
routes*

COAL

HERRING

HERRING

RYE

Lubeck

SLAVES

SLAVES

Nishapur

Herat

BRUGES

WOOL

Antwerp

Magdeburg

COPPER
SILVER

TEXTILES

LONDON

TIN

GHENT

Lille Liege

Cologne

WINE

Prague

SILVER

TABRIZ

ROUEN

Nuremberg

GOLD
COPPER

HIDES
WHEAT

Sultaniyah

Mosul

PARIS

FUSTIANS

TEXTILES

BRESCIA VERONA PADUA
CREMONA BOLOGNA

SILVER

HIDES
WHEAT

Isfahan

MILAN

WINE

Toulouse

GENOA

VENICE

IRON

BAGHDAD

Wasit

Yazd

SILKS

Avignon

FLORENCE

TIMBER

SILVER

CONSTANTINOPLE

SILVER

Basra

SHIRAZ

Lucca

Siena

BARCELONA

WOOLLENS

Pisa

Rome

ALUM

*COTTON
SUGAR*

Toledo

WOOL

Valencia

Palma

*WOOL
WHEAT*

NAPLES

SILKS

DAMASCUS

SPICES

CORDOBA

GRANADA

SILVER

Messina

SUGAR

Seville

SUGAR

Palermo

Mahalla Damietta

Rabat-Salé

*SUGAR
WHEAT*

ALEXANDRIA

CAIRO

FEZ

TUNIS

*COTTON
SUGAR*

MARRAKESH

Kairouan

SUGAR

Qus

GOLD IVORY SLAVES

Mecca

key to the smaller Lombard towns

Bergamo Vicenza

Pavia

Piacenza

Ferrara

Parma Modena Mantua

IVORY SLAVES

Sana

SPICES

After an absence of 600 years, bubonic plague returned to Europe in 1346. The epidemic, known to history as the Black Death, began on the lower Volga with outbreaks at Sarai, the capital of the Khans of the Golden Horde, and Astrakhan. In early 1347 it reached the Genoese trading stations of Tana, at the mouth of the Don, and Caffa, in the Crimea. From there it was carried by ship across the Black Sea to Trebizond and Constantinople, and from Constantinople across the Mediterranean to Alexandria, Venice and Genoa. By the summer of 1348 it had attacked most of the cities of Italy, southern France and Mediterranean Spain. It had also tracked across the south-west of France to Bordeaux, which gave it access to the Bay of Biscay and the sea routes to the British Isles and northern France. Before the year was out it had established itself in Ireland, the south-west of England and the valley of the Seine. In the Levant it had spread through the Egyptian delta to Cairo, and along the coast to Palestine and Syria.

Plague is primarily a disease of rodents, which spills over into human populations when the majority of the rodents have died and their fleas, which act as the injecting agent of the plague bacillus, are forced to seek new hosts. The epidemic that began in 1346 was probably triggered off by an outbreak among the ground squirrels of south Russia, whose fur provided the traders of the region with much of their stock. It became explosive when it reached the rat population of the Mediterranean littoral, whose habitat embraced both the seaports and the ships that plied between them: the ships carried the rats that carried the plague. Inland, the spread of the disease from one rodent population to another was slower and less certain: without seaborne reinforcements it sometimes petered out altogether. Conversely, it tended to hit island populations – both rodent and human – exceedingly hard.

The number of people killed by the Black Death was clearly colossal. Contemporaries usually put the mortality somewhere in the 50–75 per cent range, but it is rarely possible to substantiate their claims and difficult to know how typical the results are when we can. In England, however, records survive that show

that over most of the country at least a third of the clergy perished. This is probably the best measure we have of what happened in Europe as a whole in regions affected by the plague. It means that by the end of 1349, the fourth year of the epidemic, when most of Europe and much of North Africa and the Levant had experienced its full force, the total number of dead was of the order of 15 million.

The Black Death continued to make its way round Europe for a further four years. In 1350 the active front moved through Germany and Sweden; in 1351 it reached Poland, in 1352 Russia. The last major town to be afflicted was Moscow in 1353: there the plague killed the Great Prince, both of his sons and one of his two brothers. Finally, in some nameless hovel on the upper Volga, only a few hundred miles upstream from the spot where, seven years earlier, it had claimed its first victim, the Black Death struck for the last time. At a conservative estimate it had killed 20 million people.

This numbing figure seems to have had astonishingly little impact on the political and economic life of Europe. England and France were kicking each other to bits again within a few years; the armies were a little smaller but the national strategies were unchanged. Even more surprising is the lack of economic effects. Wages and prices appear to have shown very little change. The survivors seem to have assumed that life would now resume its normal pattern: the common people set about rebuilding their numbers and, aided by the fact that good farming land was now relatively plentiful, made a good start towards doing so.

But it wasn't going to be as easy as that. The plague bacillus had found hiding places in the countryside, and in 1357 a new outbreak began in Germany. Its advance was slower this time, but it got to most parts of the Continent over the next eight years, causing particularly heavy mortalities in the areas that had escaped the original epidemic. The overall effect was to wipe out any gains made in the intervening decade. And further epidemics were to occur every ten years or so until the end of the century, with a particularly bad one marking the year 1400. Instead of recovering, Europe's population bumped along the 60 million

line. The result was that the institutions that had managed to resist the effects of the plague in the short term were gradually undermined, and a new set of economic equations emerged, with money playing a more prominent part and labour having a higher value.

spread of the Black Death
AD **1346-53**

INITIAL FOCUS

Novgorod

Moscow
1353

Sarai
1346

Astrakhan

1349

1350

1351

1352

Tana
1347

Lubeck

Caffa

London

Cologne

PARIS

Trebizond
1347

VENICE

CONSTANTINOPLE
1347

Bordeaux

Avignon

GENOA

Toulouse

1347

Rome

Mosul
1348-9

Valencia

1347

DAMASCUS
1348

Seville

Messina

Gaza

1348

1349

TUNIS
1348

ALEXANDRIA
1347

CAIRO
1348

UPPER
EGYPT
1349

Mecca
1349

YEMEN
1351

When Philip Augustus annexed Normandy and the other English fiefs north of the Loire, he reckoned he had solved the problem of who was master: the territory remaining to the English Crown – in essence the Duchy of Aquitaine – could be picked up any time. Things didn't work out like that. As the thirteenth century wore on, the connection between England and Aquitaine strengthened, and in the early fourteenth century, when the French finally put the squeeze on the Duchy, they found themselves seriously at war. England's Edward III got off to a slow start, but a naval victory at Sluys (1340) gave him command of the Channel, and his invasion of the north of France in 1346 produced a stunning victory at Crécy, which in turn led to the capture of Calais the next year. Edward's son, the Black Prince, did even better. In 1356, at the battle of Poitiers, he turned on a much larger French army, totally defeated it and captured the French King. Four years later the English got the treaty they wanted.[1]

Two events stand out in the Islamic world: the final disappearance of the Ilkhanate and the rise of the Ottomans. The last serious contender for the Ilkhanate was assassinated in 1353: subsequently such vestiges of central authority as remained were acquired by the Jalayrids, who were recognized as suzerains by their immediate neighbours, the Muzaffarids on the east (now ruling from Shiraz) and the Black Sheep Turks on the west (though only after a conflict that ended to the Jalayrids' advantage in 1366). The provinces further east were divided between the Karts of Herat and the Sarbadars, a Mahdist sect that represents another stage in the development of Iranian fundamentalism. The Ottomans advanced on all fronts. They signalled their ambitions as regards Anatolia by occupying Ankara (1361; the move was contested by Karaman, which regarded itself as the heir of the Seljuks and had moved its capital up to Konya to emphasize the point). They also established a foothold in Europe by their seizure of Gallipoli (1354). This gave them a stake in a new game, with the Byzantine Empire as the prize. In this contest the official front-runner was still the Serbian Emperor Stefan Dushan, who had completed his conquest of northern Greece in the late 1340s. But Stefan's attempt to present himself as the heir of Byzantium failed for the one success that might have cemented the others, the capture of Constantinople. He died (1355) without even having attempted the siege, and his much vaunted empire immediately dissolved into half a dozen warring principalities. The Bulgars were doing no better, and the Latins had long since shot their bolt. The Ottomans could hardly have chosen a better moment to make their bid.[2]

In central Europe there are some positive achievements to report. Poland's Casimir III won recognition from Mazovia and conquered Galicia, successes that enable him to appear in the history books as Casimir the Great. Hungary forced Venice to yield its enclaves in Dalmatia and, on the eastern side of the Carpathians, acted as midwife to the emerging Vlach state of Moldavia.[3]

In the Maghreb, the Hafsid state split into three principalities: Constantine, Bougie and Tunis. In Spain, the kingdom of Aragon absorbed the sub-kingdom of Majorca (1354). In Scandinavia, the Danish King Valdemar Atterdag recovered the provinces pawned to Sweden and conquered the island of Gotland (1360–61). In Russia, Pskov won its independence from Novgorod (1348), and Lithuania occupied all of the Principality of Bryansk bar Tarusa (1357) and began to contest the steppe lands with the Golden Horde. In the Levant, the Genoese obtained the island of Lesbos, an enterprising young King of Cyprus established temporary control over much of the south coast of Anatolia (1361–73), and the kingdom of Armenia was all but squeezed out of existence by the Mamluks (1360; the final end came in 1375).

1. The French had more to be pleased about on their eastern border, where they had been nibbling away at the German territories on the right bank of the Rhône since the beginning of the century. All the important places, including Lyon, were now in their hands, and in 1349, by purchasing the Dauphiné, the French crown made an important acquisition on the far side of the river. The territory was bought as an appanage for the heir to the throne, hence the title of Dauphin borne by subsequent heirs apparent. It was effectively annexed in 1364. As noted already, Avignon became an outlier of the Papal State in 1348.

2. Not important, but interesting, are the Albanian principalities of the Adriatic coast. The Albanians are generally believed to be descended from the Illyrians, the native people of the western Balkans in classical times. They recovered their political identity in the years immediately following Stefan Dushan's death and, aided by an impossible geography, held on to it with surprising vigour.

3. In theory, Ragusa (modern Dubrovnik) passed from Venice to Hungary along with the rest of the Dalmatian coast, but as Hungary was satisfied with a nominal tribute, the city is shown as independent on the map.

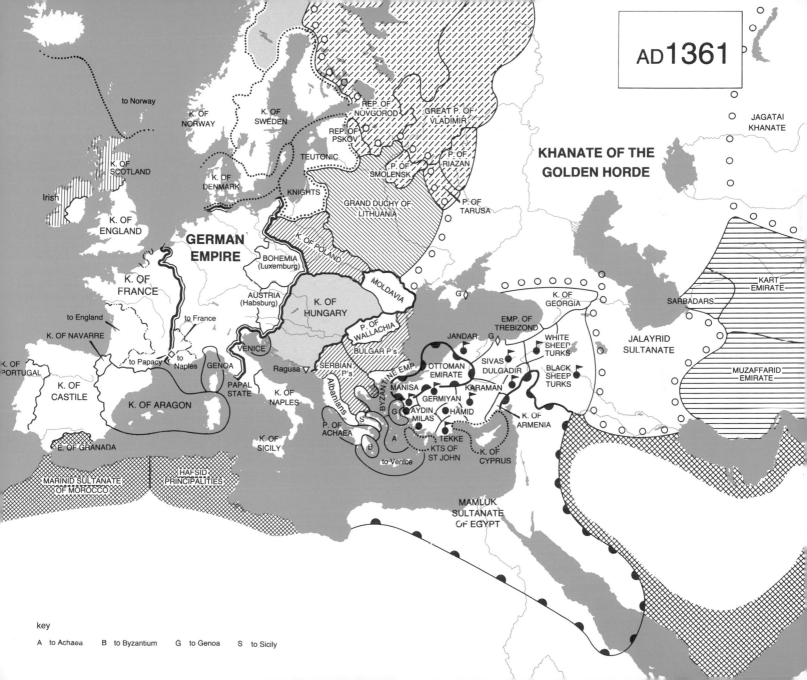

AD**1361**

KHANATE OF THE GOLDEN HORDE

JAGATAI KHANATE

to Norway

K. OF NORWAY

K. OF SWEDEN

REP. OF NOVGOROD

GREAT P. OF VLADIMIR

TEUTONIC

REP. OF PSKOV

P. OF RIAZAN

K. OF SCOTLAND

Irish

K. OF DENMARK

KNIGHTS

P. OF SMOLENSK

P. OF TARUSA

K. OF ENGLAND

GERMAN EMPIRE

GRAND DUCHY OF LITHUANIA

K. OF POLAND

KART EMIRATE

BOHEMIA (Luxemburg)

MOLDAVIA

K. OF FRANCE

AUSTRIA (Habsburg)

K. OF HUNGARY

SARBADARS

to England

to France

K. OF NAVARRE

to Papacy

to Naples

VENICE

GENOA

P. OF WALLACHIA

BULGAR P's.

K. OF GEORGIA

EMP. OF TREBIZOND

JALAYRID SULTANATE

K. OF PORTUGAL

K. OF CASTILE

PAPAL STATE

K. OF NAPLES

Ragusa

SERBIAN P's.

G

G

JANDAR

WHITE SHEEP TURKS

MUZAFFARID EMIRATE

K. OF ARAGON

Albanians

BYZANTINE EMP.

OTTOMAN EMIRATE

MANISA

SIVAS DULGADIR

BLACK SHEEP TURKS

E. OF GRANADA

K. OF SICILY

P. OF ACHAEA

S

G

GERMIYAN

AYDIN MILAS

HAMID

KARAMAN

to Venice

B

A

TEKKE KTS OF ST JOHN

K. OF CYPRUS

K. OF ARMENIA

MARINID SULTANATE OF MOROCCO

HAFSID PRINCIPALITIES

MAMLUK SULTANATE OF EGYPT

key

A   to Achaea   B   to Byzantium   G   to Genoa   S   to Sicily

The initial Ottoman advance into Europe was more remarkable for its steadiness than its speed. The 1360s were spent establishing a firm grip on Thrace, the 1370s on defending this acquisition from the Serbs and Bulgars, and the 1380s on reducing these two peoples to vassal status. Then, in 1389, the Turks acquired a leader who demanded a quicker pace, Bayezit, the first Ottoman ruler to take the title of Sultan. Bayezit opened his reign with a crushing victory over the Serbs at Kossovo Polye, the Field of Blackbirds, a subject of sad Slav songs for centuries to come. He followed this up by adding Bosnia and Wallachia to his list of tributaries (1391) and annexing north Greece and Bulgaria (1392–3). But resounding though these victories were, they were surpassed by the parallel campaigns in Anatolia, in the course of which Bayezit brought all the Turkoman emirates west of the Euphrates into his empire. The Sultan's military energies, alternately displayed in Europe and Asia, earned him the title of Yildirim, 'the Thunderbolt'. No doubt of it, he was a great warrior.

The main excitements in Central Europe at this time were dynastic. Casimir the Great of Poland, dying childless, left his kingdom to Louis the Great of Hungary (1370). Louis, however, failed to produce the son necessary to cement the union; instead he left two daughters, each of whom became responsible for a new combination. The elder, with Hungary as her dowry, married Sigismund, heir to the Luxemburg lands in Germany; the younger, who received Poland, married the Grand Duke of Lithuania. Of the two unions, the Polish–Lithuanian looked the shakier: it was initially repudiated by the Lithuanian barons, who insisted on the appointment of a new Grand Duke when the existing one became King of Poland. But the Lithuanians needed the Poles: they had lost the last of their Baltic provinces to the Teutonic Knights in 1382, and the offensive against the Golden Horde was to end in defeat in 1399. They finally decided to acknowledge Polish suzerainty, so keeping the union in being.[1]

The Hungarian–Luxemburg connection, by contrast, got off to a more positive start. King Sigismund, determined to meet the Turks head on, persuaded the Pope to preach a Crusade and sold off his initial slice of the Luxemburg inheritance to finance his share of it. As a result he was able to lead a considerable Franco-Hungarian force against the Ottomans in 1396. But if the logistics of crusading had improved – Sigismund had only to step across his frontier to confront the Turk – leadership had not. Bayezit appeared with his army while the crusaders were besieging the frontier fortress of Nicopolis. The French immediately insisted on mounting the same sort of headlong attack that had got them into trouble at Crécy and Poitiers and, once again, were first fought to a halt and then slaughtered. The Hungarians on their own could do no better, and the last of the Crusades was over almost as soon as it had begun. It had done no more than supply another battle honour for Bayezit and the seemingly invincible Ottoman army.

At home the French did better. Avoiding set-piece battles, they gradually eroded the English holding in Aquitaine, reducing it to little more than a strip along the coast. It seemed unlikely there would be much further trouble from this quarter. Less clever was the French monarchy's habit of endowing Princes of the Blood with over-large fiefs. A particularly unfortunate example of this was the appointment of one as Duke of Burgundy (B_1 on the map), for the new Duke subsequently added the County of Burgundy (B_2; a fief of the German Empire) and the County of Flanders (B_3; technically French, but in practice semi-independent) to his appanage. Positioned on the divide between France and Germany, endowed with the wealth of the Flemish weaving towns, this Burgundian domain had many of the characteristics of an independent state.

In the Mediterranean, Venice took advantage of the political fragmentation of the western and southern Balkans to gain control of Corfu and place garrisons at selected points in Albania and southern Greece. Genoa, which had been badly beaten in the fourth and most bitterly fought of its wars with Venice, was so demoralized as a result that it placed itself under French suzerainty for a few years (1396–1409). In the Baltic, the Danes were brought low by the Hansa (1370), a humiliation that made the subsequent moves towards a merger of the Scandinavian kingdoms more readily acceptable. The union of the three crowns was formalized at Kalmar in 1397. A year later, the Teutonic Knights occupied Gotland. In Germany, the Habsburgs acquired the Tyrol in 1363. The County of Provence no longer appears on the map because it separated off from the Kingdom of Naples in 1382.

Meanwhile a new power had arisen in the western border lands of the Jagatai Khanate. Of the four successor states of the Mongol Empire, the Jagatai Khanate was the least glamorous: its constituent tribes constantly changed their allegiance and few Khans were able to stay on top for long. However, in a turbulent career that started in the 1360s, one of their subordinate chieftains discovered the necessary charisma. This was Timur, the Great Emir, also known as Timur-i-leng (Timur the Lame, Marlowe's Tamberlaine). By 1393 he had added Iran and Iraq to the territories of the Khan in whose name he ruled. More importantly, he had built an army that expected to fight and win a major campaign every year.

Timur's military machine ran on plunder and, as it soon emptied any land it occupied, its needs forced Timur to look ever further afield. In 1395 he invaded Russia, seized Sarai, the capital of the Golden Horde, and let his followers gorge on the accumulated treasures of the Khanate. In 1398 he turned east and descended on India. Delhi surrendered on terms, but Timur's troops subjected it to a merciless sack all the same: its inhabitants' heads were collected into pyramids at each of the city's gates and their belongings divided among the soldiery. Back in the west, Timur picked a quarrel with the Mamluks, which gave him an excuse to pillage Aleppo and Damascus: then, on the pretext that Bayezit had refused to hand over some fugitives, he moved against the Ottomans (1402). Bayezit accepted the challenge, only to find, as he neared his eastern frontier, that Timur had got

(continued over)

1. Poland had taken a slice of Volhynia from Lithuania in 1366. Moldavia exchanged its allegiance to Hungary for a looser association with Poland a little later. Hungary also lost control of Bosnia at this time, but Bosnian independence was only briefly sustained: the Turks, as already noted, reduced the country to vassal status in 1391.

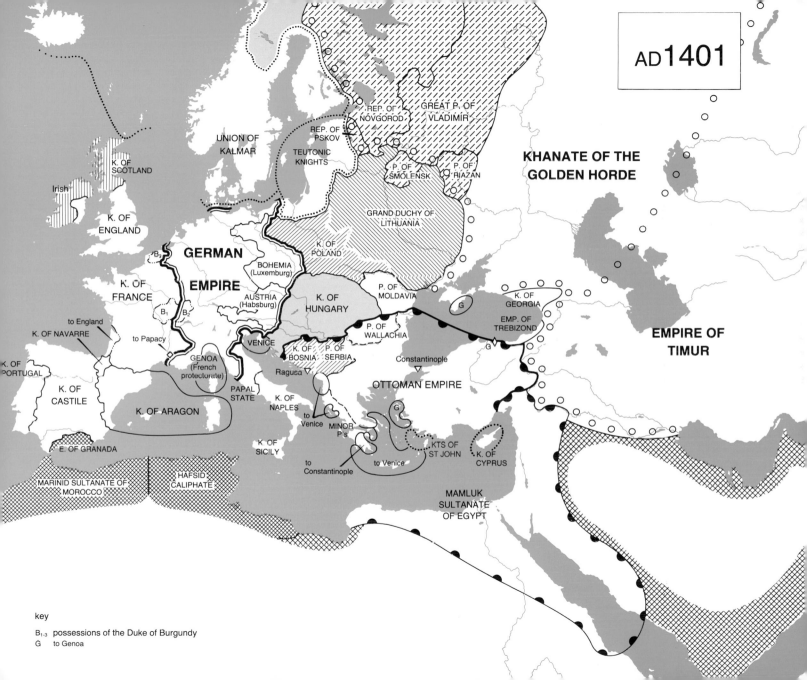

AD 1401

K. OF SCOTLAND

Irish

K. OF ENGLAND

UNION OF KALMAR

REP. OF NOVGOROD

GREAT P. OF VLADIMIR

REP. OF PSKOV

TEUTONIC KNIGHTS

P. OF SMOLENSK

P. OF RIAZAN

KHANATE OF THE GOLDEN HORDE

GRAND DUCHY OF LITHUANIA

B_3

GERMAN

EMPIRE

BOHEMIA (Luxemburg)

K. OF POLAND

K. OF FRANCE

AUSTRIA (Habsburg)

K. OF HUNGARY

P. OF MOLDAVIA

K. OF GEORGIA

EMP. OF TREBIZOND

G

EMPIRE OF TIMUR

to England

K. OF NAVARRE

B_1

B_2

to Papacy

GENOA (French protectorate)

VENICE

K. OF BOSNIA

P. OF SERBIA

P. OF WALLACHIA

G

Constantinople

K. OF PORTUGAL

K. OF CASTILE

PAPAL STATE

Ragusa

K. OF ARAGON

K. OF NAPLES

to Venice

OTTOMAN EMPIRE

G

E. OF GRANADA

K. OF SICILY

MINOR P's

to Constantinople

to Venice

KTS OF ST JOHN

K. OF CYPRUS

MARINID SULTANATE OF MOROCCO

HAFSID CALIPHATE

MAMLUK SULTANATE OF EGYPT

key

B_{1-3} possessions of the Duke of Burgundy

G to Genoa

there first, picked a route to the south and was now behind him. The Sultan led his men back to Ankara, where, on a field of Timur's choosing, Turk and Tartar finally came face to face. Bayezit's hold on the situation was slipping: the counter-march had been exhausting, water was in short supply and some of his Turcoman auxiliaries were threatening to desert. When battle was joined many of them promptly did so, leaving the remainder of the Ottoman army to be engulfed by Timur's more numerous regiments.

The débâcle at Ankara was only the beginning of Bayezit's humiliation. Taken captive at the close of the battle, he was to spend the remaining months of his life in Timur's train as the Great Emir moved slowly round Anatolia, restoring the princes Bayezit had earlier deposed and receiving the submission of the junior members of the Ottoman house. Finally, in 1404, Timur returned to his capital, Samarkand, and busied himself with preparations for his next venture, the invasion of China. Supply points were set up on the routes across Central Asia, and at the end of the year Timur himself set out for the east. To his entourage, though, it was clear that he was dying, and by the time he reached Otrar, Timur was forced to admit it too. China would not have to endure a visit from his greedy hordes.[2]

H enry V, who became King of England in 1413, decided to put an end to the quarrel between the English and French crowns by making himself King of France too. Circumstances favoured his cause. The reigning King of France was a lunatic, the Duke of Burgundy open-minded about his loyalties, and the French nobility as confused as ever about the difference between tournaments and tactics. At Agincourt (1415), the most famous of all the encounters between

English bowmen and French knights, Henry won the crushing victory he needed to complete the demoralization of the French court. Five years later he was recognized as Regent of the Kingdom and heir to the throne. The last prize eluded him: he died a few months before the French King, and it was the infant Henry VI who became the first monarch to rule both England and France (1422). In fact, only half France was Henry's: south of the Loire the repudiated Dauphin had established an opposition government, and if he wasn't able to win any battles, eventually Joan of Arc won one for him (1429). It was enough to sustain his claim to the whole kingdom.

A few years before Agincourt, eastern Europe had been the scene of a battle with similar epic overtones. At Tannenberg (Grunwald in Polish history books) the Teutonic Knights confronted an invading Polish–Lithuanian host: the result was total victory for the Poles and Lithuanians and the end of the Order as a military power (1411). The vast army assembled by the allies – it included Russians from Smolensk (now incorporated into Lithuania), Tartars from the Black Sea steppe and mercenaries from Bohemia and Silesia – could not be held together for a war of conquest, and the subsequent peace merely confirmed Lithuania's recovery of Samogitia, the province dividing Livonia from Prussia. None the less, the battle marks a true watershed, the end of the second German *Drang nach Osten* and the beginning of the ebb tide.

Among the potentates pressing Poland to make peace was Sigismund, now Emperor of Germany as well as King of Hungary. This suggests he was cutting a fine figure, but in truth the more titles Sigismund acquired the less effective he became. The acquisition of the Crown of Bohemia (1419) heralded a particularly bad spell. It was a straightforward part of the Luxemburg inheritance and should have provided him with a useful power-base. Instead, a misguided attempt to suppress the Hussite heresy provoked a blazing revolt and the appearance of a nationalist Czech government that Sigismund proved quite unable to topple. Eventually, in 1436, the year before his death, Sigismund was allowed to enter Prague and mount the throne, but for most of his reign Bohemia brought him nothing but humiliation.

Considering that Timur had ignored every instrument of government except terror, it is remarkable how well his empire held up after his death. His son Shah Rukh maintained control over the whole area between the Euphrates and the Tarim basin, and if some of the western feudatories, most notably the Black Sheep Turks, proved disobedient from time to time, they were always brought to heel in the end. It is true that there were no more of the vast plundering expeditions that had characterized Timur's heyday, but then Shah Rukh's neighbours took good care not to provoke him. The Ottomans, for example, always addressed him in the most respectful terms, and, though they quickly drew the western half of Anatolia into their empire again, they left the more eastern emirates alone. Better put up with pin-pricks from the Emir of Karaman than conjure up another storm from the east.

In Europe, the concessions that the Ottomans felt it appropriate to make in the aftermath of the Battle of Ankara proved of short duration. Byzantium got Salonika back for a few years, while Wallachia, Serbia and Bosnia each recovered their independence only to lose it again in the 1420s. By 1430 the Ottoman frontier was back where it had been in 1401. In as-yet-unconquered Greece, the Byzantines managed to absorb the last remnants of the Principality of Achaea (1428–32); the Aegean islands had already transferred their allegiance to Venice (1418).

Venice, in fact, was experiencing a highly successful start to the fifteenth century. The misfortunes of Hungary and Bosnia enabled her to recover the Dalmatian littoral (1409–20), and the weakness of Milan permitted some unexpectedly easy gains in Lombardy (1404–26).

In Russia, the Golden Horde was now clearly losing its grip. The Circassians of the Caucasus recovered their independence, and the Uzbeks of the trans-Ural steppe established theirs under a Khan of their own choosing. In the Mediterranean, Sicily reverted to the Crown of Aragon (1409), and the Portuguese seized Ceuta on the Moroccan side of the Straits of Gibraltar (1415). In the Netherlands, Burgundy acquired Holland and Brabant (B₄ on the map).

2. Timur was a devout Muslim, and it is ironic that few of his blows landed on the enemies of his faith. The best he could do was ransack Georgia every time he passed by, which was often enough to make Georgia a pretty miserable place, and, as a footnote to his Anatolian campaign, expel a Christian garrison from Smyrna.

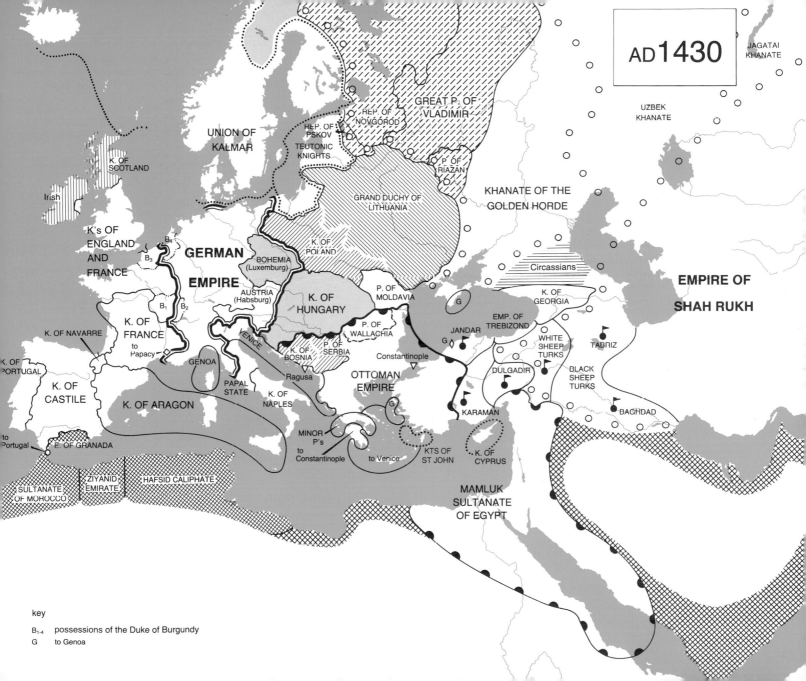

AD **1430**

JAGATAI
KHANATE

UZBEK
KHANATE

GREAT P. OF
VLADIMIR

UNION OF
KALMAR

REP. OF
NOVGOROD

REP. OF
PSKOV

TEUTONIC
KNIGHTS

P. OF
RIAZAN

KHANATE OF THE
GOLDEN HORDE

K. OF
SCOTLAND

Irish

GRAND DUCHY OF
LITHUANIA

EMPIRE OF

K's OF
ENGLAND
AND
FRANCE

B₄

B₃

GERMAN

EMPIRE

K. OF
POLAND

Circassians

SHAH RUKH

BOHEMIA
(Luxemburg)

AUSTRIA
(Habsburg)

K. OF
HUNGARY

P. OF
MOLDAVIA

K. OF
GEORGIA

EMP. OF
TREBIZOND

G

B₁   B₂

K. OF
NAVARRE

K. OF
FRANCE

to Papacy

VENICE

P. OF
WALLACHIA

JANDAR

G

WHITE
SHEEP
TURKS

TABRIZ

GENOA

K. OF
BOSNIA

P. OF
SERBIA

Constantinople

DULGADIR

BLACK
SHEEP
TURKS

K. OF
PORTUGAL

PAPAL
STATE

K. OF
CASTILE

K. OF ARAGON

Ragusa

K. OF
NAPLES

OTTOMAN
EMPIRE

KARAMAN

BAGHDAD

to
Portugal

E. OF GRANADA

MINOR
P's
to
Constantinople

G

to Venice

KTS OF
ST JOHN

K. OF
CYPRUS

SULTANATE
OF MOROCCO

ZIYANID
EMIRATE

HAFSID CALIPHATE

**MAMLUK
SULTANATE
OF EGYPT**

key

B₁₋₄   possessions of the Duke of Burgundy
G   to Genoa

England's attempt to dominate France was only realistic so long as it had Burgundy's backing: when Burgundy changed sides, which it did in 1435, the English position immediately started to crumble. Paris was abandoned the next year, and, though Normandy and Aquitaine were retained until the late 1440s, the end of the decade saw these provinces slipping away too. Cherbourg, the last foothold in Normandy, fell in 1450; Bordeaux, the capital of Aquitaine, in 1453. Of all England's possessions on the Continent, only Calais remained.

The fate of Bordeaux was sealed by a French victory at Castillon, in which the English were pricked into an unwise attack by French artillery fire. This is the first instance of guns playing a decisive part on a battlefield, for though their use is recorded a century earlier (at Crécy, by the English) the early models took too long to reload to be of much use tactically. Where guns had already established a dominant role was in siege warfare, and castles and walled towns that had previously held out for months or years were now regularly taken in a matter of weeks. If Castillon gives 1453 a claim to be the year in which the gun came of age, the claim is underlined by a resounding success in the more familiar role of siege engine. In April 1453 the Ottomans brought an outsize battery to bear against Constantinople's land walls, the famous line of 200 towers that had remained unbreached since its first building ten centuries earlier. Eight weeks of bombardment reduced a long stretch to rubble, and, at the end of May the Turks poured in.

In a sense it was an anti-climax. The fall of the city was long overdue and, if it hadn't been for the battle of Ankara, could well have been achieved by Bayezit fifty years before. Moreover, Constantinople was a city of the second rank by this time: most of the streets through which the Turks stormed in triumph had been deserted generations before and were now no more than grassy lanes connecting the few still-populated areas. But Constantine's city was important for more than its venerable past: it occupied a key position in the eastern Mediterranean, and even the husk of it was of immense value to Christendom. The news of

its sack shocked the west, uneasily aware that its sins of omission and commission had contributed to the result. Now Constantinople was to be great again, but this time as Istanbul, capital of the Ottoman Sultans, the inveterate enemies of all Christian enterprise.

The capture of Constantinople was the first major undertaking of Sultan Mehmet II, better known as Mehmet Fatih, 'Mohammed the Conqueror'. During his long reign (1451–81) he conquered much else besides Constantinople. He annexed Serbia, most of Bosnia, and all the little principalities of southern Greece (1456–68). He reduced the Genoese possessions in the Crimea and brought the local Tartars under his suzerainty (1475–8). He conquered Jandar, Karaman and the pathetic little Empire of Trebizond, and confined the White Sheep Turks to the area east of the Euphrates (1461–73). In peninsular Greece, the Venetians managed to hang on to most of their strongholds, but islands too close to the mainland often proved vulnerable to Mehmet's armies: he lifted Lesbos from the Genoese in 1462 and Euboea from the Venetians in 1470.

In eastern Europe the map was simplifying. The Polish–Lithuanian union became fully effective in the reign of Casimir IV, who used his superior resources to force the Teutonic Knights to surrender much of Prussia and do homage for the rest (1466). He had already obtained a slice off the tip of Silesia (1457) and later, when the Ottomans started to advance against Moldavia, received the voluntary submission of this border state (1485). Further east, Ivan the Great, the first of the Muscovite Great Princes to use the title of Tsar, annexed Novgorod (1478). He also refused the Golden Horde its customary tribute and faced down an attempt to extract it by force (1480). In this defiance, of course, he was much aided by the fragmentation of the Horde, which led to the appearance of local khanates in the Crimea (1441), and at Kazan (1445) and Astrakhan (1466).

Changes in western Europe include both major and minor adjustments. The King of Denmark acquired Holstein (1460) but had to cede the Orkneys and Shetlands to Scotland (1468). Sweden edged out of the Union of Kalmar (1448). England, as well as losing her fiefs in France, saw all Ireland, bar the district

immediately dependent on Dublin, slip from her grasp. France did extremely well, not just against England but against England's erstwhile ally, the Duke of Burgundy. Success in this quarter was greatly facilitated by the reckless behaviour of the fourth Duke, Charles the Bold, who tried to link up and then expand his scattered domain. After some initial success he got embroiled with the Swiss, who inflicted two sharp defeats on his over-extended forces (1476). The following year he lost his life attempting to relieve a garrison he had placed in Nancy. King Louis XI of France, who had been subsidizing Charles's enemies all along, immediately occupied Burgundy, both Duchy and County, and though he failed to win Flanders – Charles's daughter preserved the northern part of her inheritance by marrying the Habsburg Archduke Maximillian – the Burgundian state had been effectively cut off at the knees. Four years later, Louis got an additional sweetener in the form of Provence.

Spain was making equal progress, though this isn't something you can deduce from the map. The key event was the marriage of Ferdinand of Aragon and Isabella of Castile in 1469. The two of them began the reduction of the Emirate of Granada in 1481, a process completed by the capture of its capital eleven years later. Ferdinand was later to annex Naples and Navarre. As a result their daughter would inherit all the Spanish kingdoms bar Portugal, plus Sardinia, Sicily and Naples.[1]

1. Naples had been conquered by Alphonso of Aragon in 1442 but separated off again sixteen years later to provide a kingdom for his illegitimate son, Ferrante.

Other events that resulted in boundary changes on this map include the division of the Timurid Empire into two separate principalities, the collapse of the Uzbek Khanate (1471) and the disintegration of the Luxemburg domain after the death of the luckless Sigismund (Bohemia eventually passed to a Polish prince, Silesia and Lusatia to Hungary). The Venetians picked up the Ionian Islands (1482), and the Portuguese added Arzila and Tangier to their Moroccan enclave (1471).

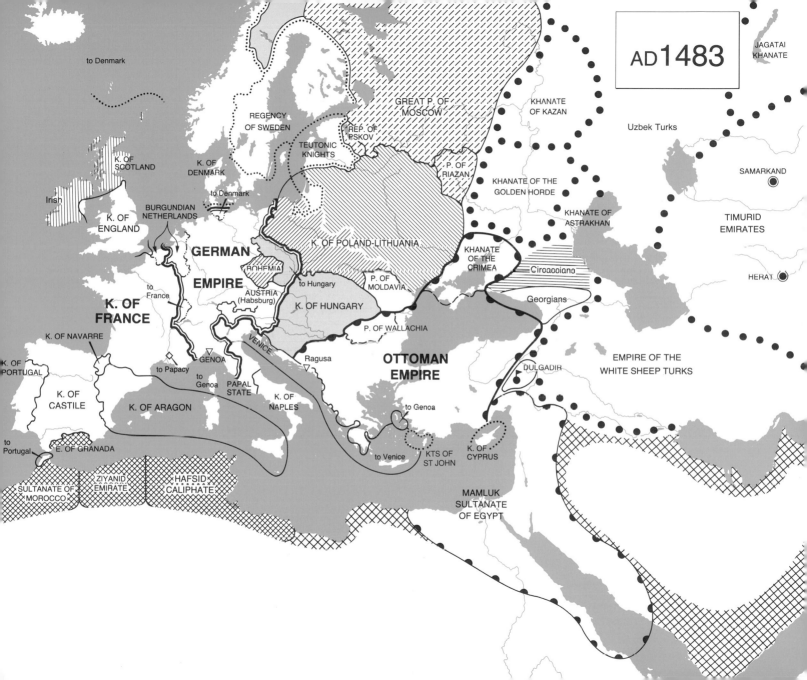

AD1483

to Denmark

JAGATAI
KHANATE

GREAT P. OF
MOSCOW

KHANATE
OF KAZAN

Uzbek Turks

SAMARKAND

REGENCY
OF SWEDEN

REP. OF
PSKOV

TEUTONIC
KNIGHTS

P. OF
RIAZAN

KHANATE OF THE
GOLDEN HORDE

TIMURID
EMIRATES

K. OF
SCOTLAND

K. OF
DENMARK

to Denmark

KHANATE OF
ASTRAKHAN

Irish

K. OF
ENGLAND

BURGUNDIAN
NETHERLANDS

HERAT

GERMAN

K. OF POLAND-LITHUANIA

KHANATE
OF THE
CRIMEA

Ciroaooiano

EMPIRE

BOHEMIA

to France

to Hungary

P. OF
MOLDAVIA

Georgians

K. OF
FRANCE

AUSTRIA
(Habsburg)

K. OF HUNGARY

K. OF NAVARRE

VENICE

P. OF WALLACHIA

EMPIRE OF THE
WHITE SHEEP TURKS

K. OF
PORTUGAL

to Papacy

GENOA

to Genoa

Ragusa

OTTOMAN
EMPIRE

DULGADIR

to Portugal

K. OF
CASTILE

PAPAL
STATE

K. OF
NAPLES

K. OF ARAGON

to Genoa

E. OF GRANADA

to Venice

KTS OF
ST JOHN

K. OF
CYPRUS

SULTANATE OF
MOROCCO

ZIYANID
EMIRATE

HAFSID
CALIPHATE

MAMLUK
SULTANATE
OF EGYPT

After half a century at Avignon, the Papacy was forced to acknowledge that the vast majority of the faithful wanted a return to Rome. Urban V made the move in 1367, setting up shop in the Vatican because the traditional papal residence, the Lateran Palace, was too dilapidated to be usable. But it wasn't just the Lateran that was run down: the whole town was a mess, and unruly with it. After three years' residence, Urban decided that it was impossible to conduct the Church's business in such a place and went back to Avignon. Seven years later his successor, Gregory XI, tried again, only to come to the same conclusion. This time, however, the outcome was different, for Gregory died before he was able to get his bags packed. The Roman mob seized its chance, forcing the election of an Italian, Urban VI, who, whatever his failings in other directions, was committed to staying in the city.

As it turned out, Urban's failings were considerable. The cardinals in particular found it difficult to deal with a Pope who was constantly threatening them with physical violence. Within a few months the entire college had fled Rome, revoked Urban's election, and voted in a more mannerly prelate, the Frenchman Clement VII. The Romans, of course, stuck by their man, and eventually Clement and the college of cardinals were forced to withdraw to Avignon, where the French government was offering support. Urban VI, with a second set of cardinals entirely of his own making (and of whom he later murdered five) celebrated by making a promenade of Italy. Most of Europe recognized him as the lawful pontiff, but the Neapolitan Angevins and the Scots, political allies of France, preferred Clement, as did Aragon and Castile.

So began the Great Schism. Neither side would give an inch, and whenever a Pope died his cardinals promptly replaced him. This went on for thirty years, until finally public opinion forced the cardinals to do what they should have done in the first place, summon a General Council of the Church. The Council met at Pisa in 1409, where it declared both existing Popes deposed and elected a new one of its own. However, as it lacked the means to make its depositions effective, the end result was simply three Popes instead of two. A new Council meeting at Constance (1414–17) did better. One Pope abdicated voluntarily, another withdrew to Spain, where his support gradually ebbed away, while the third was forced to stand down after a trial that left many puzzled as to how he had become Pope in the first place.[1] The way was clear for the selection of a new pontiff who could end the confusion as to who was Pope and where he was to be found. The Council's choice fell on a Roman nobleman, Oddo Colonna, who unsurprisingly chose Rome as his pontifical seat. He entered the city, as Martin V, in 1420.

This time the return to Rome was a success. It coincided with an extraordinary upsurge in the visual arts in Italy, a conjunction which greatly aided the Popes in their task of turning Rome into a city that a Pontiff could be proud of. By the end of the medieval period, which in terms of this map means the pontificate of Sixtus IV (1471–84), the job was well in hand. Sixtus had his off moments. He tended to get too deeply involved in the less savoury aspects of Italian politics (he was certainly privy to the attempt to assassinate Lorenzo the Magnificent in Florence Cathedral in 1478), and he played the game of family favourites a little too vigorously (he made six of his nephews into cardinals, including one who was only 17 at the time). As against which there is the Sistine Chapel, which Sixtus began in 1471 as the meeting place for future conclaves and which ultimately was to shed a lustre on the Renaissance Papacy that no misdeeds could tarnish.

While the Papacy surrounded itself with secular glories, the assets of the Eastern Church were dwindling fast: each decade the Ottomans gobbled up another of its lands. By the 1430s, things were so bad that a Byzantine Emperor decided on the ultimate sacrifice: he journeyed to Italy and placed himself and his people under Papal authority. The pay-off was a promise from the Pope to organize the Crusade so clearly necessary if Byzantium was to be saved. Nothing came of this charade. The days when the princes of the west allowed the Pope to direct their armaments were long since gone, and, even with the Turk at the gate, the people of Constantinople refused to renounce their religious identity. With neither side able to deliver, Byzantium fought and fell in its ancient faith. Thereafter, the only lands that remained both free and Orthodox were, in ecclesiastical terms, provincial: Georgia, the Romanian principalities, and Muscovy.

1. This was the John XXIII of whose trial before the Council Gibbon wrote: 'the most scandalous charges were suppressed; the vicar of Christ was only accused of piracy, rape, sodomy and incest.'

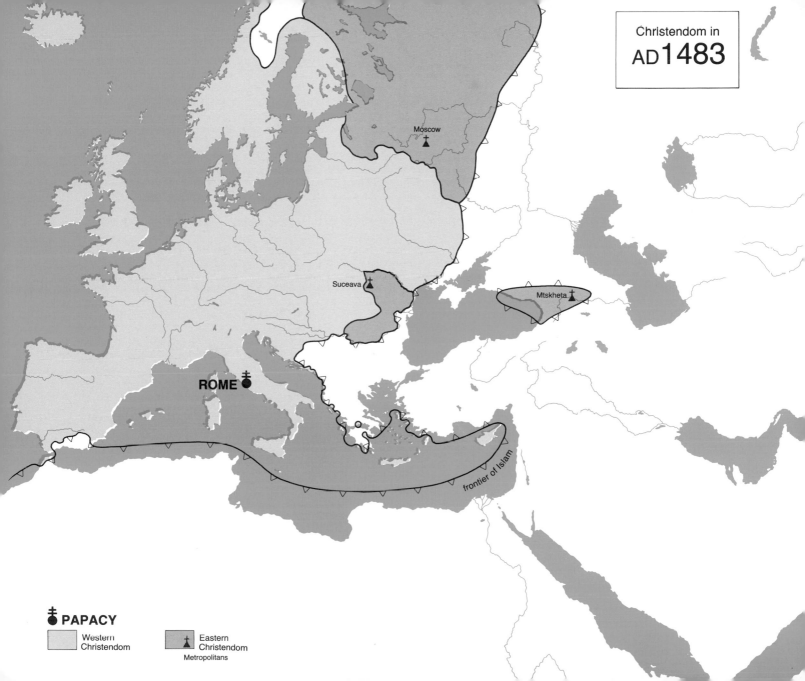

Christendom in
AD **1483**

Moscow

Suceava

Mtskheta

ROME

frontier of Islam

PAPACY

Western
Christendom

Eastern
Christendom
Metropolitans

By the late fourteenth century the European economy had entered its 'plague mode': money was relatively abundant (because plague had reduced the number of people but not the amount of bullion) and wages were high (because labour was now relatively scarce). Consequently, ordinary folk were considerably better off than they had been before the Black Death, with real wages up by as much as 50 per cent. Productivity gains reinforced the trend. Now that there was no longer the same pressure on the land, resources could be concentrated where they were most effective. And high wages encouraged the use of labour-saving machinery. This helped keep working-class incomes up when, as happened after 1400, plague outbreaks started to peter out at an earlier stage in their development and, as a result, population figures began to creep up again. The Black Death had initiated a virtuous economic cycle.

If this was true for the man behind the plough, it was equally true for the man in the street. Though the towns suffered terribly from plague, they usually succeeded in rebuilding their populations in a decade or two and often proved able to add to them. In western Europe the urban sector was actually larger in 1483 than it had been on the eve of the Black Death, which, considering that the total population was still below the pre-Black Death figure, translates into a significant rise in town-dwellers as a proportion of the whole – from 2.25 per cent to 3.25 per cent, according to the database used here. Of course, some towns lost out. The Flemish textile industry continued to contract, partly because the market was now smaller, more importantly because the English were making up their wool into cloth before exporting it; as a result, the population of Ghent fell by a fifth and that of Bruges by a third. Genoa and Siena were smaller too, having lost market-share to Venice and Florence. Pisa, sapped by malaria, no longer makes the map at all; neither does Avignon, dwindling since the departure of the Pope. But the successes far outnumber the failures. The cities of the late fifteenth century had more people at work, for better wages, in a greater variety of jobs than ever before.[1]

Like the agricultural sector, the urban economy benefited from technological changes. In stark contrast to the early medieval period, when changes were few and introduced so gradually that there seemed to be scarcely any difference in lifestyles between one century and the next, the instruments of peace and war were now changing so fast that each decade produced significant advances.

A good example is the mechanical clock, invented some time around the year 1300. In its original form, this was a large iron structure installed alongside the church bells that it used to mark the hours. There was no way a passer-by could tell that the bell was being rung by a machine rather than a monk. Gradually the mechanism was refined. Gear-cutting was improved, which meant that the wheels could be smaller, which in turn meant that they could be driven by less ponderous weights. It became possible to put clocks in living rooms, and these domestic clocks were given faces so that time could be told between the hours. By the early fifteenth century, some of them were so finely made that they could be driven by a steel spring. The machine that had been too heavy for a man to lift was more than halfway along the road to the pocket watch.

A similar process of refinement and miniaturization was at work on another western invention, the gun. The initial impulse had been to make guns bigger so that they became more efficient at what they did best, which was knocking down walls. But the converse of this trend was more important in the long run. Engineers would soon learn to build fortifications that could stand up to prolonged bombardment, but the arrival of the first small arms transformed the battlefield forever. These, not the big bombards, were the weapons that Mao was referring to when he said 'All power grows from the barrel of a gun'.

The gun and the clock are good examples of the evolutionary processes that shaped technological change: a host of inter-related advances in metallurgy and craftsmanship lie behind their slow but steady development. But the fifteenth century also has a perfect example of the opposite process, the technical revolution. Whereas the prototypes of the clock and gun go back to the early fourteenth century, and their progeny, the portable watch and the first effective

small arm, the arquebus, didn't appear till the beginning of the sixteenth, the western printing press was designed, developed and deployed within twenty years. And whereas the credit for gun and clock lies with half a hundred forgotten craftsmen, the printing press was the work of one man, Johann Gutenberg. He invented the method of casting type that was the key to the whole process, adapted press, paper and ink to his needs, and got the system up and running by 1454. Single-handed he had created both a new industry and an instrument for further change.

While Europe forged ahead, the Near East stood still or even slipped back. Egypt, for example, which had been exporting paper to Europe in the eleventh century, was importing it from Italy in the fifteenth.[2] Another of its exports, alum, lost its market when the Italians opened up better quality deposits, first in the Aegean (at Phocaea, on the mainland opposite Chios, at the end of the thirteenth century), then in Italy itself (at Tolfa, near Civitavecchia, in the Papal State, in 1462). But the Egyptians weren't too troubled: they still had a monopoly of the spice trade, and that kept their balance of payments comfortably in the black. And, with 50 per cent of Europe's export to the Levant still consisting of silver, it has to be admitted that it was Europe's mines, not its manufactures, that settled the bill.

This makes it appear that each side was simply exploiting its geographical luck, with Egypt taking advantage of its position astride the spice route and

(continued over)

1. Within the Netherlands the recession in the south was partially offset by an expansion of the shipping industry in the north. Dutch shipbuilders produced better designs than their Hanseatic rivals, and by the end of the century four out of every ten vessels entering the Baltic were in Dutch ownership. Even the fish deserted the Germans. For reasons unknown, the herring catch in the Baltic fell off sharply in the early fifteenth century. This put the European market at the disposal of the Dutch, who took in most of the North Sea catch.
2. Paper was first made in China in the first century AD. Knowledge of the process passed westward along the silk route, reaching Samarkand by the middle of the eighth century. From there it spread rapidly through the

(footnote continued on p. 106)

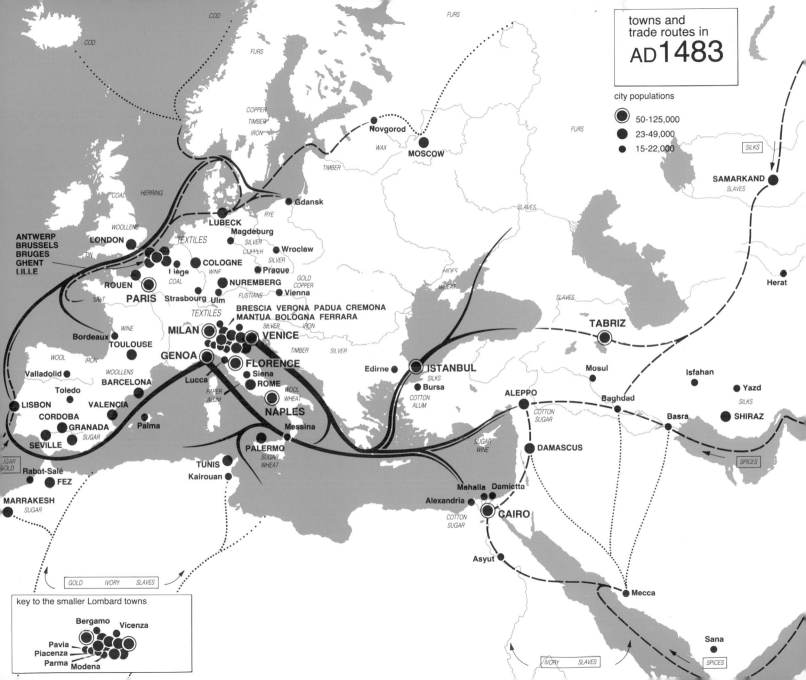

towns and trade routes in AD 1483

city populations
- 50–125,000
- 23–49,000
- 15–22,000

COD

COD

FURS

FURS

COD

FURS

COPPER
TIMBER
IRON

Novgorod

MOSCOW

WAX

FURS

SILKS

SAMARKAND

SLAVES

Gdansk

HERRING

RYE

SLAVES

Herat

LUBECK

Magdeburg

WOOLLENS

SILVER

Wroclaw

SLAVES

COAL

LONDON

TEXTILES

COPPER

SILVER

TABRIZ

ANTWERP
BRUSSELS
BRUGES
GHENT
LILLE

Liège

COLOGNE

Prague

GOLD
COPPER

HIDES

Mosul

Isfahan

TIN

ROUEN

WINE

NUREMBERG

WHEAT

Yazd

COAL

PARIS

Strasbourg

Vienna

Ulm

FUSTIANS

BRESCIA VERONA PADUA CREMONA
MANTUA BOLOGNA FERRARA

SILVER

ISTANBUL

Baghdad

SILKS

TEXTILES

SILVER

ALEPPO

SHIRAZ

Bordeaux

WINE

MILAN

VENICE

TIMBER

SILVER

Edirne

SILKS

COTTON
SUGAR

Basra

TOULOUSE

GENOA

FLORENCE

Bursa

COTTON
ALUM

SPICES

Valladolid

WOOL

IRON

Lucca

Siena

WOOLLENS

ROME

SUGAR
WINE

DAMASCUS

Toledo

BARCELONA

PAPER
ALUM

WOOL
WHEAT

SALT

LISBON

VALENCIA

NAPLES

CORDOBA

Palma

Messina

GRANADA

PALERMO

SUGAR

SEVILLE

SUGAR
WHEAT

Mahalla

Damietta

SUGAR
GOLD

Rabat-Salé

TUNIS

Alexandria

CAIRO

FEZ

Kairouan

COTTON
SUGAR

MARRAKESH

SUGAR

Asyut

GOLD   IVORY   SLAVES

Mecca

key to the smaller Lombard towns

Bergamo   Vicenza

Pavia

Piacenza

Parma   Modena

Sana

IVORY   SLAVES

SPICES

Europe benefiting from the silver ores contained within its mountains. But the Europeans were clever as well as lucky. By the end of the fourteenth century the mines had been, in terms of the technology of the time, completely worked out, and the situation in Europe was no different from that existing in Asia: the shafts in the Harz and the Alps were as silent as the long-abandoned workings in the Caucasus and the Pamirs. But in the 1460s the development of new procedures plus heavy investment in new machinery enabled the Europeans to bring their mines back into production again. They made their luck.

Of all the technical advances made in Europe in the course of the fifteenth century, the one that probably made the most important contribution to this process of wealth-creation was the development of the three-masted ship. Known in the Baltic as a hulk and elsewhere as a carrack or nao, the three-master had double the cargo-carrying capacity of the single-masted cog: on average it carried 300 tons against 150 tons for the cog. The result was a dramatic fall in costs and a real change in the nature of the west European economy. Traditionally, imports had tended to be items that were obtainable only from abroad: pepper was imported from India because it didn't grow in Europe, ivory from Africa because Europe had no elephants. If there was a local source it was always preferred, even if it was a very poor one. The advent of the carrack changed this. Previously, the demand for salt in the countries surrounding the Baltic had been met from deposits at Luneberg, just inland from Lubeck. But as the cost of bulk transport fell, the Lubeckers found it worth their while to sail to the mouth of the Loire, where they could buy better salt at a lower price. At the same time, they began to handle increasing quantities of Swedish iron. Most of the iron Europe used was still produced from local ores, and this remained true to the end of the fifteenth century and beyond. But the proportion acquired through international trade was rising, and out of a total consumption that can be roughly estimated at 100,000 tons a year, well over 10 per cent now came from outside the area of consumption. Another commodity that benefited from reduced shipping costs was coal. The mines in the north of England had been supplying

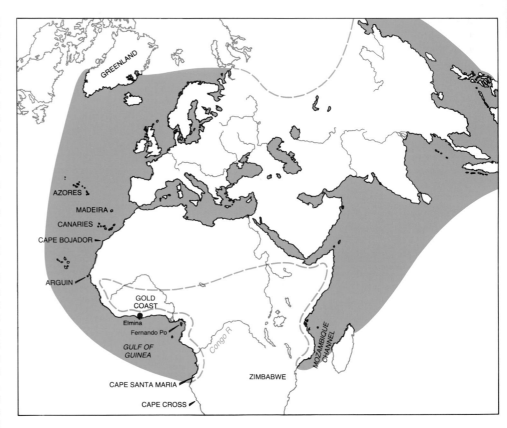

FIGURE 5 *The world as perceived in the West in AD 1483.*

Spanish sovereignty over the Canaries, originally contested by Prince Henry, was finally conceded by Portugal in 1479. As the map shows, the entire archipelago lay within the known world in 1483, but this doesn't mean that every island had been conquered: the outer members of the group remained in the possession of their original inhabitants (the Guanche, a Berber people) till the 1490s.

Other points to note are the disappearance of the Greenland settlements, which had succumbed to Inuit attack (the west settlement in 1340, the east in 1418), and the extension of Arab navigation to the Mozambique Channel (in the thirteenth century; the attraction seems to have been the gold exported, albeit briefly, by the Shona Kingdom of Zimbabwe). Two increments to the known world that are not shown (because they lie off the map) are Japan ('Cipango') and Java. European knowledge of them was pure hearsay and amounted to little more than the fact that they were large islands lying off the east coast of Asia. They deserve a mention, however, because their names were bandied about by those with geographical axes to grind, most notably Columbus.

London's domestic hearths since the end of the thirteenth century. By the late fifteenth century coal was being marketed on both sides of the Channel, with Liège competing directly against Newcastle.

Cutting costs was not the only thing that the three-master could do: it could also keep at sea longer than earlier craft. This opened up various possibilities, of which one of the most intriguing was the exploration of the Atlantic coast of Africa. Initially, interest focused on the Canaries, which had been rediscovered in the fourteenth century: several of the nearer islands were successfully colonized in the opening years of the fifteenth. Subsequently, Prince Henry of Portugal decided to finance an investigation of the African coast south of the Canaries. His idea was to establish contact with the gold-producing area of West Africa and so cut out the Berber middlemen who currently monopolized the region's output.

The trouble with this stretch of the African coast was the prevailing wind. It blew in the right direction for the outward journey, but it blew so steadily that there seemed no hope of ever getting back. For twenty years Prince Henry paid out for expeditions that never got any further than Cape Bojador. But his time and money weren't wasted. Gradually, Portuguese navigators learned how to chart a return leg that took them far out into the Atlantic before 'running down the latitude' of their home port. This wide excursion explains why the discoveries of these early years, Madeira (1418) and the Azores (1431), lie far from the African coast that was the programme's ostensible target. And once Prince Henry's captains were confident that they could find their way home – and their confidence was improved by the fact that they were now sailing caravels, lateen-rigged three-masters that could steer five points into the wind – they returned to their original objective. In 1434 Gil Eannes rounded Cape Bojador, and over the next ten years he and his compatriots charted the entire stretch of coast between Bojador and Arguin. From Arguin it proved possible to tap into the trans-Saharan trade, so that by 1457 the Portuguese crown was getting enough gold to mint its first gold coin, the cruzado. Add the income from the developing sugar plantations on Madeira, and Prince Henry's venture may even have been in profit.

Whether it was or not, a Lisbon entrepreneur, Fernão Gomez, thought that one more push could turn it into a real money-spinner. After Prince Henry's death he entered into negotiations with the Portuguese crown and eventually obtained an agreement, signed in 1469 and running for five years, that granted him monopoly rights over whatever he might find beyond Arguin. In return Gomez undertook to explore 100 leagues (300 miles) of coastline each year and make an annual payment of 500 cruzados into the treasury. It was a gamble that paid off magnificently. In 1471 one of Gomez's captains reached the Akan coast, the back door to the West African goldfields that everyone had been dreaming of. The Portuguese thought that their discovery meant that they had established contact with the Kingdom of Ghana – Guinea in contemporary spelling – hence their use of the terms Guinea Coast and Gulf of Guinea, but in fact there was never any connection between the medieval Ghana, a kingdom restricted to the Sahel, which had anyway disappeared by this time, and the Akan coast (the colonial Gold Coast, modern Ghana). No matter: by rounding the bulge of Africa and reaching the Gulf, Gomez had done his bit for geography and made his fortune to boot. He had also given his countrymen a new goal to pursue, the circumnavigation of the African continent. The reward for this feat would be entry to the Indian Ocean and an end to the Arab monopoly of the spice trade.

Gomez used the remaining years of his contract with his customary vigour. At first it looked as if he was heading for a second triumph, as if a straight run east would bring the Portuguese to the Indian Ocean within a matter of weeks. But beyond Fernando Po – an island named for one of Gomez's captains – the coast was discovered to turn southward and continue south for hundreds of miles. The circumnavigation of Africa, if it was feasible at all, was going to take more resources than anyone had bargained for.

Portugal's King John rose to the occasion. He opened up his royal purse, commissioned a fleet and established a permanent base, the Fort of St George of the Mine, on the Akan coast. The mine referred to was imaginary, for the natives got their gold from alluvial deposits, but the fort, its title simplified to El Mina,

provided a base both for the gold trade and for the further exploration of the African coastline. The captain charged with the second task, Diogo Cão, reached the Congo River (now the Zaire) and Cape Santa Maria in the course of his first voyage of 1482–3. There was still a long way to go, and Cão would not complete the journey: he died on his second voyage and was buried at the furthest point he reached, Cape Cross. But other navigators were already at sea preparing for the ventures that would give man his first true measure of the globe. Bartholomew Diaz, who had sailed in the expedition that established El Mina, was ready to take up where Cão had left off: he would find and round the Cape of Good Hope in 1488. And Christopher Columbus, a Genoese captain who had settled in Madeira, was trading at El Mina only a few years after Diaz was there. He was equally determined to break through the horizon that had marked the limits of the medieval vision and had even more radical ideas as to how to go about it.

ADDITIONAL NOTES

AD 1071 *(footnote continued from p. 60)*

possession but a fief for which the King of England had to do homage to the King of France.

This is the language of feudalism, the system that had evolved from the idea of knight-service for land introduced by Charles Martel. The concept made it possible, though far from easy, to run a state that had no revenue, the catch being that the obligation of knight-service in the feudal system was owed to the local lord, who might well have reservations about his own obligations to his king.

Another point to notice on the map is that although Muslim Spain is still shaded as Arab, which was what most of its rulers claimed to be and some of them, like the Emirs of Zaragoza, were, most of them by this time were of Berber stock.

AD 1212 *(footnote continued from p. 70)*

windfall that momentarily freed him from the cashflow problems that increasingly beset the German Empire.

It is a telling measure of the Empire's failure that, at a time when the west was shifting from the feudal system of tithes and obligations to a money economy that favoured settlements in cash, the Imperial exchequer was unable to make anything of the opportunity. In fact, the income of the German crown, far from increasing, was diminishing, and was to reach zero in the next century. By contrast, Philip Augustus fussed over the tax base of the French monarchy to such good effect that he had doubled his income by the time he mounted his successful attack on the English fiefs in France. By the end of his reign he had nearly tripled it.

Some other points deserve attention. In north-east Russia, Vladimir began to encroach on Novgorod's fur-trade outposts. In Spain, the Christians gained a great victory over the Almohads at Los Navos de Tolosa (1212). Aragon lost Provence, but gained some fiefs in the south of France. In Anatolia the Seljuks of Rum extended their control over the entire interior and reached the coast on the south-west. The Shah of Khwarizm brought order out of chaos in Iran and even managed to expel the Qarakhitai from Transoxiana.

AD 1346 *(footnote continued from p. 81)*

fellow prisoner Rusticello of Pisa. Rusticello was a professional writer, quite unable to give Marco's story the straightforward telling it needed. He mixed up things Marco had seen for himself with things about which Marco had only hearsay knowledge, adding stock battle scenes and fables taken from his own romances whenever he thought the text needed enlivening. The result, pitched in the no-man's land between fact and fantasy, is a tragic mess, about as useful as the contemporary world maps produced in monasteries to illustrate bible stories. When you think of what the two of them could have produced . . .

AD 1483 *(footnote continued from p. 102)*

Islamic world (Baghdad *c.* 790, Cairo *c.* 800), then more slowly to Europe via Spain (twelfth century) and Italy (thirteenth century) to France and Germany (fourteenth century).

This seems an appropriate point to mention four other Chinese inventions that provided starting points for the West's technological take-off: the crossbow, the compass, gunpowder and woodblock printing. The crossbow was developed in China in the second century BC; the western contribution was to increase its power by making the bow of steel. The floating compass is first mentioned in an eleventh century Chinese encyclopedia; a century later it was in use in Europe, where the addition of the compass card, which greatly enhanced its utility, was made in the 1290s (possibly at Amalfi). Woodblock printing was developed in China in the eighth century. The Chinese system was used by the Ilkhans in Persia, whence the use of block-printed playing cards spread to the West. The Chinese even experimented with movable type but never developed it into a practical technology, and Gutenberg's system owes nothing to their experiments. Gunpowder is first mentioned in a Chinese alchemical treatise of the ninth century AD, but in a form which burnt rather than exploded. As such it found its main application in rockets. There is good evidence that the Chinese military made use of 'fire lances', in which the jet of a fixed rocket was directed at the enemy, but there is nothing to indicate that they ever evolved any form of gun.

INDEX

The letter-number combinations refer to the index map overleaf.

PENGUIN BOOKS

Published by the Penguin Group
Penguin Books Ltd, 80 Strand, London WC2R 0RL, England
Penguin Putnam Inc., 375 Hudson Street, New York, New York 10014, USA
Penguin Books Australia Ltd, Ringwood, Victoria, Australia
Penguin Books Canada Ltd, 10 Alcorn Avenue, Toronto, Ontario, Canada M4V 3B2
Penguin Books (NZ) Ltd, Cnr Rosedale and Airborne Road, Albany, Auckland, New Zealand

Penguin Books Ltd, Registered Offices: 80 Strand, London WC2R 0RL, England
www.penguin.com
The Penguin Atlas of Medieval History first published 1961
The New Penguin Atlas of Medieval History first published 1992
19 20

Copyright © Colin McEvedy 1961, 1992
All rights reserved
The moral right of the author has been asserted

Filmset in Linotron Times by
Rowland Phototypesetting Ltd, Bury St Edmunds, Suffolk
Manufactured in China